PRAISE FOR

KANYE WEST OWES ME $300

"*Kanye West Owes Me $300* might be the funniest rap memoir ever. . . . It's a classic LA redemption story of an artist narrowly missing stardom and failing at his first dream, but surviving to write his own second act."

—*LA Weekly*

"Triumphantly funny . . . Karp has a gift for crafting portraits of hip-hop stars that are as funny and revealing as they are succinct, and his take on a pre-fame West is funny but also, like much of the rest of the book, surprisingly emotional and poignant. . . . A book that is something special."

—*The A.V. Club*

"Funny, irreverent . . . There's plenty of juicy anecdotes, celebrity gossip, and shady industry dealings."

—*GQ*

"Hilarious."

—*Harper's Bazaar*

"If the title doesn't grab your attention, the story definitely will."

—PopSugar

"The funniest person I follow on Twitter finally got smart and wrote about his unlikely—and hilarious—odyssey as teenage rapper Hot Karl. Karp's sharp wit and gossipy giggles keep you turning pages, but what lingers is the story of a survivor. This book should be mandatory reading for anyone who has ever wanted to be famous."

—Kevin Smith, *New York Times* bestselling author of *Tough Sh*t*

"If I had kids, I'd read passages from this to them at night. Rap careers definitely haven't been explored from this perspective, and I'm excited to see the ripples. Jensen's gonna make some enemies, though. I've been on television."

—Hannibal Buress

"I remember hearing faint whispers about a white kid on the West Coast who got, like, the craziest deal ever from some radio freestyles or some shit. But we never saw anything concrete, so I assumed he was hip-hop's Bigfoot and left it at that. Who knew it was real??!!! This is the story of the rap game's Sasquatch."

—Bun B, Grammy-nominated rapper

"Jensen's story is so funny and so well written that it's impossible there's any truth to it."

—Kay Cannon, writer, *Pitch Perfect* and *30 Rock*

"Sure, everyone is curious to know what it's like to be a white rapper, but only Jensen Karp has the wit and humility to reveal what it was like to get knocked down by the music industry, dust off his Cross Colours, and keep moving."

—Paul Scheer

KANYE WEST OWES ME $300

KANYE WEST
OWES ME
$300

AND OTHER TRUE STORIES
FROM A WHITE RAPPER WHO
ALMOST MADE IT BIG

JENSEN KARP

FORMERLY KNOWN AS "HOT KARL"

THREE RIVERS PRESS
NEW YORK

Photography credits can be found on page 301.

Library of Congress Cataloging-in-Publication Data
Names: Karp, Jensen, 1979–
Title: Kanye West owes me $300 : and other true stories from a white
    rapper who ALMOST made it big / Jensen Karp.
Description: First edition. | New York : Crown Archetype, [2016]
Identifiers: LCCN 2016009737 | ISBN 9780553448153
Subjects: LCSH: Karp, Jensen, 1979– | Rap musicians—
    United States—Biography.
Classification: LCC ML420.K1605 A3 2016 | DDC
    782.421649092—dc23
LC record available at http://lccn.loc.gov/2016009737

ISBN 978-0-451-49887-8
Ebook ISBN 978-0-553-44816-0

PRINTED IN THE UNITED STATES OF AMERICA

Book design by Anna Thompson
Cover design by Christopher Brand

10 9 8 7 6 5 4 3 2 1

First Paperback Edition

For my mom and dad,
always my biggest fans

CONTENTS

PARENTAL
ADVISORY
EXPLICIT CONTENT

EVERYTHING you're about to read actually happened. A few small details have been changed to either build a little creative context or to keep someone anonymous, but even Melissa Joan Hart did that in her memoir, and what's good for MJH is good for me. Also, like Bill & Ted attempting to finish a term paper, I have manipulated time for storytelling purposes. In case any of these disclosures now has you questioning whether my book is worth your time, I asked my mom to write a paragraph in hopes of convincing you to make the commitment. Here that is:

Jensen is an incredibly loving son who has written a very enjoyable book. When he was three years old, on a trip to the petting zoo, he played the ears of a baby goat as if they were drums and then proceeded to ask the goat its name. Jensen waited a second, looked up at his dad and me, and explained in an excited tone, "Oh right—Billy!" He smacked his own forehead like it was the most obvious answer and it was just plain stupid to ask a goat such a question. This is the exact same way I feel about you second-guessing his book. Thank you.

—Haroldine Gearhart, July 5, 2015

You heard the woman.
Enjoy the book, Billy.

KANYE WEST OWES ME $300

"YOU have three brain tumors, but I'm really only concerned with one of them," the doctor said in his grimmest tone. "The other two seem insignificant."

"Like Destiny's Child?" I asked, proving I had no idea how to handle serious things.

No laugh.

I don't blame myself for making light of a critical medical moment. I still blame myself for thinking the doctor would understand the complexities of Destiny's Child in the 2000s.

It had all started about a week earlier when, at twenty-nine years old, I woke up with a ringing in my ears that didn't disappear for six hours. Worried, I made an urgent appointment, and after a standard checkup, my doctor told me that a shot of cortisone would ease what he thought was just inflammation. I sighed with relief, ready for the next small physical ailment that would throw me into a tailspin. (A month earlier, I had Googled "rickets" when I thought my bones seemed tired.) Knowing my hypochondriac tendencies and my overall state of panic, my doctor suggested that the ear ringing might actually be a blessing. It meant that my insurance company would pay for an MRI/brain scan, which, he explained, was always a good thing. "Why not get it?" he asked. "It's available to you, and they're usually expensive." And although this theory would be awful when applied to many things (drugs, semiautomatic weapons, pet lions), I understood the logic.

Soon after the scan, when a nurse called to let me know the doctor wanted to go over the results, I halfheartedly said, "Sure, put him through." She explained he was very busy and needed to set up a time for me to come into the office. And like a clueless third-grader who keeps asking questions about the stork even after he watches porn, I missed the point completely. "Well, if he's so busy, let's make it even easier by doing it over the phone," I suggested. Her voice got lower, quickly revealing that things were about to suck, and the words "Listen, you need to come in" dragged out, seeping through the telephone line and into my ear. I said, "Sure," hung up, and then somehow stopped myself from typing "nearest cliff to jump off" into MapQuest.

Once in the office, I watched the doctor's mouth slowly move as he explained the three "white spots" he'd found on my midbrain, a section in charge of sleeping, walking, and alertness, among other things. So, no big deal, just TOTALLY ESSENTIAL ACTIONS NEEDED TO LIVE. It all got rather blurry at this point, but I found out that the spots' placement made them inoperable. If the surgeon strayed even a little, I'd incur significant damage or become a vegetable. He suggested I see a neurologist, as if I were graduating to a new level of difficulty, like when you beat *Super Mario Bros. 2* and start playing the one where Mario dresses up like a flying squirrel. But no matter what the doctor said, or how he sugarcoated it, all I heard was, "It's time to go home and plan your funeral." (For the record, I'd like to be carried into the service while WWE superstar The Undertaker's music plays.)

I felt doomed, mostly because my family is riddled with cancer. In my immediate circle, we have just under a dozen cases, including my father, who passed away during his second bout. So if your office has a cancer pool, I'm a good pick. (Also, you work with assholes.) My family is to cancer what the Kardashians are to black boyfriends.

Living with that kind of medical uncertainty is something you can't really prepare for. Sure, a neighbor, or your friend's great-aunt, or the relief pitcher for the 1985 American League champion Kansas City Royals, Dan Quisenberry, might die of brain cancer, but not you. And in the rare case that you do face this type of horrible revelation, you assume you'll pass out or scream, or that your entire life will "flash right before your eyes," because that's what happens in movies. So, that's what I planned for. I got sweaty. I felt the tears well up. I even felt light-headed.

But above all else, I couldn't stop thinking about one thing—not a bucket list or the family members I'd leave behind or why they keep making those awful Fantastic Four movies. My brain zeroed in on one small patch of time from my youth, when I tried my hardest to become, of all things, a famous rapper. My years as "Hot Karl" were repressed memories at this point in my life, but as soon as I heard what sounded like a death sentence, my thwarted, long-abandoned career was once again front and center. My father, whose life-ending cancer haunted me while I awaited diagnosis, had encouraged me during our last conversation to finally accept my extraordinary story, hoping I could come to terms and eventually live without regret, something he wished he had done sooner. I'd assumed I'd have time to face that demon down the road, but now I encountered an urgency I had never seen coming. I knew the Hot Karl story needed closure.

You see, I came extremely close to the entire world knowing every word to my songs, but, near the finish line, things didn't necessarily fall into place. In fact, my past as a signed rapper is sort of like that song "Detroit Rock City" by KISS. It's a totally upbeat and rocking anthem, but in reality about a city that's depressing as fuck.

As crazy as it sounds, I was raised a suburban Jewish kid in the San Fernando Valley yet found myself rapping alongside Kanye West, Redman, will.i.am, and Fabolous. Names like Mack 10, Suge Knight, Justin Timberlake, Enrique Iglesias, and Christina Aguilera considered themselves fans of my work, yet I looked more like a rapper's accountant than a rapper. I was signed to Interscope Records at nineteen and accumulated more than $1 million rhyming words, but you've most likely never heard of me. It's still hard to believe some of the situations I encountered during my brief, yet unimaginable, stint in the music business. I had the time of my life in studios and exclusive clubs, and most of all onstage, but for the past decade my attitude toward Hot Karl, the alter ego I adopted on a whim, has been like that of a stripper who moves five towns away to raise her new child. I didn't want *anyone* to know.

In my youth, every Tuesday I obsessively searched through the new-release bin at a local record store, trying to get my hands on the next big rap song before it blew up, learning everything I could about groups like Digable Planets or Naughty By Nature or Mad Kap, even though no one around me really gave a shit about my discoveries. Hip-hop was nowhere near the global phenomenon it is today, but to me it's always been the *only* music that mattered. How I found myself hobnobbing among rap's elite and watching hip-hop history unfold right in front of my own eyes, I'll never fully understand, but the least I can do is talk about it now. This book has finally allowed me not only to recount this period of my life, but also to give it the ending it deserves. Consider this the bonus track to an album you never got a chance to buy.

And as it turns out, after a few years of tests and constant monitoring, the Tumor Board at Cedars-Sinai came to a conclusion: my brain tumors are harmless. And even though they would still need to be closely observed for the rest of my life, the doctor thought they might even be juvenile tumors that had stopped developing in the 2000s and have no relevance in present day—like Papa Roach.

When I shared the good news with my mom, she cried, letting me know that she had prayed and knew it would all work out in time. She went as far as to suggest that these juvenile tumors may have given me a mental advantage as a kid, or even helped me as a writer today.

"Maybe these tumors are what make you so smart, Jensen," my mom brainstormed. "You were always intelligent. They wanted to move you to the gifted program as a kid. They said you were the real bright spot and everyone around you just wasn't as good."

"Like Destiny's Child?" I asked.

No laugh.

1

STRAIGHT OUTTA CALABASAS

I spent most of my '80s childhood in a California suburb called Calabasas, which is about thirty minutes to four hours outside of Los Angeles, depending on what time of day you're driving. In the past few years, this small town has become synonymous with the Kardashian family, since that's where they live, film their TV show, and most likely sacrifice innocent children in return for fame and riches. It's not necessarily how I want my hometown to be remembered, but since other notable local heroes include the Menendez brothers and Elizabeth Berkley, I guess it could be worse. It's always funny to me, though, that a Christian-Armenian family of superficial superstars has become the symbol for this exclusive San Fernando Valley neighborhood, since 95 percent of the area is actually Jewish. I'll give you $100 if you can find fifty names that don't end with "–stein" or "–berg" in my high school yearbook. And even though I look like Zach Braff eating matzo, I'm actually only half-Jewish. My mother is Catholic and Armenian, so maybe I *am* more Calabasas than I want to believe.

My parents sure had a sense of humor.
I'm talking about the bowl cut.

While I spent most of my time in this posh, yet tacky, city, I actually lived in a neighboring town called Woodland Hills. Look at it this way: if Calabasas is Mark Wahlberg, I grew up in his brother Donnie. We're technically related, but different in so many ways. Lower- to middle-class homes make up Woodland Hills, while most of Calabasas consists of guard-gated mansions. Many of my friends had last names that also appeared on food products in our kitchen or in the credits of Academy Award–nominated films, so my dad's hard work as a car salesman stood out among the parents at my school. I was only able to attend Calabasas High School because my mom worked nearby and told the admissions department it would be a hassle to drive me to my local school every day, which at its core makes no sense but weirdly got me a permit. My parents knew that schools in rich neighborhoods got more funding, and despite Puffy asking us to vote or die, this fact hasn't changed since the '90s.

Growing up, I always felt like an outsider looking in. When classmates had basketball courts in their backyards or got BMWs with bows tied around them for their sixteenth birthdays, I could only laugh. My parents did all they could to get me everything I wanted, but I was always conscious of keeping my expectations in line with my own life, not my friends'.

In the early '90s, as I approached my thirteenth birthday and bar/bat mitzvahs became a weekly occurrence, I knew I was in for some real Great Gatsby shit. Each family had to one-up the next, paying no mind to budget, modesty, or even religious tradition for this initiation into adulthood. On the other side of the spectrum, I ended up having my thirteenth birthday party in the upstairs banquet room of a local taco spot that had a DJ booth, a dance floor, and "Kids Eat Free Mondays." Not only that, but when you don't have a bar/bat mitzvah, you miss out on endless gifts and around $3,000 in cash from your friends and family. I'd sit at these things, listening to Noah's Torah portion, depressed and jealous, imagining all the Cross Colours and Air Jordans I could buy with that money. I wasn't exactly dancing the hora in excitement. But it was at one of these bar mitzvahs, as I sat, filled with envy, at my assigned table, that my life would take a surprise turn into the world of rap music.

My cousin first introduced to me to rap in 1989, when I was nine years old. I remember him showing me the album covers for Slick Rick's *The Great Adventures of Slick Rick*, UTFO's *Doin' It!*, and 3rd Bass's *The Cactus Album*; the artwork alone drew me in. Then he played me the music, and I've been obsessed ever since that first needle drop. He was six years older than I was, and because of the age gap he had access to all the age-restricted records I couldn't buy. But, strangely, the curse words weren't the hook that drew me in, unlike most of my friends who were jonesing for the forbidden and laughing every time Too $hort mentioned a blow job.

While I may not have directly related to rap, as an outsider I understood the passion at its heart. In the same way I get emotional while watching *Rudy*—despite the fact that I only played a total of five minutes on my winless freshman football team—the angst, dejection, and political commentary in golden-age rap songs spoke to me. Now, I clearly didn't have the same struggles as Public Enemy or Grandmaster Flash. And many rappers, like Ice Cube and X Clan, made music specifically, and in most cases correctly, criticizing my race. Still, I was hooked on this alternative to the cookie-cutter suburban lifestyle around me. I knew rap music wasn't mine, but I loved the art form dearly and tried to find common ground where I could.

I would study and dissect each lyric, and the eventual music video on *Yo! MTV Raps*, like I was Ralphie decoding a secret message during an Ovaltine radio spot. I thoroughly examined every issue of *The Source*, cutting out pictures of my favorite MCs to tape onto my wall for worship. I focused on albums like Run-

D.M.C.'s *Raising Hell* or LL Cool J's *Bigger and Deffer*, mesmerized by the hard-hitting lyrics and aggressive production. Those songs cleared the way for acts like Beastie Boys, 2 Live Crew, Roxanne Shanté, DJ Jazzy Jeff & the Fresh Prince, Biz Markie, and EPMD to enter my lexicon, and there was no turning back. Rap music was still something a white kid had to actively search for; nowadays it's hard to find a white kid without their own mixtape. While my classmates were engulfed in things like Little League, karate, and ballet classes, I was trying to figure out where I could buy sunglasses like Kool Moe Dee's or what size Adidas I could comfortably wear without laces. It was my hobby at a time when most of the people around me didn't even know rap existed.

When I performed "You Be Illin'" for my third-grade talent show, one teacher asked my mom, with a straight face, "What type of music is this?" Some classmates weren't as innocent with their questions. When I started writing my own rhymes in the sixth grade, almost everyone ignored me, and when they did eventually pay attention, it was to call me "wigger" and keep moving. But no matter what they said, I confidently wore my baggy JNCOs and that one T-shirt with Bugs Bunny and the Tasmanian Devil wearing their clothes backwards without a care in the world.

This backfired on the last day of sixth grade, when I was chased around school by fifty other male students who ridiculed my love of black culture, hip-hop, and dancing. They yelled obscenities and "Vanilla Ice!" at me as I tried to find refuge in different spots on campus, but they'd eventually find me and start yelling again. The most offensive part about the attack was that I hated Vanilla Ice. But I didn't expect them to respect my preference for credible hip-hop over commercial rap, let alone give me a second to explain the difference. Luckily for me, the bell rang and summer vacation started. I continued to write my own songs, and, that next year when I returned to the same school, I not only became friends with many of those bullies, I formed a rap group with one of them, one of only a handful of black kids in my entire middle school, Rickye. We called ourselves X-tra Large, which, yes, was a reference to our dick size.

Even in third grade, you have to respect my rapper pose.

Maybe secretly I did wish I was the kid in the chair being hoisted above his friends and family at every bar mitzvah I attended that year, but the one thing I openly loved about them was that the DJ would always end up playing rap music. Yes, we'd have to sit through "Celebration," "YMCA," and "Unchained Melody," as well as the instrumental Muzak they played when food was served, but as the evening went on, the parents would sit down and the party would quickly turn into an episode of *The Grind*. Most of my peers were into rock music, from softer glam bands like Poison to harder metal like Sepultura, which is as likely to get people dancing at a bar mitzvah as *Mein Kampf* on tape. Since the DJs hired for these things were in their early twenties and from Hollywood or the greater Los Angeles area, they were itching to play Heavy D & the Boyz, De La Soul, and Dr. Dre, just as much as I was itching to hear them. With dances like the Cabbage Patch and the Robocop becoming popular, mostly with white suburban girls, you could look forward to a nice set of hip-hop, even if "Ice Ice Baby" and "The Electric Slide" had to be the entry drug. New York had the Tunnel; we had the Rosenthal reception.

And this one specific bar mitzvah I attended in 1991 was no letdown, as many current rap songs got spins. But it wasn't until a few songs in, when Black Sheep's "The Choice Is Yours" played, that I sprang up from my seat, ready to do the Running Man. It was my favorite song at the time, and I couldn't help but rap along to Dres's words, which I had already studied to the point of knowing where every syllable and breath was supposed to sit. The MC must have seen my attention to detail, because he feverishly ran over to ask if I could do it into the microphone. I said sure, both because I was in the zone and because I didn't understand how to avoid being bullied. But thanks to years of rapping into my bedroom mirror and pretending I was on Soul Train, I spit the verses with ease. The MC was visibly impressed and pulled me off to the side, just as the grandparents came up to light candle number eight.

Most of my gimmick at the time was that no rapper in the

world looked like me. I was a clean-cut, scrawny twelve-year-old, a better fit for a Boy Scouts meeting than a Big Daddy Kane concert. And because of that fact, the MC knew he was on to something. He immediately asked for my parents' phone number, and after proving to them he wasn't going to molest me, a man named Demetrius Cash became the official manager of X-tra Large.

Demetrius was one of the first black adults I ever interacted with. As crazy as that sounds, it's true. My grandfather, who was raised in Iowa, told stories of seeing a black man for the first time in his late teens at a supermarket. He asked his father why that man was "made of chocolate," which, although innocent, does seem like something only a Sacha Baron Cohen character would say. While I was not as isolated as my grandfather had been, not one school I attended, from kindergarten to twelfth grade, employed a black teacher. A common nickname for my hometown is still "Cala-blackless." It's the Utah Jazz of the San Fernando Valley. My family never really traveled beyond Nevada for vacation either, so even though I was wildly obsessed with music largely made by black rappers, I had very little firsthand experience with minorities in general.

I still don't know if Demetrius Cash was actually born with that money-centric last name, but he was so convincing—and confident in my abilities—that I would've believed anything he told me. He was around twenty-one years old and dressed strictly in silk button-ups and Z. Cavaricci jeans, constantly looking like he was auditioning to join Jodeci. He was as skinny as a twig, but heavy in bravado and charm. After the bar mitzvah where he approached me with the mic, he'd call my house every day, detailing his plan to make X-tra Large a household name. Another Bad Creation and Kris Kross were at the height of their popularity, with more obscure, and hardcore, kid groups like Da Youngstas and Illegal also releasing music—so there was an obvious spot in the marketplace for our act. Demetrius Cash was ready to lead me and Rickye to that Promised Land.

Demetrius immediately rented a dance studio and started holding rehearsals, focusing on dance routines instead of songs, while at the same time coming up with a plan for our show. Even though I never took a formal class, hip-hop dancing came to me naturally. I would watch videos from Bobby Brown and the *In Living Color* Fly Girls, then emulate each dance step almost perfectly. Demetrius was transforming X-tra Large from a pipe dream into a full-fledged group, and we gladly followed his lead. The only rule I was adamant about, as the duo's main songwriter, was that Demetrius couldn't give any input or critique on our lyrical content. It's a demand that seemed rather pretentious for a twelve-year-old, but I always knew my words were important.

There were a few outstanding issues with X-tra Large, however. Even though we'd decided what our first album cover would look like (us standing in the middle of a Parental Advisory logo holding our crotches) and what we'd wear for shows (button-up shirts and ties), we didn't actually have any songs. I had notebooks and notebooks full of lyrics, but no beats, so X-tra Large was technically shit out of luck unless we decided to become slam poets.

To address the fact that we didn't have our own instrumentals, we planned to open with two crowd-pleasers by current artists (the Black Sheep song that Demetrius discovered me mimicking and the then popular Kris Kross hit "Jump"), not unlike karaoke. Then we'd surprise everyone with our new, and only, original song, "Killin' at the Playground," a scathing diss I wrote about Another Bad Creation, a popular kid-rap group founded by Bell Biv DeVoe member Michael Bivins. In the song, I relentlessly made fun of ABC's names, music, style, and, yes, penis size. I had nothing against them, but I knew my real talent rested in rhyming aggressive insults, emulating battle raps I had heard from rappers like KRS-One and Tim Dog.

I also knew that targeting groups at the top of the charts would be an easy way to garner attention without much experience or music of my own. We found an existing instrumental that heavily sampled the S.O.S. Band's "Take Your Time (Do It Right)" and decided it would be the perfect beat for "Killin' at the Playground," a song where I, as a preteen, claimed, "Iesha, I had her, she's nothing," thereby celebrating the fact that I fucked the fictitious girlfriend the group sang about on their biggest hit. Bob Dylan I was not. No matter what came out of my mouth, though, X-tra Large was ready to take the stage. We had Demetrius. We had fully realized dance routines. We had an original song that could get us beat up. We had a lot of Cross Colours. And I had a partner who would, Demetrius excitedly explained, give me the "street cred" I needed.

Rickye Kidd lived really close to a freeway. I remember that because when I first visited his place in the seventh grade, he informed me that that's "how you can tell if someone is poor." If I felt the economic and racial divide of Calabasas, Rickye was plagued by it. Living in a small apartment on the border of Calabasas, he was raised by a single mother after being deserted by his dad at an early age. While we played *Lakers versus Celtics* on Sega Genesis, he revealed that his parents were never married, which was a situation I had never heard of before. He was one of the shortest kids in our grade, standing under five feet tall, but he looked like, and had the tenacity of, a bulldog.

When we hung out, I'd notice the stares. Mall employees would shadow us closely in stores, as his skin color appeared to pose a shoplifting threat. When this happened, Rickye would whip around and angrily ask if something was wrong. When the startled clerk answered no, Rickye would turn to me and nicely ask if I wanted to leave with him, and I would. His unwavering confidence made him a bully at times, especially when he'd been part of that mob chasing me around school. But no matter how hard he tried to act, his big infectious smile and flattop—a perfectly groomed cross between Kid from Kid 'n Play and the top of a mushroom—quickly let you know his ferocious growl was actually that of a puppy dog.

Rickye's mother's main goal was to make life easier for him, which explained the relentless hours she worked as a doctor's assistant in order to live in a specific zip code and assure him better schooling. She would wake up early every morning to make him breakfast and iron and starch his color-matched T-shirts and long shorts. She also always made sure he had the new Air Jordans for every basketball season. My mom remembers trying to set Rickye's mom up on a date just to give her a break from parenting, but she told my mom she didn't really want to bring a man into her life until Rickye was an adult.

X-tra Large in da house!!!
(My parents' house. That was our fireplace.)

Rickye's mom was determined to raise him right and got ir-ritated when I would write curse words into songs, making sure they were delegated to my parts. My mom's only rule, on the other hand, was to try and avoid the f-word, a guideline I was willing to follow, since she had to drive me to every rehearsal. In turn, Rickye played the Vinnie to my Treach or the Phife to my Q-Tip, delivering hard-hitting lines I wrote for him but leaving the quotable punch lines for my animated voice. Rickye was just as impressive of a dancer as I was, but we both knew that seeing a suburban white kid master the Roger Rabbit was a more arresting visual than his own footwork. Talent didn't really matter with my gimmick. Demetrius knew I needed Rickye, though, almost twenty years before Dr. Dre had to tell us it was alright to love Eminem and before T.I. had to endlessly defend Iggy Azalea. Kidd X, the name Rickye took on to honor Malcolm X, helped the audience digest my foreign presence.

Demetrius was connected with West Coast hip-hop, so he got us opening slots on a few local shows, including a performance before Ice-T's Rhyme Syndicate and Tone Lōc, who was fresh off the success of "Wild Thing" and "Funky Cold Medina." The opportunity to rap onstage felt like a dream come true, but to be

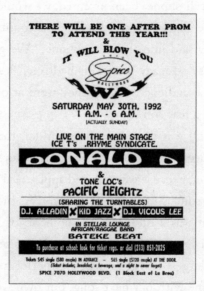

My mom kept every one of my show flyers, including this first one. It would be funny if one of you guys prank called her one day saying you're with the Rock and Roll Hall of Fame and need the collection for display.

in the same conversation as some of my idols was mind-blowing. So after months of rehearsing, two children in neckties took to the stage in the heart of Hollywood (chaperoned by their parents, standing sidestage), at a packed Club Spice on Vine, to perform two songs everyone knew and one song that made fun of Michael Bivins's meal ticket. We were excited and nervous, but believed the months of practice would pay off.

The two cover songs bombed right off the bat, most clubgoers probably wondering if the organizers found us on a street corner outside the venue. As the second song ended, I noticed the lackluster response and started to regret everything Demetrius had planned. Had cell phones been invented, we would've seen a few hundred people checking their Facebook accounts at once. The DJ sarcastically said into the microphone, "We gotta get them done, 'cause it's waaaaaay past their bedtime," leading to a few laughs from the audience. While they were at our expense, at least they were a reaction.

When the DJ was done belittling our act, there were a few seconds of silence, which was just enough time for us to catch our breath. However, because we expected applause at this point, the stillness wasn't something we'd planned for. As the awkwardness built, I knew it was a life-or-death moment for X-tra Large. I hadn't endured years of insults for liking rap to be ignored now, in front of the largest crowd I might ever perform for. We had to impress everyone with our next song, our own work, and I had to leave no survivors. I entered a zone—one I would encounter a few other times in my career—and, in the most arrogant tone I could muster at the age of twelve, quickly improvised, "Alright, this one I wrote a long time ago. It's called 'Killin' at the Playground.'" (Small note: I hadn't written the song "a long time ago," mostly because I WAS TWELVE. I had actually written it that month, but I heard Johnny Cash say something like that once and I always thought it sounded cool, so it just came out.)

I knew as we tore through the song that our practices had paid off. Everything was executed perfectly, and I even spontaneously made a motion at my crotch when I angrily rapped, "We wouldn't be called Large if we didn't have somethin'." The other rappers waiting backstage, guys who would perform later in the night, were visibly freaking out after every punch line and yelling at Demetrius to "get the whiteboy a louder mic." The audience was applauding every time we went at Another Bad Creation, each line getting meaner and meaner as we emulated and satirized gangster rap to get our point across. Halfway through the song, I looked at Rickye, and, on mic, said, "We did it, man." Demetrius, who stood behind us onstage, knew we were on fire, and I started to feed off his energy as well. I felt electric, jumping around the stage, finally finding the confidence I'd showed for years in my bedroom. To close the song, Rickye and I had dance solos, because that's what happened in the '90s, and during my routine, the rappers, now enthusiastically pumping their fists and smiling, chanted "Go, whiteboy!" at the top of their lungs. I executed moves I hadn't even tried before. I was like *Teen Wolf*, but for rap, not basketball, and, thanks to my Armenian heritage, just as hairy. When the song ended, the room erupted.

Well, that's what I assume, because right when I finished dancing, we were quickly escorted out of the building, unable to bask in the glory. Because no matter how ill we were, twelve-year-olds weren't allowed in a bar.

We were the highlight of the show, and both Ice-T's camp and Tone Lōc's friends immediately bum-rushed us outside, asking about working together. I couldn't believe what I was hearing as one industry professional after another came up and told us how great we were. It felt like every guy who approached us was vying to take us under his wing. The offer that stood out most was from Donald D, a rapper himself and a member of the Zulu Nation and Ice-T's Rhyme Syndicate crew, who was allegedly cowriting a lot of Ice-T's raps. Donald told us he would help develop our act, along with contributions from other Rhyme Syndicate members like DJ Aladdin, Evil E, Hen Gee, and eventually Ice-T—so in essence, we would become their hip-hop apprentices. Soon after that show, we distanced ourselves from Demetrius, who admitted that we might need someone with a little more experience. Although he was the first real source of encouragement for my talents, I never saw or worked with Demetrius again.

Starting that next week, my mom would drive us out to Hollywood on weekends to hang with Syndicate's gangster rappers. We would sit around Donald D's studio, recording on tracks for the first time and learning how to properly write songs. It was like if Def Jam ran a summer camp. At first, my mom would stick around as we worked, fearful that if she left it would quickly turn into a scene from *New Jack City*. The Syndicate guys would laugh, telling her not to worry and to let us have some creative space. Funny enough, the one time she did leave me alone to pick up lunch, a guy showed me his gun and Donald D taught me what a condom was.

About two months into working together, and with a few songs now under our belt, Rickye and I were starting to feel confident, so Donald set up a photo shoot to get some promotional shots. He explained the importance of these pictures: they'd be the first thing prospective fans would see as music started to roll out. He emphasized how critical it was to get them right, especially since I was a new face to rap, and even pushed our parents to make sure we got our "beauty rest" the night before. Rickye and I were excited, considering that the moment we had formed the group at our school's pep rally, we'd predicted what our first photo shoot would look like. When we arrived at Donald's apartment the day of the shoot, it felt nothing like our prophecy.

Two weeks had passed since the infamous 1992 Los Angeles riots, all sparked by racial tension from the Rodney King verdict. There were days of looting, arson, and fights, spreading across most of the city, even causing the National Guard to protect our local shopping mall all the way in Woodland Hills. Fifty-three people were killed, over two thousand were injured, and there was in excess of a billion dollars' worth of damage to the inner city. So when Donald informed us that we'd be driving around South Central LA, taking pictures in front of burned-down businesses and rubble, Rickye and I were visibly uncomfortable. We both called the suburbs our home, and I knew as a middle-class white kid, this was probably too much. I expressed concern to my parents as the edginess of the photo shoot escalated, but Donald assured us we didn't have anything to worry about. He claimed to be our "hood pass" and promised this was the way to go. When all was said and done, he was wrong.

The scrapped photo shoot depicts Kidd X and me in the middle of South Central Los Angeles, holding bats and wearing beanies and surrounded by debris and ashes. I still have nightmares about the confused, and angry, looks we got from passersby. Donald directed us from behind the camera to look tough, even having me stare down the camera with a frown, an unbuttoned shirt, and a baseball bat in one setup. As if that wasn't bad enough, he had us pose with crowbars, pretending to break open the window of a deserted liquor store. Despite his enthusiasm, I

Oh, you thought I was kidding?

realized that our ideas for X-tra Large didn't match Donald's. I begrudgingly posed for the photos, but I explained to Rickye on the way home that this might not be for me. I realized we had picked the wrong management company and longed for the days of Demetrius. Even at twelve, I knew, like a prepubescent Pitchfork critic, that this "lacked credibility."

We did record a few more songs for the Syndicate guys (including a Christmas track I hope no one ever releases, even ironically), and I ended up only meeting Ice-T once in passing, so over time everything started to feel slightly weird—the start of a consistent pattern in my hip-hop career. Once the mainstream controversy over Body Count's "Cop Killer" took center stage, a duo of dancing and rapping interracial kids in suits didn't seem like a good fit for Rhyme Syndicate anyway. Donald D swore he knew that gangster talk from innocent young boys would sell, but I just didn't want to know who was buying.

Only a few months after we met him, Donald D abruptly stopped returning our calls, which were getting more and more frustrated on our end. Somewhat scarred, I would cautiously wait years to professionally rap again. Our dreams of becoming famous disappeared for the time being, and X-tra Large once again became two unknown students who bragged about having huge dongs in Calabasas, California, the hometown of the Kardashians.

The only things that had hits in this picture were the baseball bats.

"KILLIN' AT THE PLAYGROUND" LYRICS, 1992

(written by 12-year-old Jensen Karp)

(intro)

This one is dedicated to all the mental hip-hop midgets,
  Another Sad Creation . . .
Swinging the trigger of the gat, small little young guys make
  you wanna shoot that,
XL is in the house to set the record straight, finally ABC gets to
  see their fate,

We hate to see you dancing and jumping around, I shoot my
    gat at the playground,[1]
You know what I'm saying . . . awww, chorus time.
(Baby, we can do it.)
Killin' at the playground, it's the K to the I to the double L-I-N,
    killin' at the playground is what I'm saying.

Now that we got rid of the intro,
It's about time we loosen up and let go, boomin' out the stereo
    Dolby style,
If you don't like it return it for a free trial,
Kill at will, everybody's at a standstill,
Before you get another top-ten hit, you better grow,
Chris, Mark, Red, Dave, Ro.
Ro?
Where the hell'd you get your name?
Were your parents watching hours on the aisles of *Soul Train*?
You may think you're playing our game,
Ha ha, I bet Lil' Dave ain't just a clever name,[2]
We see you at the AMAs, lookin' like straight gangsters,
But you're just damn pranksters,
Boyz II Men wins, you wish,
Like Cypress Hill said, you dug your own ditch, ditch, ditch,
    ditch.
(Baby, we can do it.)
Killin' at the playground, it's the K to the I to the double L-I-N,
    killin' at the playground is what I'm saying.

---

1   Always a stickler for authenticity in rap, I also looked to shock or cre-
    ate a stark comparison between my words and my age/innocent look.
    Mentioning a gun is something I never did once I started really "song-
    writing," but I knew this would catch any casual listener's attention at
    twelve, so I approached it like writing an action movie or a parody of
    gangster rap in the '90s.
2   Dick joke #1.

Hey, Dallas, get your hands off TLC,
I want 'em saved up for the Younger MC,[3]
Always playing basketball, like to see you shoot,
You could be Spud Webb and I could Manute,
You're about three-two, if you're lucky three-three,
I'll still block the hell outta you, it doesn't matter to me,
I'll be sinking every shot, makin' triple doubles,
ABC—you're in trouble.

(Baby, you can do it.)
Iesha, Iesha, don't wanna meet cha,
Iesha, Iesha, don't wanna meet cha,
Iesha, Iesha, don't wanna meet cha.

Iesha, I had her, she's nothing,
We wouldn't be called Large if we didn't have somethin',[4]
To make her feel nice we're saving up our pennies,
All I had to do was take the tramp to Denny's,[5]
Alright, we're being harsh, alright, we might not mean it,
We might end up being friends, I guess that's how we'll leave it,
For now we say PEACE, we're out the door,
Call us a little later if you wanna hear some more.

---

3   I was going by the name Younger MC, a play on the then popular and
    Grammy-winning rapper of "Bust a Move." It was the first of many
    bad monikers I would sift through before finally landing on Hot Karl,
    the worst of them all. Also, I'm saying I would fuck all of TLC here,
    and I couldn't even produce semen yet.

4   Dick joke #2, and the biggest reaction we got at the live show. Watch-
    ing the video now, I did a weird "grab my dick" dance while spitting
    the line, which made my parents super uncomfortable/proud.

5   I remember meeting Donald D that night, and him saying he thought
    Demetrius wrote this line for me. He said it was too "gangster" for a
    twelve-year-old. I told him I wrote the song alone and I'd never let
    anyone touch my lyrics. Ever. Donald looked at me with a genuine
    need for an answer and asked, "Who the fuck are you, kid?"

2

(818) MILE

AFTER my brief experience with X-tra Large, my love for hip-hop never waned, but my interest in the industry itself straight-up disappeared. Through the rest of middle school, I realized it was easier to blend in with my classmates if I stopped rhyming loudly near my locker or trying to debate with random people whether Cappadonna was an actual Wu-Tang member.

In 1994, when I finally got to high school, I hoped things would change with age. I assumed that with puberty my classmates might also gain a tolerance for other people's interests, or at least notice the revolutionary work taking place in the rap world during an era now widely considered its golden age. I was wrong. My school's principal asked me to perform at a school dance on a bill that would include my grade's resident rock band—coincidentally the younger brothers of eventual hometown heroes Incubus—and I happily obliged. Two songs in, the entire gymnasium was chanting "Fuck rap!" and I walked off the stage, defeated. I decided to accept that because I was an average white kid, I wasn't allowed to participate in rap music, a ridiculous idea driven home by the school's white quarterback, who asked me why I even tried to write rhymes, since "rap is for blacks."

Sure, I look as suburban as a cul-de-sac, but I was low-key furious that the photographer couldn't get my Ice Cube Predator shirt into the frame.

I mostly kept the passion to myself from that point on, but every so often, when a student would transfer from a public high school in the city and claim to rap, someone would wake me from my slumber. I'd be forced to battle him and embarrass the transfer beyond healing, then return to my cage and focus on the baseball team or after-school tutoring. I was basically Woody Harrelson in *White Men Can't Jump*, but for rapping in front of wealthy white kids.

Since the early days of ridiculing Another Bad Creation in *X-tra Large*, I always knew battling was where I was my most comfortable. I excelled when freestyling off the cuff and disrespecting people's skills, wardrobes, and hairlines. I'd even talk about moms if I knew it would make me the undisputed winner. I was just as influenced by Don Rickles as I was by Grand Puba. But finding a battle wasn't quite as easy for me as winning them.

Since I didn't have any classmates who shared my desire to attend rap concerts in the 818 area code, I had to make friends from nearby cities just to drive me to shows where groups like A Tribe Called Quest or Tha Alkaholiks performed. I knew that in those concert parking lots, or somewhere in the audience, I might find a cypher—a spontaneous circle of MCs taking turns rapping—and that it could turn into a battle. At one house party, when I was fifteen years old, in the less affluent and more rap-friendly neighborhood of Canoga Park, I went head to head with a rapper named Frog. Of the dozens of infamous stories going around about him, none were about how polite or nonviolent he was. I remember one tale about how he knocked every tooth out of a kid's mouth during an altercation at a pickup basketball game—every single one. He supposedly counted before he left. But he was a rapper who reportedly had some skill, so despite my parents' investment in retainers throughout my childhood, I had to put my teeth on the line.

Whatever fear I had about battling Frog took a backseat to adrenaline the moment I walked up to the DJ table and started rhyming into the microphone. I knew he depended on intimidation to level the playing field between us, but in duels like these I felt completely invincible. Over the instrumental to Group Home's "Livin' Proof," and wearing a brand-new Alonzo Mourning Hornets jersey I had ordered from an Eastbay catalogue the week before, I systematically degraded every aspect of his existence. I attacked everything from his dirty sneakers to his dismal dental records, noting, "So many pearly whites in your mouth, good grief / Even a shark would say 'That's too many teeth.'" The audience laughed loudly at every punch line and winced after every insult, while Frog sat and took each one with the closest thing to a smirk he could muster. When it was his turn to rap, he was adequate enough to avoid boos, but forgettable enough to make the outcome indisputable. When the dust cleared, I had beaten Frog hands down, and although I'd shown no mercy in mocking him, he seemed to take the defeat in good spirits. He shook my hand, smiled, and then left the party.

Happy with the aftermath, I went on to celebrate my victory with a few friends who couldn't believe the degree of Frog's humility. But ten minutes later, while one partygoer was regurgitating his favorite lines from the battle back to me, out of the corner of my eye, I saw Frog return, now wearing a Jason mask and holding a machete. AN ACTUAL MACHETE. He didn't run back into the party or even seem angry (something I convinced myself of despite not being able to see his face), but there he was, a man in a serial-killer mask, flashing a big-ass knife and calmly stalking the exit. I didn't want to show any fear, assuming he could probably smell it like a pit bull—I also knew that kind of reaction would hurt me in a future rematch—so I just politely asked the homeowner if there was a second exit. I snuck out a back door, walked about seven city blocks to the closest pay phone, and called my mom for a ride. Frog could have just been messing around, and I may have been the Valley's most promising rapper, but at that exact moment, I was a scrawny dweeb who had just run for his life after a battle so his mom could pick him up outside of a Vons supermarket. Still, despite my physical retreat, I had another win, even if I forever had to watch my back for a vengeful masked man with a sword.

The Frog battle wasn't the only time my mom had to rescue me after I rapped at a party. Soon after this victory, my Canoga Park High School friends invited me to DJ with them at an all-ages nightclub. In addition to rapping, I gravitated toward the world of turntables and vinyl, since it was considered a core element of hip-hop and gave me another excuse to look for new rap songs all the time. Also, it was an easy way to make sure I'd get the chance to rap at any party, since I'd be the guy controlling the music and, more important, the mic.

DJ Just Hit Puberty on the ones and twos!

This specific party would take place in Van Nuys, which, like most neighborhoods, has its good and bad areas. Make no mistake about it, though: this party was definitely in a bad area. My father had sold cars in Van Nuys for most of my life, so I was good at determining the neighborhood's safety as you traveled through it. I knew that if I told my parents where the party was, they would've forbidden me from going, even scoffed at the mere *thought* of me attending. But since hip-hop parties were hard to come by in Calabasas, and I was genuinely infatuated with being around rap at all times, I decided I had to lie to my mom and dad.

While some of my friends misinformed their parents about their whereabouts nightly, I had never lied to mine before. I mostly agreed with their stance on things, and, honestly, I was kind of a square. But I knew I'd get the chance to rap at this party, and maybe even battle, so I decided I had to approach things a little differently. And just like that, a good kid went bad. I told my parents the party was in Agoura, an always-safe neighboring area best known for its horse property. I never expected my parents to find out the truth, let alone witness firsthand the depth of their son's lie.

The night ended up being pretty awesome. Sure, a party in Calabasas might play "Tootsee Roll" by 69 Boyz or even "Funkdafied" from Da Brat, but that night in Van Nuys, we all took turns spinning less commercial records like "Wrekonize" by Smif-N-Wessun, "Drink Away the Pain" by Mobb Deep and Q-Tip, and almost every song from *Only Built 4 Cuban Linx*, the recently released debut solo album from Wu-Tang member Raekwon. Some of my friends even breakdanced. I also got to rap when one guy stepped up to battle. Unfortunately, he wasn't very serious, marking the night's only small letdown. Everything was working out, especially since I made sure to pay close attention to my beeper, just in case my parents wanted to check in. I doubted they could tell the difference between a pay phone in Van Nuys and a pay phone in Agoura, so I didn't see any way this night could backfire.

As the party calmed down at midnight, I decided I wanted to play some R&B records, so I started for my car to get the designated "Slow Jams" crate, worried only about what SWV song I would play first. I didn't get too far, as one partygoer near the door warned me, "You might not want to go out there, people are about to fight." I thanked her for the warning and turned back to tell my friends, when I heard three loud bangs. I had never heard gunshots before in my life, but I immediately knew what was happening. The entire party hit the floor, ducking for cover, as I ran to take shelter near the DJ booth. I heard more blasts—five or six in a row this time. Mista Grimm's "Indo Smoke" continued to play loudly, creating a weird soundtrack among the screams and explosions. I sat terrified, looking up every few seconds to see what was happening near the door, and caught a glimpse of someone walking through the party with a gun in the air. I assumed it was security, but wasn't sure. Another shot. One of my friends rolled over to where I was huddled and decided to sit directly in front of me, promising that a bullet would hit him first, an act of kindness I still tear up about. It was chaos and it felt like it would never end. One drunk girl near us yelled, "Who cares? We're all going to die anyway." I felt my pager vibrate. It was my mom.

When the gunshots stopped, people started to emerge from

their hiding places. I noticed a group of guys near the entrance frantically attending to their friend, who was bleeding profusely from his head. There was no way he was still alive. Some of my friends took off before the cops arrived, but between my heavy DJ equipment and an illogical fear that I'd be framed for the murder, I stuck around for questioning. It became a locked-down crime scene, and since we were told that getting statements from every single clubgoer would take around five hours, I knew there was no way I could hide this from my parents. I asked a policeman if I could use the pay phone to call my mom and dad. He looked at me with a straight face and asked, "What the hell are you doing here, son?"

When my mom answered the phone, I immediately yelled, "Don't be mad at me," which is always a foolproof way to make sure your parents will be mad at you. I told her the story and gave her the real address of the club, along with the only information I had at the time: we'd probably be getting out around 6:00 a.m. She was quiet and listened to every word, meaning she was more concerned than angry, which hurt even more. My parents left the house immediately. Around 4:00 a.m., police brought me into a room with two other randomly selected partygoers to give our accounts of what we saw. One of the guys I was grouped with wasted no time in divulging that he could point out the gunman. He described what he looked like and how the gunfight started, and also said he saw someone "throw a grenade." The cops tried their hardest not to laugh, but it was obvious they didn't believe him. Yet he kept repeating the same thing: "I saw a grenade, man." They asked us a few more questions, then cleared us to leave, knowing that if we *were* the actual gang members involved in the shooting, we'd have taken off hours ago. They also informed me that I wouldn't be able to get my car until the next afternoon, since it was only feet away from where the victim had been shot. They added, "You're lucky though; the car next to yours has bullet holes."

I walked outside and immediately saw my mom and dad, terrified in their robes, talking to cops and holding our family Shih Tzu. Not exactly a scene from *Boyz n the Hood*. We didn't talk much on the ride home, but I did tell them about the grenade guy. They didn't think it was as funny as I did.

When I woke up the next afternoon, my parents went into detail about their disappointment. They knew why I'd lied, admitting they would've never let me go to that party, but were still surprised by my dishonesty. I repeatedly apologized, saying this was the first time I'd ever lied to them and promising it would never happen again. They knew this type of behavior was out of character, so they decided not to punish me, understanding that the trauma I'd gone through most likely scared me off attending another party in that area. They were right. They drove me to pick up my car from the crime scene and then to the closest police station to claim my seized DJ equipment. In the end, I knew what I'd done was wrong and was happy to have such a supportive and caring duo for parents.

That night my mom and I watched the news coverage of the shooting, now being described as a standoff between rival gangs that left one man dead and a few injured. No arrests had been made, and there were no credible leads. But at the end of the

KANYE WEST OWES ME $300

story, as a small footnote, the news anchor explained that the shooting created standstill traffic in Van Nuys for hours when police blocked off the street after finding a grenade near the club. The bomb squad was called in to investigate, and the grenade was deemed "a dud." The newscaster joked, "That's lucky for everyone at that party, isn't it?" I was immediately grounded for two weeks.

———

A much safer battle from my high-school years involved an aspiring rapper whose real name I don't think anyone knew. The biracial transfer student was given the nickname Toothbrush because he walked around campus with, you guessed it, a toothbrush in his mouth. Its purpose wasn't to tend to the dental hygiene that my prior victim, Frog, clearly ignored. He instead sported it for the same reason Nelly wore that stupid Band-Aid on his face: for the sake of fashion. Twenty years later, toothbrushes and Band-Aids are yet to catch on, and for good reason: they both look really dumb. Toothbrush fancied himself to be more than just a trendsetter, however. He also believed he was a freestyle rapper, a title I too had publicly claimed that month, when I turned sixteen and ordered a personalized license plate that read FRSTYLE. Since most people in Calabasas thought the plate meant I was a swimmer (I was not), I knew it was the safest way I could represent my passion in this atmosphere. But when the student body figured they could pit me against the cocky new kid with a dental utensil in his mouth, and I heard from multiple sources that Toothbrush was proclaiming he could beat me, I knew what I had to do.

The battle was set for lunchtime; we would meet at the school's upstairs quad, right near the lockers. The news traveled rapidly. Kids whispered the details to each other in the hallways, making sure everyone would be present for the anticipated bloodshed. My peers may not have talked about, or praised, my abilities often, but when they did, they agreed I was nothing to fuck with.

When the time came, I was the first to arrive at the designated area. I quietly paced, listening to my Walkman and going through possible rhyme schemes in my head.

Chew on a toothbrush / get crushed . . . (no)

Is it that you have plaque? / oral fixation, sucking on a ball sack . . . (no)

Not the answer / transfer . . . (maybe)

Here to explain / why no one knows your name . . . (eh)

When I eventually looked up from my lyrical meditation, I saw two hundred kids huddled around me, ready for the throwdown. Toothbrush arrived a few minutes late, noticed the crowd, and looked stressed. I didn't give him an opportunity to back out, quickly setting up how the contest would go down. I announced we'd have two rounds, with a possible tiebreaker, and since I considered the high school to be my home turf, I'd go first, an idea that Toothbrush quickly agreed to.

I started slow, focusing on my own skills with jabs like, "We know I'm gonna win, we can state that shit as fact / Like Biff Tannen made a bet from a future almanac." The crowd grimaced, catching the *Back to the Future* reference and realizing I wasn't there to play games. As I gained momentum, it became obvious that Toothbrush knew his days were done, as he slumped lower and lower with each put-down. "If we compared this battle to LL and Kool Moe Dee / I'm LL Cool J, you're a kid who bought his CD." He never expected this type of venom from a kid sporting reading glasses, corduroys, and New Balance. I knew he was against the ropes, so I pushed harder with an even more intense string of insults. "You challenged me to a battle after talking lots of smack / Since you're new to this school I hope you didn't unpack / 'Cause when this is said and done I promise you just one fact / Whatever school you transferred from, well I'm sending you back!" The audience hit a decibel level that kept me from hearing my next line. Like when I performed "Killin' at the Playground" at Club Spice years earlier, I entered an unstoppable zone. Even if Rakim had magically stepped out of a nearby locker as my next opponent, I would've been like, "Sure, and who's after him?"

As I wound down my first round, I compared our battle to the Mike Tyson/Peter McNeeley fight that had happened just days before, where Tyson, in his first fight out of prison, pummeled a scrub in eighty-nine seconds. "When this shit is done, we won't be friends, do you feel me? / That's like Mike Tyson making plans with Pete McNeeley." I knew I had landed the knockout blow. I was an animal at feeding time, finally able to display the skills I had been perfecting over the past two years mostly in private, or at least miles away from my high school campus. Still fueled by adrenaline, I stared at Toothbrush, waiting for him to rap, as the entire crowd sat in silent anticipation. When he did start, I immediately wished he hadn't.

Toothbrush wasn't only a bad rapper; he was hardly intelligible. He mumbled and coughed and made up words. It genuinely felt like he had never rapped before. The crowd that had just celebrated every word I said now laughed uncontrollably at his attempt. And not the good type of laughter. I felt bad, immediately realizing Toothbrush wasn't being an asshole; he was just trying to seem cool and getting called out for it. I don't think he realized how competitive this battle would actually be, or had even been sure it would happen. I looked like a member of the school's math club, and it's not like we went to the school in *Fame*, where kids musically competed every day. He was in over his head.

Right when I was about to step in to stop the bleeding and shake his hand, I felt someone grab at my neck and start violently pulling me from the circle. My instinct was to fight back, assuming Toothbrush's friends had just jumped me—a cardinal sin in battling—but I quickly realized I was being manhandled by an adult. Luckily, right before I started punching wildly, I saw it was a teacher, who believed he had just broken up a brawl. I tried to explain the innocent reality—we were just rapping—but the teacher assured me I couldn't get out of this one. As he dragged me out of the crowd and toward the principal's office, where I was convinced I would be suspended for the first time in my academic career, Toothbrush jumped in front of the teacher and blurted out, "He's telling the truth." The teacher, now somewhat embarrassed, noticed everyone around him saying the same thing and decided to let me go. He admitted he had no idea what we were talking about, genuinely asking, "Why would you be rapping at each other?" as he tried to decipher exactly what this Jets vs. Sharks musical nonsense was. Eventually, he told the crowd to disperse, and everyone calmly went their separate ways. I went to thank Toothbrush, but he ignored me and went to eat lunch alone.

Even though the win was painfully lopsided, I was proud of the newest notch in my undefeated belt, especially since it would become part of my high school's folklore for the next few years. However, when I realized I hadn't seen Toothbrush for weeks after the battle, I started asking around. I learned that he transferred soon thereafter, returning to a nearby alternative school for troubled youth, which bummed me out. No matter how adamantly I rhymed about him leaving Calabasas High, I didn't actually want him to leave. That was always my favorite part about battle rapping; you can say whatever you want for the sake of winning, but there's an understanding that when it's over, you respect your opponent. You don't mean 90 percent of the shit you say. It's all in good fun. I wondered if I would ever be able to explain this to Toothbrush.

Years later, when a coworker realized he knew someone I'd gone to high school with, I didn't recognize the name. Like many failed attempts at the Name Game, I figured that would be the end of our discussion. But when he explained, "He said you'd know him as Toothbrush," I lit up. I wanted to know everything. What was Toothbrush doing now? Was he doing well?

Did he bring up the battle? Has he been slowly stalking me in hopes of eventually murdering me and scattering my fingers and toes throughout our high school's campus? He informed me that Toothbrush was actually recording music, now part of a group mostly focused on R&B. When my name was mentioned in passing, he told our mutual friend that he'd transferred from my high school because "kids didn't really like him," but gave no other details.

I felt relieved that Toothbrush was doing well, putting to rest any fears that the thrashing he took that day sent him into a tailspin of shame that ruined his life forever. Maybe he'd even forgotten it happened. I asked the guy to say hello for me, forcing my coworker to laugh and admit he was surprised I was being so nice. "He said he killed you in a battle and that you never rapped at your high school again," the coworker said with a shit-eating grin on his face. Toothbrush even assumed it was probably one of the worst days of my life. I felt my competitive rage return, ready to pace angrily and come up with a dozen new disses, then roam the globe looking for a man performing R&B and chewing on an old toothbrush. But now an adult, I calmed down by remembering that he'd also stopped the teacher from dragging me into the principal's office, saving me from another awkward situation with my already-suspicious parents. I laughed and said, "Yeah, well, you win some, you lose some," and walked away, knowing damn well that "Hey, Toothbrush, I have a big correction" easily rhymes with "made you quickly transfer schools like it was witness protection," and that he'd better not test me again.

3

THE BEST PHONE CALL

MY rap career in high school was sporadic after the Toothbrush battle, even when some of my classmates finally started gravitating toward mainstream hits like Tupac's *Me Against the World* or Warren G's "Regulate." I'd rap over beats on an eight-track recorder at home and stockpile lyrics for when I was challenged again, but my surroundings just didn't allow for much else. I retreated into hip-hop hiding, accepting it'd be difficult to find anyone in Calabasas as passionate about rap music as I was, lost among headbangers in Megadeth T-shirts and surfers blasting Sublime in the high-school parking lot.

It wasn't until I went to college that I found myself surrounded by a more culturally diverse, and accepting, crowd. It was 1998, and the Abercrombie scene had just started to fully embrace hip-hop without judgment. College parties played credible rap songs like Big Pun's "Still Not a Player" and tracks from Jay Z's *In My Lifetime, Vol. 1*, and I was finally able to connect with people who celebrated hip-hop in the same way I did. Jeep Cherokees driving down fraternity row were no longer *just* playing Dave Matthews Band's *Crash*; they also blasted The Lox, even if they had to turn it down at stoplights.

Here I am with my mom and dad the weekend I moved into my freshman dorm. I was happy to have them both there, especially since my mom blocked my wallet chain in this photo.

And in a more welcoming place, on the campus of USC, I began to feel more confident about showing off my surprising talents. I started performing wherever I could in college, whether it was at campus coffee-shop open mics or frat parties. I didn't quite know yet what role rap would play in my life, if any, but I knew I was developing a distinct voice and was yet to lose a battle. Unlike any rapper before me, I was wearing slick button-up shirts and slacks, a style that was slightly influenced by the movie *Swingers* but that also made me look like the coolest member of an R&B-themed bowling league. As I reentered the circuit, I was having consistent fun with music for the first time since the riot photo shoot and searching for anyone willing to go to battle.

One night around this time, at LA's now defunct Key Club, I took on almost a dozen different MCs onstage and devastated them one by one, until I was alone, daring members of the audience to step up and press their luck. No one else would take the challenge. Earlier that day I may have studied for hours on end, hoping to pass a Spanish 201 class, but like Sylvester Stallone turning his hat around in *Over the Top*, that night I became a real competitor, unwilling to be overpowered by anyone.

Seeing a white guy in a battle was still a rarity in this pre-Eminem era—even if nowadays it's the norm—and I was the only Caucasian onstage that night, making me look like Christian Laettner on the 1992 USA Dream Team. You'd think looking like the Verizon guy would have made me an easy target, but when the audience expects very little from you, it's simple to blow their minds. Also, every opponent's joke about my appearance came off as predictable and hacky. You can only exclaim "Look at this Jewish nerd!" once, because I'd extinguish it with "You think I'm a Jewish nerd? Ha, that's funny / Who the fuck you think manages your favorite rapper's money?"

My parents were also attending most of my scheduled battles, something I assumed I didn't share with other rappers of the day, like Mos Def or JT Money. I remember seeing my father move closer and closer to the stage one night as I racked up victories, assuming my verbal attacks would result in an eventual beatdown that he'd have to break up. Most rappers had a posse of bodyguards; I had a nervous dad. When he saw everyone hug in the end, rap music became even more confusing to him.

Once 1999 came around, I started to become slightly obsessed with the craft. I would sit in my dorm room for hours, with five or six magazines opened to random pages around me, picking apart each photo with specific freestyle lines, pretending they were all willing participants in a fictitious battle. Then I'd flip all the pages and start over. I treated battling like a sport and pretended a prizefight loomed in the distance. It was my *Rocky* montage, and I was getting strong now.

When I was challenged by an MC named Titanic, I was able to quickly conjure the line, "Not even sure why you showed up, when it's obvious you'll lose / They call you Titanic 'cause hundreds of men went down on you." And just hours after the famous golfer died in an airplane accident, I freestyled to a less talented rival, "Stop now before you get hurt / Your whole style should never take flight like Payne Stewart." My reputation as the college's on-call rapper started to build, and so did the body count of MCs I left behind. When I went up against a guy named Marc Luna and felt the audience slowly turning against me, I realized something remarkable and spit one of the most creative lines I ever freestyled: "Now I know you got lines and you think that you the man / But keep in mind your name backwards spells out Anul Cram." I dropped the mic. He never recovered.

And compared to high school, the response to my abilities at USC was incredible. Girls started to show interest after seeing me onstage. I'd come home from battles with messages from sorority girls wanting to hang out after getting my number from the university directory. Fraternities were fighting over me, hoping I'd eventually be rapping at their house parties and making fun of rival frats. What once was my embarrassing parlor trick was now my ticket to popularity.

Battling at a house party, telling my opponent that although he seems like a nice fellow, I think I'm a more competent MC. I'm kidding: I'm probably saying he's a shitty rapper and has a tiny dick.

When not in competition, battling was seeping into my real life. It was hard to break the feeling, like when you play *Grand Theft Auto* for hours, then have to drive your actual car. I had to bite my tongue when a store clerk looked like "a homeless Vince Vaughn" or when a classmate had bad enough acne that I could rhyme "second-place fail" with "checkered face Braille." But no matter how hard I trained, I never could have imagined the career I was building up endurance for.

Although battle rapping was my true passion at the time, I didn't really see how I could earn a living being mean through rhyme. (Some competitions would offer a few hundred dollars as prize money, but it's not like So So Def Records set up a booth at USC's job fair seeking "sick lyricists.") Instead, I had attended USC with the hope that I could turn my interest in writing into a Hollywood career. When I was a teen, in between memorizing Black Moon and Organized Konfusion lyrics, Martin Scorsese and Coen brothers movies captivated me just as much as the videos on *Yo! MTV Raps*.

So in an attempt to work in that industry, during my junior year I secured an internship as a director's assistant on *Viva Rock Vegas*, the prequel to the live-action *Flintstones* movie. You probably haven't seen it, and that makes sense, but I treated that shit like I was in charge of delivering camera lenses to Orson Welles on the set of *Citizen Kane*. I would take a full schedule of college classes in the morning, then speed down to Universal Studios, where production was centered, then back to USC or Hollywood to find a battle. No one at *Viva Rock Vegas*, or any of the contacts I was making in the movie industry, knew anything about my double life as a lyrical destroyer, and I liked it that way. I was nervous they'd hear me insulting some poor kid's mother for being "an example of human waste / Give or take eight pounds, she's *Hairspray*-era Ricki Lake," then fire me for being an insensitive asshole.

Now imagine me telling this part of the story huddled around a fire with a bone pierced through my nose, because it's important to note that back in 1999, there were no iPods or satellite radios yet. Because I had a daily commute to the *Flintstones* gig, I was forced to listen to terrestrial radio. Yes, with the commercials and everything. Radio stations like Power 106 and The Beat in LA, and Hot 97 in New York, set the trends in the urban-music landscape because they were basically the only shows in town. This was especially the case in Los Angeles, where I found myself gridlocked in traffic for a majority of this drive. Regional captivity made listening to the radio a big deal, and that's how I got a second chance at rap stardom.

—

Created by West Coast radio personalities Nick and Eric Vidal, DJ brothers collectively known as the Baka Boyz, the World Famous Roll Call was a daily on-air competition where four or five aspiring MCs would call in and compete against each other with witty battle-rap lines over an instrumental beat. The listeners would then vote on who came back the following weekday as champion, and that winner's reign would continue until they were defeated. It started in the early '90s and became a staple on Los Angeles radio, then spread to other cities, including New York, where it was also incredibly popular. Supposedly, rapper The Game competed when he was young, way before he ever told us "How We Do."

As a kid, a little bit before the X-tra Large era, I was going by the name Shucks (a reference to the "Aw shucks" vibe I gave off to rappers before I devoured their souls) and had started competing in the Roll Call occasionally, later actually winning once in ninth grade. But the real battle back then was against my nerves, so much so that you'd hear the tremble in my voice when

I rhymed. I had no problem stepping onstage to open for Ice-T's crew as a child, but I had given the Roll Call such importance that I was terrified. My friend Ali had strung together a few consecutive wins once, and I couldn't have been more jealous. But my dreams of finding stardom through a somewhat forgettable radio contest had faded away once I made the decision to focus on fitting in at high school. I had never really thought about entering the fold again, but when I heard the Baka Boyz announce they were looking for Roll Call contestants on my way home from work in 1999, after I'd watched Stephen Baldwin play Barney Rubble for hours on end, I knew it was time for my trembling, and now slightly deeper, voice to be heard once again.

When I was younger, it had been almost impossible to get through on the station's hotline once they started requesting Roll Call challengers. In all honesty, I spent maybe 15 percent of sixth grade listening to a busy signal. So when I got through on my first attempt that day, almost ten years later, I was startled. The show's producer, J-Love, who had now been screening high quantities of shitty rappers for years, answered with just the order, "Rap now!" I quickly fell into line, freestyling out, "Any other rapper is getting jumped over like hurdles / I keep it underground, next to those four mutant turtles." I started another bar but was abruptly put on hold without a response. It left me slightly nervous that he had recognized that fearful preteen who sounded like a rapping Katharine Hepburn and hung up, assuming I would crack on live radio.

He did eventually come back to ask my name, and that's the exact moment I froze. I hadn't planned on the station picking up the phone, let alone inquiring about my name, so I stumbled with the answer. I knew that if I said Jensen and then fucked up, everyone would know who it was. I'd hardly be able to hide behind my strange name. I'd throw away any credibility I had built in campus competitions, and kids from Calabasas would finally have the validation they needed for pushing me to hang up the mic in high school. Had I known how big of a deal this one decision would become, I would've made damn sure the first thing that came to mind wasn't "Hot Karl," a slang term for shitting on someone's chest during sex.

And just like that, I was Hot Karl. It was a dumb term I had heard thrown around a frat house by dudes, right in the mix with other acts you won't find in the *Kama Sutra* like a Dirty Sanchez or Donkey Punch. Although chosen randomly, the name actually made sense. My whole life, after I annihilated rapper after rapper, people would say, "You just shit on that guy!" I had now unintentionally picked a moniker that confirmed their claim. Within seconds of rechristening myself, I was live on air, going back and forth with the Baka Boyz as the last contestant of the day.

The Roll Call had a call-and-response format, where the DJs initially asked your name with their own set rap ("One for the trouble, two for the rhyme / It's the Roll Call, who's on that line?") and you responded with your own two lines as an answer. Then the DJs asked for your location ("That sounds cool and that may be / Where you calling from, what city?") and you would rap back with another two bars, somehow incorporating your hometown into the lyrics. The goal was to be as skilled as possible, using humorous punch lines to assert your dominance over whoever else was rapping that day. Obviously, you couldn't see what your competition looked like, so you had to be creative with your attacks. I knew a little rust would be unavoidable for my return to the Roll Call, but also figured I'd be better than any contestant they'd find, as long as I kept the nerves at bay.

So I wasn't surprised when I was crowned that day's winner with my big line, "I can take you down with many styles fast or slow mo / 'Cause my skills are more 'N Sync than those five singing homos." It wasn't anything to brag about, especially with its embarrassingly homophobic insult, which is a cornerstone of battle rap and one of the many archaic practices still seen in the culture today (I see you too, misogyny). As gross as it was, I was coming back the next day for a possible second win, a goal that seemed attainable now, especially since they gave me a private winner's phone number to avoid the dreaded busy signal of my childhood.

I was ready for whatever competition the Roll Call would bring my way, but didn't expect much to come of my new endeavor. At most, it was a goof, something to laugh about in a few days when I was dethroned and back to focusing on making endless copies of the *Flintstones* script. I didn't plan on telling any of my college friends about the win, or on turning it into a tool to bring attention to a music career. I just thought it seemed like fun. Even when I completed an entire week of consecutive victories, starting a streak rarely heard on the Roll Call, I still prepared myself for it to end at any moment. But it didn't. I may not have seen it coming, but this was the start of something big. Very big. Even bigger than *Viva Rock Vegas*.

4

MACK 10'S BRIEFCASE

BEFORE I knew it, two weeks had passed, I had ten wins under my belt, and I was becoming a bit of a radio phenomenon. My voice had stopped trembling, and I wasn't just winning; I was pulverizing rappers with perfect wins, instances where every caller voted for the same contestant. The Baka Boyz started advertising the Roll Call earlier in the day, replaying my appearances with a promise that "LA's most talked-about rapper" would be competing later, which made me laugh while I was fetching coffee on a movie that would later be nominated for four Razzies. The Baka Boyz quickly took an interest in learning more about Hot Karl, uncharacteristically interviewing me after victories, but I continued to keep my identity secret, mostly in fear that my bosses would find out, but also in case I eventually embarrassed myself. Eric and Nick were even taking bets from listeners on whether I was black or white.

I'd usually perform the Roll Call from my dorm room, getting home just in time from class or work, but on some late *Flint-stones* nights, I would have to lock myself in the script closet and hope no one walked by to hear me scream rhyming insults into an office phone. The Baka Boyz started to have me freestyle to an instrumental of their choosing for extended amounts of time after my wins, forcing me to use an indoor voice to avoid suspicion from nearby coworkers. It truly was a pathetic sight, as the phone's cord would travel from my desk right into a closed closet, like I was dialing 911 and hiding from home invaders, or a teenage girl talking to a boy her parents forbade her from seeing. I was lucky my competition would never see my hiding place, because "You ain't the hottest / You should just come out

until I tattoo Karl on my dick, keep my
name out of your mouth!
Marlee Matlin as you hype
now
Dexter Manley = Ghost write
they say in strip clubs
Stat Kat in Opp Attract

Although I never wrote down Roll Call lyrics,
during class I'd scribble ideas to use later. Here's a
note card that references beloved deaf actress Marlee
Matlin, as well as keeping my name out of your mouth
until I tattoo "Karl" on my dick. I genuinely hope those
two things had nothing to do with each other.

the closet" may be the easiest, and most perfectly homophobic, battle knockout ever.

I had tied the all-time record for most perfect wins in a row as I entered my third week of victories. The Baka Boyz invited me into the studio to compete until I was dethroned, an invitation that was rarely handed out, but also an obvious roadblock in keeping my identity secret. I contemplated sending in an actor to announce that I was terminally ill and could only rap over the phone from the hospital. I even visited a local costume shop to browse masks, but realized I would probably never win again if muffled by the latex face of Richard Nixon. I knew that no matter how hard I tried to avoid it, my anonymity was up. I would also have to start perfectly timing my *Flintstones* job so I could avoid traffic and make it to the studio, which sounded like a *Mario Kart* level of stress I wasn't thrilled to face.

But when Monday came along, I finally stepped foot into the radio station I had basically taken hostage for weeks, and the studio exploded in surprise. The Baka Boyz tried their hardest to explain my physical appearance ("He's just . . . a huge dork"), but they couldn't stop laughing at me and their own shock. I wore a bright Hawaiian shirt and sported the thick, black-rimmed eyeglass style I still wear today, looking more like a member of Reel Big Fish's horn section than the vicious battler they expected. Even corporate executives from the station came out of their offices to get a look at the rapper who had redefined the Roll Call for almost a month but looked like he'd also do your taxes.

I'd be lying if I said I didn't know my ultra-whiteness was a major element of my appeal. That's something I knew even during X-tra Large. There had been white rappers before me, some of whom I openly idolized, like MC Serch, the Beastie Boys, and Everlast—and Eminem was slowly gaining momentum during my breakout—but I still knew I was different from everyone else. I rapped only about what I knew, which for me was a suburban, pop culture–riddled life that, although familiar to most of the white fans flocking to hip-hop, had not yet been represented in the genre. Where 95 percent of rappers were talking about guns or jewelry, I was referencing the girls in my high school who got nose jobs, or spitting stupid lines like, "I'm too obnoxious to be called conscious / I drive a rape van like the white B. A. Baracus." On the Roll Call, and throughout the years I was actively pursuing a career in hip-hop, I regularly heard the phrase "a white rapper who acts white," which is coded in racism and, beyond that, just dumb.

I grew up loving rappers like Biz Markie, Doug E. Fresh, and the Fat Boys—guys who had fun and didn't care about acting tough—and I wanted to bring that back. I called myself "the Jewish Jay Z," sampled Hall & Oates, and name-checked Dave Eggers. I wasn't making a racial statement; I was being honest. It's really all I could be. I was happy the listeners were appreciating the perspective.

The Roll Call just got easier from that point on. I was experiencing an unstoppable stretch, racking up wins from inside the studio and trying my hardest to create entertaining radio. I brought in piñatas for the DJs to break if I won, and when they did, porn magazines came flying out. For one victory, I brought along USC sorority girls to boo after my opponents' lyrics and applaud after mine. I concocted ridiculous similes like "So, here's your warning, at least half of y'all been told / I'm just like Lil' Bow Wow but white, Jewish, and old" and "You can't get at me, you ain't getting raw / 'Cause you're uneven like Wilson Phillips on a seesaw." I still didn't see Hot Karl as a long-term endeavor, but if this hobby was to play out publicly, I wanted to have fun with it.

I was still able to keep my burgeoning rap life secret from my bosses at *Viva Rock Vegas*, but my classmates at USC were starting to catch on. As much as I tried to maintain a low profile, students would sometimes see me in the quad and yell "Hot Karl!" and I even reluctantly signed an autograph during an International Relations lecture. The university asked about my availability for the school's annual Spring Fling concert, and I ended up opening for Naughty by Nature, who called me "the future of hip-hop" during their set. Vinnie even said, "Eminem better get his running shoes." Things got chaotic once I hit six weeks of uninterrupted Roll Call victories, and I was just too busy juggling the radio appearances, my junior year, and my internship to even notice what was going on around me. But no matter how excited USC was about their newest musician, no one was prouder than my mom.

Ever since I was a kid, both my parents had been incredibly supportive of my love for hip-hop, and I always assumed they were three or four of my daily Roll Call votes. But it was my mom—a singer who toured with the USO during the Vietnam War and wished she had taken her career further—who ended up being my biggest fan on the radio. While I avoided any and all conversation that could expose Hot Karl's identity to anyone, she always seemed just one step away from hiring a skywriter. I've joked that if she were Peter Parker's Aunt May, the police would've arrested Peter the day after the spider bit him.

My mom was proud and I appreciated that, but when our local dry cleaner wished me luck on the Roll Call, I knew she would make an awful candidate for the CIA. Another stop on her National Hot Karl Publicity Tour was the local shipping supply spot. She rented a mailbox there and would stop by throughout the week to pick up packages. When she casually dropped my accomplishments into a conversation with the store's owner one day—and by "casually" I mean the same way people drop that they spent a semester of college abroad—she realized the woman also had a rapping son: well-known Inglewood gangster rapper Mack 10.

When my mom told me that Mack 10 would be listening to that night's Roll Call, I obviously had a few questions for her, starting with "HOW THE FUCK DO YOU KNOW MACK 10?" She explained her earlier run-in, which meant that my mom knew more Bloods than I did. Even though the added pressure of Mack listening in didn't help my nerves, I notched another perfect victory, followed by an off-the-cuff freestyle that included the impromptu line, "I'll battle on the radio, battle at a show / Either way I run through lines like Bo Jackson in *Tecmo Bowl*," which ended up being the most quoted lyric I ever spit on the airwaves. I left the station feeling like a winner, ready for another weekend off, entering an unprecedented seventh week in a row—and that's when Mack 10 called my cell phone.

"I liked your raps, so I got your number from your Moms," Mack 10 said to me in a soft tone. I safely guessed this was a sentence he'd never said before. The man who once rapped "Addicted to crime, so I stay in the mix / With a love for hoochie chicks and pullin' jewelry licks" couldn't have been more polite. He kept repeating the *Tecmo Bowl* line, in total shock that it was actually freestyle. He asked where I'd be in a few hours, and I told him I planned on spending the weekend doing chores at my parents' house in Calabasas. "Like every other rapper," I joked. Unfazed, he asked for the address and told me he'd see me soon. I assumed when most people heard that from Mack 10, they feared for their lives, while my mom just wanted to know if she should make him a sandwich.

When he pulled up in a Rolls-Royce, smoking a cigar and holding a briefcase, I assumed my neighbors were all just going to pack up and move. Mack and I sat in my living room, feet from where I'd watched *Punky Brewster* as a child, and talked about Hot Karl. He admitted he had only heard that day's Roll Call, but needed no more convincing; he was already a die-hard fan. He explained his current situation at Capitol/Priority Records, and how because of his success with the supergroup Westside Connection, he could sign a rapper quickly—and he believed Hot Karl was the next worldwide superstar in hip-hop. Since this wasn't my first run-in with a gangster rapper promising riches, I was skeptical. That is, until Mack placed his briefcase on my mother's coffee table and exposed $50,000 resting inside.

"Look at this as a signing bonus," he went on to explain as I wide-eyed the contents like the Goonies when they first see One-

Eyed Willy's ship. In an interview about that night, he would later casually drop the gem "I think that's just what I had on me at the time" when asked why he brought that specific amount to my parent's house.

If I signed that night, he promised me more money, as well as an appearance on the upcoming Westside Connection album and a song with T-Boz from TLC, his wife at the time, which sounded awesome but also seemed super awkward. I had seen enough of Suge Knight on *Behind the Music* to know that if I made a deal right there, things wouldn't end well. I thanked Mack for his confidence in me, but admitted the attention given to my hobby was still a bit overwhelming. I needed some time to think it over, and he politely said he understood my stress. He closed the briefcase and walked back to his car, which was worth more than my parents' yearly salaries combined.

I waved good-bye, not believing the surreal shit that had just happened. Before Mack drove off, though, he rolled down his window and yelled "Karl," a name I hadn't really heard much of yet, but would hear for years to come. I turned around, hoping he would just make it rain out his driver's-side window, no matter how I'd responded to his proposition. Instead, he offered advice that forced me to realize just how much my life was going to change.

"Do me a favor," he asked. "Stop calling it a fucking hobby. You about to be a millionaire, playboy."

With that, Mack 10 drove off and I went back inside my parents' house to do laundry.

5

TYRESE ISN'T HAPPY

DESPITE having had the opportunity to pocket $50,000 in cash a few days earlier, that Monday I returned to school, my internship, and the radio station, still pinching pennies to exist. Final exams were steadily approaching, and I had already broken the radio station's previous record for most consecutive Roll Call victories by over a month—hitting around forty consecutive days—so I wasn't sure I could maintain my hunger to keep participating. I told J-Love that I wanted to "pull a *Seinfeld*" and leave while on top, and that I planned on retiring at the end of the week.

He passed along those words to the Baka Boyz, and when I got to the studio that day and saw a management contract near the microphone, I was shocked and flattered. The DJs had never managed an artist before but explained that they'd partner with their own management team—a company that represented names I didn't recognize, except for Jennifer Beals from

Flashdance—and learn as they went. They'd been LA's premier radio personalities for years, so their connections were important, especially since radio was still the most crucial outlet for breaking a record.

As a child I had just hoped the Baka Boyz would answer my phone call, and now they were trying to run my career. I didn't know what would happen once my Roll Call reign ended, and I had no idea if anyone actually cared about Hot Karl, but I figured an opportunity this big was worth exploring. I told them I'd think it over, and I included the line "Might retire on Friday, let my career start to swell / Or end up just handing out free demo CDs like AOL" during that day's victory.

I walked out of the studio with their contract in hand and decided to treat myself to a taco at a nearby stand while I waited for rush-hour traffic to die down. As I sat and stared at words like "term period" or "commission"—terminology I had never seen before this proposed agreement—I finally let the prospect of this new career path settle in. It was then that I heard some kids at a nearby table start talking excitedly.

"He's the best rapper I've ever heard," a female teenager explained.

"Does he have any songs out?" a guy who seemed to be her boyfriend asked.

"No, he's just been on the radio for weeks. His name is Hot Karl and he's incredible."

I knew they had no idea that the unassuming, pale motherfucker in the booth next to them, gnawing on a shrimp taco, was the Hot Karl they were talking about, so I took it as a sign.

I thought to myself, "Holy shit, a lot of people *are* listening." But I couldn't commit to *any* contract until I actually came to grips with what was unfolding around me. I knew the Baka Boyz' hearts—and wallets—were in the right place, but it all just seemed too early to limit myself to anything. I had been living in a bubble during the Roll Call explosion, too busy with college and work to understand how many people had actually been exposed to Hot Karl.

I decided to call J-Love from the car to ask for advice. As producer, he was the guy making sure I got on the radio every day, and we had forged a close friendship during the streak—so I knew he'd be honest. He understood my trepidation, reiterating that Nick and Eric only wanted to help but that it might be best to not lock myself in anywhere yet. After the small pep talk, I knew my instincts were right. I would become a "professional rapper," but I'd at least learn the landscape before I put my trust in anyone or anything. I told the Baka Boyz my decision and they seemed to totally understand, saying they'd still be willing to take me around to their connections. If anything were to come of it, I'd owe them their deserved commission or, in hip-hop terms, "have to break them off." As I celebrated Y2K and readied myself for a life without the Roll Call, it seemed everyone loved Hot Karl. Well, everyone except two guys.

———

No matter how hard I trained to become a freestyle champion, the act itself wasn't easy. There are always shortcuts and tricks of the trade, but the pressure is real, especially when you're head to head with another skilled MC who's waiting for you to slip, stumble, or stutter. Once the Baka Boyz started having me spit an entire verse after my wins, everything changed. Not only did I have to bring eight lines for the normal call-and-response contest, but I also needed to produce somewhere between sixteen and thirty-two bars every single day for my victory lap. I wasn't able to write all these out, mostly due to lack of free time, but also because that was kind of cheating in the early 2000s.

While "freestyling" has since become a term for just rapping an orphaned written verse over a random beat, it used to mean that you rapped impromptu off the top of your head, improvising almost every line. I hate to sound like an old man here and say that we had it harder, but . . . we had it harder. Sometimes I was centered and on my game, while other times I definitely wasn't. Without written verses to fall back on, I often just called an audible mid-line and hoped I fell on my feet. I usually nailed my landings, but during my third week of wins, when I found myself starting a verse with, "Excuse this next line, 'cause it may start some beef," I had no endgame. It was such a clear setup for a punch line, like when Jay Leno used to say, "Did you hear about this?" and follow it up with some hack bullshit he wrote in a Studebaker. But as those words came out of my mouth, I knew I had nothing. As I grasped for anything, the stanza became, "Excuse this next line, 'cause it may start some beef / But I'd rather kill myself than ever have a song with Tyrese."

To be clear, I have nothing against Tyrese Gibson. It was only a few years after the Coke commercial that introduced him to the world, and he had just released his first album, a record that went on to go platinum and win a Grammy. (Small note: The Ramones never won a Grammy. It's just a fact that seems relevant here.) I can't tell you if I had heard any of his songs at that point, but I knew his name rhymed with "beef." And I found it humorous that I would rather take my own life than step foot into his studio. The Baka Boyz immediately started laughing. They understood how ridiculous and random the line was, which is something I can't say for the three people who called me over the next hour asking why I hated Tyrese so much.

At first I admitted the truth to my friends: "Honestly, his name rhymed. That's it." But as the inquiries kept coming in, including an e-mail from an underground hip-hop site asking for a comment, I realized I should be having more fun with our supposed bad blood. So I fabricated reasons, from saying Tyrese stole my girlfriend to saying he cut me off in traffic, causing a flat tire. The weird part is, people believed me. So when I walked into the studio the next day, I had every single word that rhymed with "Tyrese" on tap, ready to go. And just like that, "People wanna know why I had words about Tyrese / Trust me—he knows, and I'll see him in the streets" came out of my mouth FOR NO REASON AT ALL. Again the Baka Boyz couldn't stop laughing, probably because they saw the absurd face I made when attempting to threaten an R&B singer "in the streets." As I left the studio, three calls turned into six, and one voice message from my mom asked me to stop antagonizing "Tyreef." But the concern only fueled my fire, and I saw no end in sight for this silly conflict with "Black-Ty." It became a harmless part of my daily Roll Call folklore—until, supposedly, Tyrese found out.

I strutted into the studio during week four, head held high and ready to add another victory to my tally, when I noticed J-Love's concerned face. He immediately pulled me into a side office and whispered, "Tyrese isn't happy." My immediate reaction was not concern for my health but concern for how quickly I could get the phrase "Tyrese isn't happy" onto T-shirts to sell to fans. J-Love saw me start to laugh and cut me off with a sentiment I first heard from Mack 10 in my parents' driveway but would encounter consistently throughout my attempt to become a professional rapper: "You may want to start taking this serious." He explained that Tyrese hadn't actually heard anything I said, but a friend told him that someone on the radio had a problem with him. The Baka Boyz assured him it was all in good fun, but Tyrese didn't seem to comprehend any part of it. He, understandably, had no idea who I was, yet I was assuring Los Angeles that he knew why I wanted to beat him up. So J-Love made me promise to calm it down, and I obliged.

But that day, during my freestyle session, after long consideration and at a loss for words again, I decided that no matter how much I appreciated my well-being, I wasn't done with this stupidity. Halfway through my extended rap session I rhymed, "I promised I'd stop bad-mouthing Tyrese like I've been / But that's hard for me, I'm a bad actor just like him." J-Love shook his head, trying to hide his laughter, and I continued to make fun of Tyrese for the rest of my Roll Call reign, and maybe ten other times on songs I recorded throughout my career. And weirdly, I never heard a word from Tyrese, probably because he didn't actually care, or because J-Love had just been fucking with me. But despite the silence, I still found it necessary to clear the air, even if it was years later.

Fast-forward six years to when Tyrese would often get manicures and pedicures next door to a place where I worked, which is a sentence that should've gotten me a book deal on its own. One day, I watched as a white Rolls-Royce pulled into our parking lot and the man I had methodically dissed day after day, song after song, stepped out and made his way to the adjoining nail bar. Without any real preparation or plan, I instinctively yelled his name, and thus began one of the most awkward exchanges of my life.

JENSEN: "Tyrese!"

TYRESE: "Yeah?"

J: "Hey, man, I just want to say I'm sorry."

T: "Sorry for what?"

J: "It's not important. I just think it's worth saying. You literally did nothing."

T: "What?"

J: "Nothing. Loved you in *Baby Boy!*"

I walked back inside my office with a skip in my step, and Tyrese could not have looked more confused. He looked around nervously, waiting for Ashton Kutcher to pop out and expose a camera, but instead, after a few seconds, he just made his way into the salon without any further fanfare. I figured that exchange was the amends I needed to make, and the less he knew about it, the better. Poking fun at Tyrese wasn't one of my more admirable moments as Hot Karl, and in the end, he actually seemed like a nice dude. Unfortunately, his name just rhymes with "beef." And honestly, had I known he got weekly mani-pedis, it would've ended like Biggie and Tupac.

Not all of my tense encounters with celebrities were as nonchalant, or as insignificant to my career—especially the one with the other guy who seemed to dislike Hot Karl. When talking about music in the early 2000s, it would be hard not to mention the industry's version of herpes simplex 2: Fred Durst. No matter how hard you tried to get rid of him, he was gonna pop up in some fashion over and over again. He had found astounding success with Limp Bizkit and become an efficient Interscope music executive, signing both mediocre (Puddle of Mudd, Staind) and impressive (Kenna, She Wants Revenge) acts to his own label, Flawless Records.

Fred was the poster boy for the music-industry gold rush, selling over forty million records worldwide and scoring three Grammy nominations. (Small note: Jimi Hendrix was only nominated for a Grammy once. It's just another fact that seems relevant.) Limp Bizkit's sacrilegious cover of George Michael's "Faith" to the braggadocio bullshit of "Rollin'" is the musical equivalent of seeing old pictures of yourself wearing Hammer pants in the '90s. I recently visited a Hard Rock Cafe and saw one of Fred's signature red baseball caps immortalized under glass, and I immediately feared that the Hard Rock curators weren't actually interested in rock 'n' roll history; they were just hoarders. But to his credit, there were few rock stars bigger than Fred Durst in the year 2000. So during my Roll Call days, when I first heard he was interested in signing me to his record label, I was ready to learn more.

My connection to Durst began a week or two into the Roll Call, when I had been thrilled to hear that Limp Bizkit's DJ, DJ Lethal, was a Hot Karl fan. Lethal first jumped on the scene as part of the Caucasian trio House of Pain, a rap group that heavily influenced my love for hip-hop and helped me understand my own place within the genre—so he'll always get a pass. (Like how Tara Reid was in *The Big Lebowski,* so I still follow her on Twitter.) When that group went their separate ways, he quickly joined a rock band, a trend I can happily say faded away rather quickly but really worked out for DJ Lethal. A mutual friend set up a meeting, and without any time wasted, I was making music at his studio in the Valley, just blocks away from my parents' house. We created a song that would later make its way onto my demo tape and help cement my record deal, but at the time we were just two guys fucking around. Lethal was also part of a weekly LA radio show on a rival of the station where I was battling every day, airing his episodes on Sunday nights. So when he told me he'd be playing one of our songs on his show, I knew that meant even more exposure.

Since it would be the first time I'd have an actual song on the airwaves, rather than just my battle lyrics over someone else's beat, I alerted all of my friends and family and told them when to listen. My grandma, who didn't fully understand the Roll Call and what my success on it meant, was thrilled to finally comprehend this milestone and excitedly told me she'd be listening. My mom, who up to this point had taped—and announced to anyone within a fifty-foot radius—every one of my Roll Call wins, was basically one step away from transcribing the song in case someone she knew was hard of hearing. While I was usually nervous about the live nature of my battles, I felt relaxed and confident in this case. I didn't even need to be in the studio or on the phone. Halfway through the show, DJ Lethal announced an "exclusive" song he was excited to play, and I could hear the sound of everyone I knew pressing record on his or her tape player at the same time. He had the "first song ever" from LA rap phenomenon Hot Karl and would play it next, but first, he wanted to welcome this week's special show guest, his bandmate Fred Durst.

I had no prior warning of Fred's appearance but figured it was perfect timing, since I had just heard about his interest in me. They warmed up by asking Fred about his recent tour and the upcoming MTV Video Music Awards, questions I'm sure he answered with a perfectly measured amount of angst, while I waited patiently with bated breath for the debut of my songwriting skills. After about ten minutes, they introduced my song and asked Fred if he had heard of Hot Karl. Fred said something along the lines of, "Yeah, he's got all the buzz right now. I'm excited to check this out," and just like that I had an epic introduction from the man who penned "Nookie," a setup I couldn't have paid for. The first few notes of my song played, and I just sat back and smiled. A shot-in-the-dark phone call to a dumb rap contest, from a suburbanite who once sharted in sixth-grade PE and as a result had his mom pick him up from the nurse's office, had turned into a song dope enough to play on LA radio. My mom called me freaking out about the track, like it was Marvin Berry calling his cousin Chuck during the Enchantment Under the Sea dance. Everything sounded perfect, and I felt well on my way to a professional level for the first time since the false start I'd had with Rickye as a child. Then the song ended and they asked Fred Durst what he thought.

"He's a huge nerd. It's not for me. He's not going anywhere," Fred Durst said without a hint of sarcasm in his voice.

I could feel the silent shock in the studio, even through the radio. I tilted my head slightly, pretending for a second I had misheard his statement but knowing damn well I hadn't. Fred went on to insult me, and imitate my voice, as the show's hosts defended me. They went to a commercial break without any sign that Durst was letting up, and now I was fuming. Did this piece of shit just halt my career before it even started? The man who in 1998 performed atop a giant toilet at Ozzfest had made himself the gatekeeper of hip-hop, and, for some unknown reason, he had just announced he wasn't letting me in. As I stared at my radio, stunned by what had just unfolded, my phone rang, finally breaking the coma. It was my ecstatic grandmother, so happy she had just heard my song and oblivious to what Fred had just unleashed. To be honest, I'm not 100 percent sure she was even listening to the right station, but at that point I didn't care. I thanked her politely, hung up, and plotted my next move. The show was still on a commercial break. Not knowing what Fred would say next, I decided to take matters into my own hands and dialed into the station. I tussled with a busy signal for a few minutes until Lethal picked up.

"Put me on the air," I demanded.

Lethal sensed my rage. I could hear him walking into another room to avoid Fred hearing.

"Dude, he doesn't mean it," Lethal explained.

"Fuck him, he doesn't mean it," I shouted back. "If he wants a battle, he found one."

I spoke with a real Tony Soprano confidence that clashed with the 125-square-foot dorm room and thrift store ALF slippers I found myself in at the time.

Lethal said he believed putting me on air with Fred was a bad idea, given my current state, but that he'd talk to him and make things right. I heard the call-waiting alert on my phone and put Lethal on hold, only to hear my mom, confused, on the other line.

"Who's this Fred Durst?" she asked in a disgusted tone more warranted when talking about child molesters and serial killers than rock stars.

"He's a rock guy. I'm on the other line with them right now."

"You are?" she asked. "How'd you get through? I've been trying for five minutes."

"Wait, what? Why are you calling them?"

"To yell at him. How dare he?"

Fearing for even more damage to my career, I begged my

mother to stop calling. I could only imagine the field day he'd have with her.

"They'll know it's you, Mom," I said, annoyed, hoping to knock some sense into her.

"I was going to use a fake voice," she said in a voice that was clearly fake in the same way that Kermit the Frog and a bunch of Muppets in a trench coat were clearly a fake tall man.

"Mom, do not call them," I demanded.

She promised she wouldn't, so I returned to Lethal's line. He assured me he'd fix the problem and begged me to just stay tuned.

"You two will live in perfect harmony," Lethal promised.

"FRED CAN NEVER BE IN HARMONY. HAVE YOU HEARD HIM SING?" I yelled, to remind him that I'm always ready to battle.

I listened closely as the final commercial faded out.

"So before we went to break, Fred had some things to say about Hot Karl, a rapper whose first song we debuted here on the show," Lethal announced, like he was about to apologize for a weatherman yelling "fuck" after being stung by a bee during a live broadcast. "And now Fred wants to say something."

"Yeah, man, I was just messing around," Fred said politely. "I just want him to diss me next. He's gonna be a big deal. I'm trying to make him famous. I may even sign the kid."

I let out a sigh of relief, marking some closure to this weird turn of events.

"Yeah, we got a lot of callers mad at you, dude," Lethal informed Fred Durst. "One man said you were fat and knew nothing."

Fred joked that he wanted none of that, and they went on to the next song, leaving a potential Hot Karl beef in the dust. I was finally feeling relaxed when my phone rang. It was my mother.

"I'm happy that all worked out," she proclaimed. "He said he might even sign you."

"I'm not interested. I mean, he seems like a psychopath."

My mom quickly responded, "Yeah, and he's fat and knows nothing," in an obviously fake voice.

I prayed the radio station didn't have caller ID.

———

No matter who did, or didn't, appreciate my newfound career, it was time for my run on the radio to come to an end after almost two months of domination. So, for my final appearance on the Roll Call, the Baka Boyz arranged for an All-Time Roll Call Championship at an El Torito restaurant in West Covina. The idea was to bring together past champions in front of fans and have us compete against each other, leaving just one past winner victorious with the undisputed title. When I first heard the idea of a Roll Call with a live audience, I wondered who would even care to see it. Before YouTube, rap battles were confined to cyphers, surrounded by thirty-five onlookers yelling "Ooooooooh" at the end of every punch line and trying to start an actual fight. They took on a real *Fight Club* vibe, so much so that one of the more infamous New York competitions ended up co-opting that name soon after. Battling was one of hip-hop's best-kept secrets, so I couldn't help but wonder how far the whispers could travel for this blockbuster Roll Call.

I convinced a few friends to make the trip with me, both for moral support and to keep me busy in case only eight people showed up. On the drive there, I practiced tirelessly, hoping that the weeks of dedicating my time to a few minutes of regional radio would actually result in some sort of title in the end. Between Mack 10's ridiculous offer, the Baka Boyz' management aspirations, and the unknowing young couple at the taco stand talking about me, I was now willing to see rap as more than a hobby, but for now this win was all I had my sights set on. As we pulled into the parking lot, I immediately noticed a crowd of maybe a hundred people lined up outside the restaurant, one holding a sign that read FUCK TYRESE. My friends were thrilled by the unexpected crowd; I was just nervous I'd lose.

Most were in attendance just to see what I looked like and were shocked to see me emerge when it was my time to rap. One guy actually yelled, "Is Hot Karl John Cusack?" Although I was only one of a dozen MCs competing that day, it felt like everyone was just waiting to hear what I had in store for the championship round. The Baka Boyz had set me up to rap last, giving me the final word, and I didn't disappoint. I ended with the line "You can't battle Hot Karl, what's that about? / You ain't doing nothing, like A. C. Green in a whorehouse," a reference to an NBA player who had recently announced that he was a virgin, and the restaurant went ballistic. I hadn't heard that type of reaction since I dismantled Toothbrush during lunch break. There was no doubt that I had won the title as I ominously mean-mugged the crowd and gave exuberant high fives to the front row, like I'd just 360-dunked on Kevin Garnett.

As a lifelong fan of the Roll Call, I felt like I had just made history. The Baka Boyz had me perform my usual victory lap, but this time going down the line of past victors and dissing them one by one. They assured me they'd cut to a commercial break so I could curse in front of the audience without worrying about affecting the station. When I got to a young boy reminiscent of middle-school Jensen, the kid who once dreamed of participating but only got busy signals, I pulled no punches. "You shouldn't even be here, all your wins were shit / You're a kid allowed to battle 'cause of a mom's permission slip." I called another past winner "a gay Rick Fox" because, well, that's what he looked like. The place erupted again. I'm not sure I've experienced that type of validation from anything I've done since, and it's safe to say I probably won't ever again.

I walked out of the restaurant understanding that my skills were no longer confined to the radio or college parties. I felt unbeatable. I still had to go run errands at the *Flintstones* production office come Monday, but for now I signed a dozen or so autographs on my way to the car, content with leaving the Roll Call and pursuing a career in hip-hop, even if I didn't know what, if anything, could happen next.

6

RAP GAME
LLOYD DOBLER

THE next morning, J-Love called to congratulate me on the victory, admitting he had never seen anything like it during his career as a radio producer. He also revealed that during my time on the show, he had been compiling a list of record executives and industry folk who had called to ask about me. However, like a teammate avoiding a pitcher during a perfect game, he had decided to keep those inquiries to himself until the streak was broken or I decided to walk away. Now that I had retired from the Roll Call, he rattled off some recognizable names as interested parties. Eminem was all over MTV, so a lot of industry types saw dollar signs without even hearing, or caring about, any of my music.

I began following up on some of the interest, which ranged from worth a second look to absolutely ridiculous. DJ Pooh, Ice Cube producer and cowriter of *Friday*, pitched the Baka Boyz an idea where I would take on an alter ego, Hot Karl the Pimp, and wear floor-length fur coats and big hats, traveling with women everywhere I went. When I asked why I would do that, I was told, "'Cause you look goofy as yourself." Manager Jeff Kwatinetz, who cofounded a company called The Firm, which represented Jennifer Lopez and Korn, seemed to be the most esteemed of the bunch, so I decided to hold off and contact him last. I hoped I would be more knowledgeable by then, but I knew damn well that no matter what happened, this situation would never make sense. In the meantime, the Baka Boyz were very close to one of the other possible suitors, Ruffhouse Records cofounder Chris Schwartz, so I decided they'd take me to meet him and be involved in any dealings that came of it. In turn, they made an appointment with Schwartz at a posh Beverly Hills hotel during his trip to LA for the Grammys.

On our drive there, I noticed a boom box in the Baka Boyz' backseat and immediately felt nervous. They explained that the portable tape player was for rapping on the spot in the meeting, which in all honesty, was my absolute nightmare. Then they informed me that Chris didn't actually have a room in that hotel; it was just conveniently located near his previous meeting. So now I envisioned myself spitting a verse, holding up a boom box like I was Lloyd Dobler in *Say Anything*, in the middle of a crowded restaurant. Despite my fears, they promised me everything would be fine since it was just for Chris, someone who *wanted* to meet me, and not like I was a street performer just asking for dollars from strangers. They also emphasized that to make it in this business, I'd have to be willing to rhyme at the drop of a hat, which seemed like a ringing endorsement for just going back to college and pretending this whole thing had never happened. But I sucked it up and we pulled into the valet line.

As we waited our turn, I noticed Missy Elliott getting out of the car in front of us. I knew it was Missy mostly because she was wearing a purple leather pantsuit with razor blades glued to almost every inch, and there was no other human being in the world who would wear that shit. The only thing that would have clued me in quicker was if she were wearing a huge garbage bag and making weird car noises with her mouth. I nonchalantly pointed her out from the backseat, almost laughing, not expecting the Baka Boyz to jump out of the car and talk to her, which is exactly what they did. Because they were an LA radio institution, everyone stopped by their show at some point to shamelessly promote their music. I figured there weren't many rappers they didn't know, at least in passing, and this theory was proven true when, one cold night on a Beverly Hills sidewalk, I shook hands with Missy Elliott.

I was introduced as Hot Karl, a name I was becoming accustomed to, and during our brief interaction, I found her to be a pleasant lady. I was starting to walk toward the lobby to find Chris Schwartz when I heard the Baka Boyz start pitching me as "the next big rapper" to Missy. Now obviously, this was an extremely nice gesture by Nick and Eric, promoting me at every turn, but like a skilled quarterback, I could predict the open hole where a defensive lineman was about to sack me and push me back fifteen yards. Envisioning the next four steps of their conversation, I knew that in just a few seconds they'd be pressing play on that boom box and something awful was going to happen: I was going to perform publicly for Missy Elliott on a Beverly Hills street corner. If I was tepid about the eventual Schwartz dinner-table freestyle, *imagine my feelings about this.* The one thing the Baka Boyz promised me was that I wouldn't feel like a street performer, and here I was about to be . . . a literal street performer.

Everything played out exactly like my nightmare. The Baka Boyz suggested I rap for her, and anxiety took over my entire body, even though "You have to be willing to rhyme at the drop of a hat" echoed through my head over and over again. We were surrounded by valets, hotel guests, and passersby, all coming and going in LA's stuffiest elite neighborhood, and I was about to pretend this intersection was *106 & Park.* Missy commented on my unorthodox appearance and admitted she didn't know what to expect, and then Eric pressed play on the portable player, an action I saw happen in slow motion. I officially sensed disaster from every angle, as the absurd notion sank in that I was about to flow for—or accost, depending on how you saw it—Missy Elliott, a musician I highly respected, as she entered her hotel for the night. Everything was happening so fast that I started rapping without really thinking, a cardinal sin in freestyling. I pretty much blacked out from that point on, but I do remember two things for sure:

#1. At some point I said, "They asked me to rap for Missy, now I gotta rock it / Who got the keys to my jeep? I bet valet's got it" and pointed to a valet guy.

#2. And this is directly related to #1: I was awful.

I'm not sure if I was expecting Missy to just start popping and locking or something, but she sort of just sat there and listened. Rather than stop and huddle around me in amazement, anyone walking by paused for a second, looked, then snickered and kept walking. For as far as Hot Karl had progressed up to this point, that night brought me right back to square one. I felt like I was a young, untalented juggler being forced onto the street by his parents to make rent and accidentally dropping balls for the uninterested. For impromptu rap to be impressive, a lot of pieces have to fall into place, and I was so uncomfortable that it showed in my performance. I couldn't even remember some of my old standbys I would use in case of emergencies. I could sense the Baka Boyz' disappointment as I wrapped up the verse and hung my head as the final word left my mouth. I immediately hoped there'd be a third *Flintstones* movie, because I had student loans to pay off and I'd just fucked my dreams. Missy wished me luck politely and walked into her hotel, luckily before I could pull a razor blade off her jacket and slit my wrists.

It makes sense that the meeting with Chris Schwartz afterward didn't feel right. He had helped develop Cypress Hill, the Fugees, and Kris Kross, but I couldn't get the Missy audition out of my head, imagining that it had looked like a homeless man competing on *The Voice*. I couldn't get my swagger back, and I came off as an insecure amateur looking for a record deal. Shockingly, Chris was still interested, though he knew I needed some work. He kindly gave me some advice that helped me over the next few years, but we never met again.

As we walked out of the hotel, the Baka Boyz did their best to make me feel better about the fumble, but I knew it was a blown opportunity. There would be chances like these again, and now I knew what *not* to do when they appeared. The valet pulled our car up, and we headed over. I was walking around to the backseat, defeated, when the valet guy walked up and handed me a dollar bill. He didn't say a word. He just ran to the next car that needed attending to. I'll never know whether I had dropped it or whether it was change I was supposed to give to Eric, but I'll always assume it was my first tip as a professional street performer and, thankfully, my last.

Meetings got easier as time passed, and I gained more experience with each introduction. I started to book shows too, especially on campus, where I was becoming the go-to guy for an opening act. Every flyer at USC for the next month included the name Hot Karl, alongside a rising student rap group called Emanon. Despite having a name unfortunately close to an up-and-comer about to take the world by storm, Emanon ("No Name" backwards) already had a small following from appearing on a short-lived reality competition show on MTV called *The Cut*, hosted by Lisa "Left Eye" Lopes. The duo consisted of a rapper and a DJ/producer, both good enough for second place on the show, forcing my favorite member of TLC to say their name a ton. They had already recorded a bunch of songs to original beats, which was more than I could claim at the time, and one surefire, crowd-pleasing cover of Biz Markie's "Just a Friend"; in performances at our college, they changed the words of the hook to, "I, I love USC, but I hate UCLA, I hate UCLA." I loved being on the same bill as these guys and went out of my way to become friends with the rapper, since I didn't really know anyone in the scene. He was first introduced to me as Egbert, but onstage he went by the name Aloe Blacc.

He's since gone on to become one of the more important voices in soul music, with hits like "I Need a Dollar," "Wake Me Up," and the TV-commercial-friendly "The Man," but at one time he was solely an impressive MC. Honestly, I didn't even know he could sing. I'm not sure he knew either. But his voice wasn't the only talent he was hiding; he was one of the most impressive scholars in his class. During summer break, while I was practicing complex patterns for rhyming "power to drop bombs" with "devour your fat moms," Aloe was dissecting frogs to cure cancer. That's not hyperbole. That was his actual sum-

At one of my college gigs, I forced my friend James to play bodyguard and wear a T-shirt that read I COULD KILL YOU IF I WANTED, *in hopes he'd protect me from lunging battle opponents, or just that gigantic looming dragonfly lady.*

mer internship. He also attended a class, made up of students hand-selected by the university's president from the top 5 percent, where former U.S. presidents and Nobel Peace Prize winners dropped in for lectures. As much as I appreciated Aloe's mic skills, every time we were on the same bill I couldn't help but think we were allowing cancer to get stronger.

In addition to the campus gigs, I was starting to get offers to headline venues around Los Angeles, even though I technically didn't have any original songs that Fred Durst hadn't shit on publicly. Decent meetings were taking place, and every one ended with someone important asking when my next show was, so I knew I needed to act fast and prove I could perform. But I also knew I was missing so many elements crucial to an impressive live show. So, while walking into a USC fraternity house one day, I noticed a guy moving records from his car and immediately asked if he was a DJ. When Brian Sanchez responded yes— before I could even test his skills—he immediately became DJ Sancho, the first component of my rap group. He would dig into his extensive record collection and find somewhat obscure instrumentals to play on turntables held up by cinder blocks in his room. Then I'd write rhymes to those beats and silently pass the song off as our own, weirdly similar to my days in X-tra Large. I never said I was proud of it, but the Hot Karl buzz was traveling much faster than the actual Hot Karl, so we didn't have much of a choice. Soon after meeting Sancho, at one of our first shows in downtown LA, we walked offstage and were introduced to DJ Muggs, a prolific and legendary producer best known for his work with Cypress Hill; a friend of Muggs had heard me on the radio and brought him to the show. When I asked him if he enjoyed the music, he jokingly said, "Yeah, the first time I heard it."

Sancho and me at a college party playing obscure hip-hop jams no sorority girl wants to hear.

With Sancho committed, and now that I'd finally, after numerous meetings, connected with a manager, I accepted an offer for my biggest gig yet. I would be headlining at the legendary Roxy on Sunset, a street where my mom, as a teenager, saw the Doors perform. She also made out with Jim Morrison that night and said he smelled like old tires, so the place held historical significance in many ways. It was also only a few blocks away from where I'd rapped onstage for the first time ever as an adolescent member of X-tra Large, a fun fact that my mom reminded me of around 100 to 125 times in the week leading up to the show.

Now keep in mind that most promoters were contacting me

through a website, HotKarl.com, that a classmate had quickly thrown together. It only displayed a logo—my name in the New York Mets font, a copyright-infringing idea that I had whipped up one night while drunk—against a stark black background. Anyone could e-mail me directly through the site but never know what I looked like, which is why many talent bookers swore I was an imposter when I showed up. One made me rap when I arrived to prove my identity, since he would have to pay me half in cash before I took the stage. So when I found out that my Roxy show had actually sold out—thanks to some radio promotion and a flyer adorned with a shirtless picture of R. Kelly announcing, HOT KARL - GIRLS 14 & UNDER FREE—I made sure the club's bouncers at least saw my picture before I arrived.

No matter how amateur our rehearsals felt, our naïveté never derailed our plan to be professionals at the Roxy, and the same could be said about our steadfast ignorance to the cease-and-

desist letter we got regarding that R. Kelly flyer. His lawyers didn't find the joke funny, but we were two college kids in a frat house juggling a Nubian Crackers beat and hoping people would think it was our own—what did we have to lose? No one had talked about money or an actual record deal since Mack 10, so Hot Karl still felt like role-playing at best, no matter what my ambitions were. Nice try, Pied Piper.

In preparation for the Roxy show, I was forcing nighttime practice sessions with Sancho into my schedule, between studying and my social life. Most of my friends thought my burgeoning side job was cool, but still a pipe dream. They were too busy surfing, taking business classes, or chugging beer to really notice, and I weirdly appreciated that. I had started dating a younger girl named Paige, whom I'd gone to high school with and who was now attending USC to play on the school's water polo team, arguably the least hip-hop sport the college had to offer. She listened mostly to Pearl Jam, so she didn't quite share my excitement when I brought her to watch me open for Kool Moe Dee. I may have been breaking into the urban-music scene, but my surroundings were like when people plan on giving leftovers to a homeless man on their drive home but then forget the food at the restaurant—very white.

Even if it was the most Caucasian fan base in hip-hop, I knew a lot of my college friends were going to fill up the Roxy, and if I wanted Hot Karl to build on the Roll Call momentum, this show could be the catalyst to do that. I knew I needed something memorable to kick off the night, especially since I assumed some industry types would be attending to see if my buzz was legit. I needed something that would tell people I was more than just a contest winner; I needed something that would make them laugh.

The night of the show, I sat backstage, waiting to be introduced, nervous that my first packed concert would end with the crowd chanting "Fuck rap!" and fifty bullies chasing me around the Roxy. Each ticket-holding member of the audience would see right through my bullshit, bum-rush Sancho for playing other people's music, and lead any interested record exec to another rapper who was actually ready for prime time. For as heralded as the show was, Sancho and I just waited alone, going through the set, making sure we knew every cue. The only time we were interrupted was when my mom walked in.

"It's packed out there," she exclaimed with an excitement that usually brings along a serious jinx. "The Osbourne kids are here."

Frustrated, I asked my mom to stop bringing up the audience. I had also heard that members of Eminem's crew, D12, would be in attendance. Any more information and I would most likely spiral into a panic attack. Despite the overpowering fear, I knew that if we followed the plan we'd concocted in Sancho's little dorm room, we'd be fine. It wouldn't matter who, if anyone, was in the audience. Right then the show's promoter walked in and gave us a five-minute warning. Somehow, over the deafening sound of my heart pounding, I was able to tell my mom to go get changed.

I was announced as "the greatest Roll Call champion of all time" *and* "the kid who played Rufio in *Hook*" to try to sustain the mystery. A lot of the crowd would be seeing me for the first time, no matter how often they'd heard my voice. Once the sound guy ended his intro by yelling "Hot Karl!!!" we let it sit for a minute, stage empty and dark, before hitting the theme from *2001: A Space Odyssey*. With that, an astronaut, helmet and all, walked onto the stage holding a flag, taking each step as if in a constant fight with gravity. The flag read HK, and we dragged out the bit to overplay the drama, hoping the now cheering crowd would assume it was me in the suit. As the beat for our first song started and the flag was finally planted in the middle of the stage, I ran out and loudly asked, "Guess who motherfucking landed?" I maneuvered from one side of the stage to the other, self-assured, influenced by every single move I'd seen during a childhood spent glued to BET. Whatever nerves I tangled with before the show disappeared as the crowd went nuts and the astronaut broke out into full dance. Our suited spaceman was throwing elbows, leaning back, and doing the Diddy Bop (or at least trying).

The voice-trembling teenage Roll Caller I once was would've been impressed as I shook hands with members of the crowd from the stage and got through each verse with more and more bravado. I'd ditched the gimmicky button-ups and now focused on vintage rock T-shirts, designer jeans, and my Peter Sellers glasses. Everything felt much more natural. And as the first song ended, I turned around and nonchalantly thanked my mom, who then took off her astronaut helmet, bowed, and casually walked offstage. During the next thirty minutes of my set, a performance I still regard as my best, I never mentioned my mom in the spacesuit again. As hoped, I'd made the crowd laugh.

My mother once asked if "she HAD to do these bits."
I said, "No . . . only if you love me."

To close the night I freestyled to Lionel Richie's "All Night Long," a beat Sancho manipulated long enough for me to diss members of the audience for a few minutes, much like I had battled magazine spreads in my room. Ironically, Nicole Richie was in the audience, but I didn't find that out until years later— otherwise she would've gotten hit with some major shrapnel too. Standing near the stage at a Hot Karl concert was a lot like sitting front row at a Gallagher show; you were probably going to get hit with some watermelon. I focused on a few pretty girls in my eyeline and even mentioned the Osbournes in passing, mostly because I had learned how a crowd reacts to celebrity targets a few weeks earlier when I was asked to perform a song at actress Kate Towne's birthday party.

When I stepped onstage to freestyle one night in some

backyard for around five hundred people, I was surprised to notice President George W. Bush's then nineteen-year-old daughter, Jenna Bush, in the crowd. I recognized her immediately, since it was right around the time she was cited for underage drinking and possession of a fake ID. Her face was all over the news. I did my normal freestyle routine but waited for my last two bars to emphasize, and end on, a punch line directed at her. As it approached, I looked at her and said, "You can try your hardest, but you can't stop the almighty / 'Cause most rappers are fake like they were Jenna Bush's ID." I got an overpowering "Ooooooooh" from the audience, and Jenna gave me one of those half smile, half "What the fuck just happened?" faces that her father ran the country with for eight years. Later I would try to go up to her and say hello, but a nearby Secret Service agent halted me dead in my tracks. When I explained I was the rapper who'd mentioned her onstage, he looked at me with a disapproving smirk and said, "I know. That's why I'm stopping you."

The evening I stepped off the Roxy stage, however, I knew I'd no longer be pigeonholed as a radio fluke. My mom, still in her astronaut suit, hugged me and admitted she couldn't believe where this whole thing was going. My father, who had videotaped the whole show from the audience—a job he would proudly possess for a dozen more Hot Karl shows—joined us and seemed to finally understand rap music in general, which was a step in the right direction. I wanted that high to last forever, not knowing where the next adrenaline rush would come from, or if it would come at all. And that's when an excited DJ Sancho stormed in.

"Holy shit, dude. A guy from Interscope Records was here. He said Jimmy Iovine wants to meet you," he revealed with a huge smile.

I knew as long as I didn't have to perform for Jimmy Iovine on a street corner, I'd be alright.

At our next show, my mom came out as "Ma Rule," holding a bottle of Cristal, sporting a dookie chain, and wearing a Ruff Ryders jumpsuit. No one can ever question this woman's love for her son.

7

CALIENTE KARLITO

AFTER the Roxy show, the industry finally started to take notice. I may not have known my intent before taking the stage that night, but I now knew what my next goal was: to sign a record deal. A few days later I was mentioned in *HITS* magazine, an industry bible at the time for A&R guys looking to sign the next big thing. I also had a meeting with Interscope founder and CEO Jimmy Iovine in the works, although when I asked his secretary exactly when this would be scheduled, she replied cryptically: "You'll know." And I finally made that call to The Firm's Jeff Kwatinetz to follow up on his initial interest. I had hoped to connect with him once I was more comfortable in the biz, but things were moving so quickly that I couldn't wait any longer. A meeting was set up for the following Monday.

Despite my best attempts at living a double life, with these big names entering the equation and my senior year of college in full swing, I knew it was time to finally leave the *Flintstones* internship behind. At this point, the office had started to hear rumblings of my flourishing rap career, but I went out of my way to keep the details, and my shit-centric stage name, something of a mystery. As far as quitting, I didn't exactly know what to say. "I'm a rapper now" felt like an odd way to give notice to your boss, but I also wanted to be honest and not burn a bridge. I read somewhere that Plies was a nurse when his song "Shawty" broke, and I've always wondered what *his* resignation sounded like. Given his career post-"Shawty," I hope he didn't leave on bad terms. I like to think he's back at work, changing someone's IV right now. But all my fears were unwarranted; when I let my supervisor know I was moving on, she thanked me and just hired one of the other two hundred idiots anxiously waiting for an unpaid PA job in Hollywood (possibly Plies).

Another new development in my busier schedule was a weekly all-ages party in Los Angeles called, in the most endearingly dated way possible, Club Bling Bling. It was thrown by a few local teenagers from one of the most exclusive and posh private high schools in LA and, make no mistake, was just a venue for underage rich kids to get drunk, dance to 2001 hits like 112's "Peaches & Cream," and hook up. Seventeen-year-olds with last names like Katzenberg and Winkler and young celebrities like Anna Paquin and the Olsen twins frequented the packed party, held at Whisky a Go Go on Sunset Boulevard. I was hired to host and subsequently battle three or four different amateur rappers each night. I had come a long way from hiding my skills in a public Valley high school, now battling multiple times a night for children of the über-wealthy.

It was as tiring as it sounds, especially since most of the young challengers would practice for weeks to take me out, while I had the disadvantage of meeting them only seconds before I had to annihilate them. The competition was never fierce, though, mostly due to my challengers' prepubescence, and I never had much fear of losing. It was just a paid gig to me, but it quickly became a highlight of Bling Bling for partygoers, right behind getting to use their older sister's ID for the first time or getting their first hand job in the parking lot. One of my more memorable lines, delivered while glancing at my watch, was "Just give me this win, we don't have to pretend / Let's judge this shit quick, his mom picks him up at 10." Most of the time I felt like Billy Madison aggressively swatting the shots of grade-schoolers, but the bloodbaths made me a shitload of new upper-class listeners, and I was fine with that.

With no camera phones or YouTube at the time, these sessions live on only as myth, even if I did rack up easily fifty wins in two months. To be honest, though, I didn't really retain a lot of memories from these nights either. They would keep me out until about midnight; then I'd have to race back to USC, grab a few hours of sleep before morning classes, and eventually end up in a studio until late at night recording tracks for a demo to bring to meetings. It became a bit robotic, but making it a routine helped me get through it all in one piece. I didn't have much time to think about the pressure I was facing at school, or the pressure I was getting to record songs as exciting as my battles. And the best news about those recording sessions, no matter how tired I ended up, was that I was finally starting to create original music I was proud of. I made a few songs with the Baka Boyz, who were still somewhat involved in my project, and a few more with DJ Lethal. But it wasn't until I tapped into my nonexistent Hispanic roots that I started to understand exactly what songwriting was.

———

Talk to any avid rap historian or even casual fan, for that matter, and you'll hear that being a good battle rapper doesn't always mean you can write a hit song. Actually, history has proven the exact opposite. Battle rappers are usually awful when it comes to making radio-friendly tunes that include hooks and structured verses (and topics other than banging another rapper's mother). It's similar to how stand-up comedians aren't necessarily known for writing great movies. They're two entirely different things. Ask Chris Rock about *Head of State*.

Proving the theory true, the first half dozen songs I made basically just bragged about how good I was at rapping, which in my defense *is* what 80 percent of all rap songs are about anyway. But to succeed in hip-hop on a mainstream level, it's about taking those raw verses and making a fully complete, catchy song with them. It's not an easy process. If it were, I probably wouldn't have written this memoir, because I'd be too busy being fed grapes by Hawaiian Tropic models or whatever shit I assume Pitbull does all day. When it came down to it, being a celebrated battle rapper is actually a disadvantage, since I knew I'd have to prove my songwriting abilities if I ever wanted any of these important meetings to actually connect. So when I stumbled across a beat that sounded like a mariachi band performing at the Apollo, all created by an unknown local producer, I knew it was my chance to write a hit.

We were right in the middle of what the industry was calling the "Latin Explosion," where Enrique Iglesias, Ricky Martin, Shakira, and Jennifer Lopez were simultaneously blowing up. Even Christina Aguilera exploited the fact that she was half-Latina and won a Latin Grammy, an awards show that debuted during my time recording these demo songs. In that initial Chris Schwartz meeting, somewhere between obsessing over my Missy Elliott debacle and staring at the boom box in a cold sweat, I heard him ask if I was Latin. I basically pointed at my nose and said no, and he just changed the subject.

But I always wondered about what would've happened if I had said yes. Would he have been excited and advised me to just mindlessly start making Latin music despite not having any evidence of my heritage? Although I never asked, I like to think that's what he was alluding to. So, when I heard the beat to what would end up being a song ridiculously called "Caliente Karlito," I knew what I wanted to do: I was going to make a Latin song. I knew little to no Spanish and figured that if groups like 98 Degrees were exploiting whatever small amount of Mexican DNA hid somewhere in their lineage, couldn't I just admit I wasn't Latin but still cash in? Because, truly, what's the difference? You're still being an opportunistic asshole, *amigo*.

The track started with a fictitious record-label A&R guy forcing me to make a Latin song, despite my insistence that the idea seemed racist. In a whiny voice, he continued to pressure me, promising everything would be alright but forcing me to strike while the iron was hot. So I caved and got the fiesta popping. My first line was "I know Latin music is hot, and the label wants a hit / But there's a problem, I don't know much Spanish," and from there I continually fumbled Spanish words, calling myself "the real *Papi Chulo*," and yelling, "Drop my chalupas!"—all bars that would make Cesar Chavez wince, especially pronounced in my extremely Caucasian accent. Lyrics like "I'm gonna keep on rapping in Latin to go platinum / So my record gets paid and played at Puerto Rican parades" got the point across perfectly, but it wasn't until I wrote the hook that I knew I was on to something.

I enlisted a female singer to come in and, with a perfect Spanish accent (she was Asian to further the joke), serenade us with, "Caliente Karlito, *no comprendo español / Gringo* acting Latino, what a *pendejo*," which translates—roughly—to "Hot Karl, doesn't understand Spanish / White guy acting Latin, what an asshole." Behind her, in the background, I mindlessly screamed things like "Play this on Cinco de Mayo," "La Bamba, Ritchie Valens," and "This is for La Raza." It was racially insensitive, sure, but not much worse than seeking fame by pretending you were raised in a Mexican household, which it seemed like everyone was doing back then.

Somehow "Caliente Karlito" quickly found itself on Napster, which at the time was not only ushering in the state of the music industry we know today but was also helping create buzz for musicians without a major label before that became the norm. At first I was concerned about the leak, since it was purely recorded as a demo, but it quickly became popular with file sharers, gaining hundreds of new fans a day. In an instance of foreshadowing, the song was commonly mistitled "NEW EMINEM SONG," which couldn't have made me angrier at the time, since I was trying my hardest to differentiate my persona. After seeing its popularity online, though, I believed I had the makings of a hit song on my hands, or at least a controversial fire starter that would cause a racial revolution. If there was any time to sign a major label record deal, it was *ahora*.

Having a song online made my Bling Bling battles even more popular; there was now a line of suckers every week who thought they could take out the champ. The whole thing was so strange. Bling Bling was like *Downton Abbey* in the sense that I was the help escorted to the family dinner table only to battle, then, when finished, hurried back downstairs to minimize my ability to pass deadly influenza to the wealthy. Truthfully, though, the girls there were so young, it was better not to converse with them anyway. And since most of the guys siphoned their parents' Bombay Sapphire and were learning what drunk felt like for the first time, I never actually felt like I was missing something I'd want to partake in anyway. I'd usually just battle, find the same bartender each week, order a soda, and roll my eyes over and over again until they got tired. So it stood out when a guy in my age bracket approached with his hand out to introduce himself.

For a few seconds I thought it was someone's older brother showing up at the club to punch me in the face for something I'd said in the heat of battle, but I quickly learned that wasn't the case. It was an Interscope A&R executive, someone I had met in passing before, now braving the tween set to watch me in action. He admitted he was blown away and recited a lyric where I compared my opponent's career trajectory to that of Dwight Gooden. I quickly remembered this guy wasn't just any A&R guy; he was Jimmy Iovine's nephew DJ, a twentysomething being primed to eventually run the entire department, if not the entire label. He had been heavily involved in the early development of Eminem, even appearing in his first low-budget music video, and was now looking to build his own roster within the family business.

Where Jimmy seemed meager and reserved in interviews, DJ was round and excited, even animated when it came to talking about rap music and sports—not yet jaded like most of the industry execs I had already met with. That night at Bling Bling we talked about the Mets, the insanity of the kids grinding around us, and my alleged upcoming meeting with his uncle. DJ was quick to make me feel at ease, assuring me it would happen but that Jimmy was insanely busy and hadn't come up for air in over a week. I nodded to show DJ I heard him over the loud music, but I knew deep down that if Jimmy really wanted to see me, he'd make the time. As we said good-bye, I thought on my toes and reached into my backpack for a new cut of "Caliente Karlito" on CD. It was the only copy I had, but I knew with a quick phone call I could get another—and who better to hear my newest song, and my most likely attempt at a hit, than my connection to Jimmy Iovine? DJ thanked me and promised he'd listen in the car, and a few seconds later I was back to being the world's most awkward chaperone and the only person at Bling Bling with the ability to grow facial hair.

That night I got back to USC around 1:00 a.m., tired but thankful for the few hundred dollars now added to my wallet. Walking into my room, I noticed a flashing light on my answering machine, a device I'm hoping you're old enough to at least know existed. I assumed it was my mother, checking in to see if anything had developed professionally since our last talk or to check up on my sore throat or to tell me a neighbor had died of cancer (those are still the only options I have with her). Or maybe it was my friend Fitz from down the hall, hoping to partake in our late-night tradition of watching *Kids in the Hall: Brain Candy* until our bodies forced us to go to sleep. However, no matter how many guesses I took, standing there exhausted, I never would've guessed what I'd hear next.

"Hi, Karl, this is Clara calling from Jimmy Iovine's office. It's currently around midnight, and Jimmy was hoping you could come by his house tomorrow, Monday night, around nine, for dinner and a movie. Let me know."

She gave her office number and instructed me to call as soon as I could and leave my availability on her voice mail. I couldn't believe my ears. Not only was the Jimmy Iovine meeting now set, but it was at *his house*. And he had a receptionist who apparently worked all night long, which seems baller but also brings a bunch of labor laws to mind. But that wasn't my concern right then. My concern was getting ready for this introduction, which seemed to have become a top priority once DJ heard "Caliente Karlito." I laid a possible outfit on the floor, like a boy getting ready for his first day of elementary school, and quickly realized that, with that action alone, I was very different from any rapper

Jimmy Iovine had met before. I doubted any members of The Outlawz adorably predetermined their outfits in anticipation of a first meeting. Yet I had come this far, still looking like Milhouse and sounding like Kermit the Frog. I accepted Jimmy's invitation and put more thought into this dinner and movie than any date I'd ever had, or any I've had since. After playing out hundreds of possible scenarios in my head, I popped in the *Kids in the Hall: Brain Candy* DVD and fell asleep, nervously praying he didn't actually think I was Latino.

A rare live performance of "Caliente Karlito,"
where I look as comfortable speaking
Spanish as that sombrero looks on my head.

"CALIENTE KARLITO" LYRICS, 1999

(19 years old)

[The intro is a conversation between a major label A&R guy and myself, where he advises me to make a song in Spanish. I quickly explain I'm not Latin, and he says it doesn't matter. He says, think Santana, Jennifer Lopez, etc. The beat kicks in and I'm freaking out, since I don't know Spanish and I know this song will come off sounding racist.]

OK, I know Latin music is hot and the label wants a hit,
But there's a problem, I don't know much Spanish,
So *señorita*, hit the speakers if you're feeling me,

I wanna come more Latin than a Ricky Martin homo tendency,[1]
So I'm gonna keep on rapping in Latin to go platinum,
So my record gets paid and played at Puerto Rican parades,
But now I advance, and hope to bring it tight, man,
While you're annoying like Rosie Perez was your hypeman,
I know I can, Hot Karl is the real *Papi Chulo*,
Come any closer I'll stick my finger up your *culo*,
Yeah, I said it, you sound like bitches up on the mic,
Your next concert should be *VH1 Divas Live*,[2]
It's the *gringo*, who brings it so, *muy gracioso*,
El naco grifo, I'm anything but bilingual,
My singles for the barrios, *vatos* in drunken stupors,
Acting like Mexican storm troopers, yelling,
  "Drop my chalupas."

(hook)

Caliente Karlito,
No compredo español (Viva gordita),
Gringo acting Latino (Rico Suave),
What a *pendejo* (What an asshole).

---

1   It wasn't only battling; in most hip-hop of that era homophobic punch
    lines were used frequently. In this case, I was just joking that Ricky
    Martin was gay years before he officially came out of the closet. Times
    have changed, and most rappers have become more tolerant (except for
    you, Marshall), but this part of my time capsule just sucks, even if I am
    kind of psychic.
2   Once an annual tradition, *VH1 Divas Live* was a televised concert
    featuring live musical performances by female superstars like Celine
    Dion, Mariah Carey, Aretha Franklin, and Shania Twain, all to raise
    money for charity and promote sisterhood. In contrast, now VH1 fo-
    cuses mostly on women who've made it their job to marry a basketball
    player.

Oh la, oh la, oh la (Livin' *la vida loca*),
Oh la, oh la, oh (This is for La Raza[3]),
Caliente Karlito (Pump up la radio),
What a *pendejo* (What? What?).

[Before the second verse the A&R jerk has returned, telling me to get more pumped up. I explain I'm trying my hardest, and he tries to motivate me some more. I say I'll try harder in the second verse.]

Doesn't it bother you, hearing me molest this language,
Right now I bet you're wishing Fat Joe was the one who sang
   this,
But it's Karl, and I'm just gonna help your career to end,
'Cause I know you ain't getting action like Jessica Simpson's
   boyfriend[4],
I'm just trying to find an ID like white kids on Alvarado Street,
So let me be, *roca adoté toda la noche*,[5]
[A&R guy: "Karl, you just said you'll be rocking me all night long,"]
FUCK, I thought I said I was trying to learn Spanish to rap this
   song,
No matter the language, don't attack the champion,
You beating me rapping, that's like Jim Abbott clapping,
I'm trying so hard to speak Spanish up in my flows,
Sounding ridiculous like Outkast's wardrobe in music videos,
I'm busting Latin flavor and for a whiteboy, that's tricky,

---

3   I included a few shout-outs to my favorite actual old-school Latin hip-hop songs, including this one to Kid Frost's regional hit "La Raza," and later nods to Lighter Shade of Brown and Mellow Man Ace.

4   One of the problems with being a pop culture–obsessed rapper is that your lyrics can be outdated in a matter of weeks. This allusion to Nick Lachey dating a virgin Jessica Simpson could not seem more ancient in 2016, like my grandparents talking about movies "before they were talkies."

5   I actually tried to use proper Spanish here and blew it, proving I really shouldn't have been doing this song in the first place.

So eat your heart out, Enrique, Marc, Ricky,
So *silencio*, and be quiet like you supposed ta',
You talk about being dope, but *y mañana es otro cosa*.

(hook)

Caliente Karlito (Play this on Cinco de Mayo),
No comprendo español (Edward James Olmos),
Gringo acting Latino (This is for Kid Frost),
What a *pendejo* (What an asshole).

Oh la, oh la, oh la (La Bamba, Ritchie Valens),
Oh la, oh la, oh (*Mi mamacita*),
Caliente Karlito (*Ay yi yi*),
What a *pendejo* (*No comprende*).

[Before the third verse, the A&R guy finally agrees this might not be
the best approach. He instructs me to just kill it in English for the final
bars. I'm excited.]

Even my mic check is doper than your whole compact disc,
And my message is positive like Whitney Houston urine tests,
For real though, a rapper who looks like Elvis Costello,
I always reach the top and you come up short like Willow,[6]
You better than me? Come on, what are you joking?
Everything that you record sounds like *Say What? Karaoke*,
You can't smoke me, you have no clue what I'm about,
You ain't doing shit like A. C. Green in a whorehouse,[7]
You have lyrics? Sure, and DJ Quik ain't dissing Dre,

---

6 A reference to the 1988 Ron Howard classic *Willow*? I'll accept my
   Peabody now.
7 Every so often I would include one of my favorite Roll Call lines into a
   song, just so they weren't lost in the abyss of forgotten LA radio. Freestyle
   battling was always a good breeding ground for possible song lyrics down
   the road, especially since only a small fraction of people heard it once.

Serious, I get busy like Kelly Price at a buffet,
My mission is to kick you straight outta the rap game,
Have you doing posse cuts with College Boyz and MC Brains,
But some still show hesitance, my styles against their preferences,
Too random of references, loaded in every sentences,
Thicker than Daisy Fuentes-es, baby, I'm outta sight,
So with all of my might, I choke players like Bobby Knight,
So, *señorita*, I want that hook lasting for days,
It's Hot Karl's cheap attempt to cash in on the Latin craze!

(hook)

Caliente Karlito (Elián González),
No comprendo español (Margaritas and Coronas),
Gringo acting Latino (This is for *Federales*),
What a *pendejo* (What an asshole).

Oh la, oh la, oh la (For spring breakers in Cancun),
Oh la, oh la, oh (Or the Donkey Show in TJ),
Caliente Karlito (And Lighter Shade of Brown),
Gringo pendejo (What? What?).

Caliente Karlito (For my high school Spanish teachers),
No compredo español (And Mellow Man Ace),
Gringo acting Latino (Cheech Marin and Paul Rodriguez),
What a *pendejo* (YA!).

Oh la, oh la, oh la (*Por favor, mucho agua*),
Oh la, oh la, oh (*Mi amore big chi chis*),
Caliente Karlito (Who am I kidding?),
Gringo pendejo.
[A&R guy: "That's the hit right there."]

8

JIMMY IOVINE'S SALMON PLATE

I didn't need a twenty-four-hour secretary to realize I had scheduled the two most important meetings of my life on the same Monday. I was set to meet with Jeff Kwatinetz of The Firm at 6:00 p.m., then make my way across town for my moment with Jimmy Iovine, completing a one-two punch with arguably the most powerful duo in music at the time. DJ called me first thing that morning to make sure I had confirmed with Jimmy and to let me know he'd be attending. He revealed that Jimmy had indeed heard "Caliente Karlito," which DJ was now calling "an obvious hit," and that the song had helped rush the meeting into existence. When I inquired about what movie theater we'd be going to, he laughed like I'd just asked how Santa is able to slide down the chimney to deliver me gifts and explained that we'd be using Jimmy's home movie theater. Ignoring my embarrassment, he asked if I wanted to get together beforehand to go over things, and I casually mentioned I couldn't because of a "meeting on Wilshire." The silence on the phone helped me realize I might have made a mistake.

DJ pointedly asked, "Are you meeting with The Firm?" leaving nothing to the imagination.

"Yeah, they wanted a meeting," I innocently answered, revealing the naive child underneath the industry buzz.

DJ explained that Kwatinetz was going to war with Interscope and attempting to bid on every artist they showed interest in for his new record label. Despite the fact that The Firm managed many of the more successful bands on Jimmy's roster, including everyone's favorite HK supporter, Fred Durst, a rivalry was ready to erupt. DJ gently inquired whether he could share this new information with his uncle, and since I saw nothing wrong with it, I said, "Sure." Then DJ started to give me directions to Jimmy's estate, and I had to pretend I didn't know where Jimmy's house was. As a die-hard Death Row Records fan, I knew exactly where I was going.

When you talk about Interscope in the late 1990s/early 2000s, it's hard not to bring up Death Row Records. Jimmy had given Suge Knight, the label's CEO, his first big break, and they made millions of dollars together on releases from Dr. Dre, Snoop Doggy Dogg, Tupac, and Nate Dogg. But, like most of Suge's business deals, it quickly went south. So south, in fact, that Suge Knight released a DVD called *Death Row Uncut* that showed clear photos of Jimmy's mansion, along with the address. It was no shock to hear that Jimmy, who lived in that estate with his young children, feared for his life based on past stories about Suge's gang affiliations. Suge's name would later be thrown around during investigations of the murders of Biggie and Tupac, and no matter how the mighty has since fallen, at one point in his career, he was the most feared man in America. He's currently facing life in prison for allegedly killing a man with his car and then fleeing the scene, but weirdly, he ended up being one of the nicest guys I ever met in the rap industry.

I mostly recorded in professional studios, ones that could be inhabited concurrently by numerous musicians—or terrifying rap moguls like Suge Knight—in separate rooms. I explain this only because I know most rappers nowadays, the type with dollar signs in their names, can do the same thing from their bedrooms and we'd hear little to no difference. But back then, before home studios, part of the fun of recording was seeing who was working in a nearby room. Occasionally, I'd find myself eating a bagel in the kitchen with another up-and-comer, like the one time I small-talked with Petey Pablo. Every once in a while, a rapper would walk, uninvited, into our studio and hang out to listen to what we were making. It was rare, but when it did happen, it always ended in a story worth retelling. And one day in 2000, while I was knee-deep in a mix for a new song, I got the most memorable, and frightening, studio visit of all.

It's important to establish Suge's history with white rappers and his reputation for uninvited studio visits before I go any further. One of the most infamous tales about the mogul involves the publishing rights to "Ice Ice Baby" by Caucasian car crash Vanilla Ice (legal name Robert Van Winkle). Soon after the track exploded, California rapper Mario "Chocolate" Johnson claimed he wrote the song for Vanilla Ice and enlisted one of his "associates," a then unknown bodyguard named Suge Knight, to deal with the disagreement. The details of the story change from person to person, but allegedly Suge Knight dangled Vanilla Ice over a Miami hotel balcony by the feet until he signed over the writer's credit.

And years later, once Suge became one of the most successful label heads in music, his reputation only became more mythical. Word got around town that Suge would just stroll into studio sessions, walk up to the engineer, and commandeer the tapes—the song was now "his." He would just sit on the product or give it to one of his other artists as a beat, but either way, it wasn't yours anymore. Like when people took candy from a baby and created that weird saying everyone uses. So to say that the music industry, and Interscope specifically, was afraid of Suge Knight would be a massive understatement.

After about two hours of pecking away at a song that day, the engineer asked, in a mysterious tone usually reserved for when someone asks if you want to see a dead body, "Do you want to know who's in the studio next door?" Intrigued, I said yes, and he leaned in to whisper, "Suge Knight."

I only read two or three of the Harry Potter books before I got bored, but I do remember that when they mentioned Voldemort, they had to say, "He-Who-Must-Not-be-Named," and it genuinely felt like Suge should've gotten the same treatment. Even if half the stories were exaggerated, where there was smoke, there was fire (not just weed). From that point on, I tried to stay in my room, hoping to get through the day's chores as quickly as possible. I wasn't willing to hang around to see if the stories were true. But as we started a final mix, with only a few minutes to go, I heard the studio door swing open and smelled what I assumed was a cigar. My nightmare had come true: it was Suge Knight.

We had just started the song, playing it loudly on the speakers for a last take, and neither myself nor the engineer looked up from the board, knowing exactly who we'd be looking at if we did. Like those two *Jurassic Park* kids hiding from raptors in the kitchen, we knew any movement would trigger killer instincts. We played dead. We didn't even breathe. I thought maybe he'd leave after the first hook or during the bridge, but for the song's entire duration, he didn't move. When the song finished, we sat for what felt like ten minutes, but was probably more like ten seconds, in complete silence.

"Was that you?" Suge asked me without ANY indication of whether my answer would prompt him to shake my hand or shank me.

I waited for a second, fully trying to figure out my options. It felt like the world's most terrifying Choose Your Own Adventure. I closed my eyes and answered.

"Yes. Yes it was."

There was a brief silence; then he took a drag from his cigar and said, "That's some good shit."

And then we chatted for a little while. He asked me about my influences and where I was from, and I asked him what he was doing next door (he was recording the album of his then wife, Michel'le). I wish I could tell you he then called me a "stupid whiteboy" and punched me in the stomach, but he didn't; he was just *really* polite. After a few minutes, he shook my hand and walked out.

I obviously never met John Wayne Gacy, but if I did, I would've either met the party clown who performed every weekend for smiling kids, or I would've met the psychopathic serial killer who buried bodies under his house and became the closest thing we have to Tim Curry in *It*. I guess it would've just depended on what day I met him. And with Suge, I bet it's the same thing. I'm not making a "Hitler was nice to dogs" argument, 'cause he is, without a doubt, a trash-can human. Obviously, Suge is nowhere near Hitler-esque—unless you listened to that MC Hammer comeback album start to finish—but I still have this one fond memory to fall back on. I caught him on a good day. And despite his DVD helping me know where to go for this Interscope meeting, I knew not to bring up this story at Jimmy Iovine's house.

Before I made my way to Jimmy's, though, I had my meeting with Jeff Kwatinetz, who also ended up being a rather nice dude. He was tall, confident, and good-looking, and had a clear ability to sell you just about anything, even a record label that didn't really exist yet. He started the meeting by saying, "Fred Durst has told me a lot about you," and I'm still not sure if that was a good or bad thing. I was quick to admit that other labels were pursuing me, and in return he promised that his new business venture had big budgets and a major interest in entering the distribution game with Hot Karl front and center. He mentioned getting Ice Cube on a song with me, which made it hard to not just stand on the table and yell, "Hand me the papers, I'll sign anything!" but somehow I remained calm.

On my way out of the office, Jeff introduced me to the Backstreet Boy who looks like a magician and then asked if I wanted to join them at some Hollywood nightclub that night. I told him I had plans, keeping the specifics secret, but that I appreciated the offer. The Firm had just acquired the forgettable '80s shoe company Pony and was preparing for its relaunch, so he handed me a gift bag of apparel (which I eventually gave to my housekeeper). Then I was on my way to Jimmy Iovine's pad.

I left The Firm with a confidence I hadn't yet felt; the unthinkable was actually looking possible. Jeff assured me that, during a time when these agreements were deep in the six figures, he would be able to compete with the big boys. I had always assumed I'd either get a record deal that was *just* enough to survive on while I produced a full-length album, or not get one at all. And I was fine with that. But now, with what Jeff told me, it was looking very probable that I'd be seeing a nice payday. So, even if at some point I blurted out "Do you think Suge could climb your security fence?" during my meeting with Jimmy, I would still have a Firm plan B.

—

Jimmy Iovine's house was big in a way that tells you his grandkids' grandkids will never have to work. He had manned security sheds around the property, with Doberman pinschers chained to some. Had I been blindfolded and brought to the house, I would've assumed a drug kingpin, suspicious of my recent decline in sales, had angrily summoned me. Sadly, I couldn't avoid embarrassing myself in front of these guards; with a straight face I said, "Hot Karl to see Jimmy Iovine." I'm surprised they didn't shoot me and search my car for that Death Row DVD. As I pulled up the driveway, I realized that Jimmy lived across the street from the Playboy mansion, a fact that seemed insane to me, a Valley kid who grew up across the street from an electronics salesman. The all-night secretary didn't seem so outlandish anymore.

Once I was escorted into the house, I found DJ waiting for me, watching *SportsCenter* and looking more comfortable in the situation than any other A&R in the company would, since he also spent his holidays there. We were in just one wing of the estate, and that alone doubled the size of my entire childhood home. He said Jimmy would be out soon, and while we waited, we talked at length about my possible future at Interscope. DJ went into a full-court press, listing the impressive lineup the label currently advertised, from No Doubt to Dr. Dre to U2 to Marilyn Manson to Jurassic 5. Jimmy treated acts like Pokémon: he collected them all. Outside of Berry Gordy and Quincy Jones, no record executive had seen success like Jimmy Iovine. Luckily, DJ admitted he saw an open roster spot for Hot Karl. And with that, Jimmy entered the room.

Hidden behind a low-riding baseball cap and an extra-large hooded sweatshirt, Jimmy made his way to the couch to shake my hand. He had the presence of one of Snow White's dwarves, almost shuffling his feet to where I was sitting. For a man with a gigantic reputation, he sure was the size of a middle-schooler. I was still dating Paige at the time, and her parents were huge Fleetwood Mac fans, a band that Jimmy was associated with for his work on Stevie Nicks's solo career (and vagina, since they reportedly dated for years). My girlfriend advised me of the love connection, suggesting that if I were to get nervous at any time during the meeting, I should imagine little Jimmy Iovine mounting sex goddess Stevie Nicks in the '80s. It was a good idea in theory, but now, with the man just feet away, the thought was only making me giggle. Where I should've looked confident, I was coming off as stoned, which he—after working with Snoop Dogg for years—may have actually appreciated. Jimmy apologized for being late, admitting he'd been getting better acquainted with my music in his office. He cut to the chase and said he wasn't interested in playing any games or delaying the movie, so he wanted to ask, straight up, what could make me part of the Interscope family tonight.

Despite all my preparation, it was a question I wasn't ready for. I sat there, a bit taken aback, without a word to say. It was the moment I, as well as basically anyone trying to kick off a music career, had always hoped for. Jimmy Iovine had been controlling music careers for years, consistently releasing albums that would go over ten times platinum, and now the man with all the power wanted me to tell *him* what to do. My mouth went dry and I stuttered. I panicked. I was in way over my head, and I immediately wanted to run back to Sancho's room and focus on co-opting other people's beats.

The silence continued until two men in suits walked in, holding plates and saving the day. Quietly, they placed salmon dinners in front of each of us and walked right out. And with that, we were joined by Jimmy's preteen son, Jamie, who'd been given my music earlier in the week and had since announced he was the "biggest Hot Karl fan in the world." He was thrilled to meet me and proclaimed that on the entire Interscope roster, he was most excited about Hot Karl and a rock group called Sev that his dad had signed earlier that year. Jimmy chuckled and let Jamie know they hadn't signed me yet. Sev was dropped from Interscope soon thereafter, so maybe Jamie Iovine wasn't quite the good-luck charm I had hoped for, but it was still obvious his dad listened closely to his opinions.

Jamie quickly left, taking his plate back to his room, and Jimmy started to pitch again. The only thing interrupting his patter was our sporadic chomping of fish, during which I struggled to build up the courage to respond. He reiterated DJ's thoughts on "Caliente Karlito," calling it a first single, and mentioned Timbaland, who was signed to a prosperous production deal at Interscope at the time, as a possibility to come in and rework it. If his initial question stopped me dead in my tracks, these words of praise had me legitimately paralyzed. He promised high-budget videos, *TRL* exposure, expensive guest rappers, and a marketing budget that would make any other offer seem minor league. I was being offered the keys to Interscope, and I'd never felt better.

Since this night in 2000, Jimmy Iovine has become one of

the most successful entrepreneurs of all time, selling mediocre headphones for outlandish prices and in turn building an empire of riches that Scrooge McDuck would consider too deep of a pool to swim in. I saw firsthand the man's ability to sell, and his fortune makes total sense. He sold me right there in the room. If anyone had a machine that could make your music career a reality, it was him, and he let you know how he'd do it with an ease unparalleled in any business transaction I've been involved in since. His track record spoke for itself.

I have to assume now, looking back, that I was getting the grade-A dog-and-pony show, but honestly, it was thrilling. Jimmy wanted to get me into the studio immediately, in both Los Angeles and New York simultaneously. He would have DJ officially run the project on both coasts, making Hot Karl the first artist to exist solely under his supervision. I would also be allowed to graduate USC, wrapping up the final forty credits needed to get my degree while crafting a major-label debut album. The promises were gigantic, as were my eyes, and Jimmy ended his speech with the inviting and important query, "Do you have any questions for me?"

I sure did.

I had to address the major fear I'd had when walking into Jimmy Iovine's house that night and contemplating Interscope Records as a whole. All you need to do is spend about thirty seconds listening to my music, or revisit the alternative title "Caliente Karlito" had on Napster, to hear a possibly major roadblock for my career as the early 2000s progressed. I sounded a lot like Eminem.

There were two different reasons for this undeniable similarity:

(1) We were both white guys who hardly disguised our real voices as many Caucasian rappers had done before us. Most white people had emulated African American rappers' affectations, which always came off as inauthentic to me and, if we can judge based on Vanilla Ice's career, most of America. An easy way to see the difference between that style and ours is to listen to a Marky Mark interview, then compare it to an interview with Mark Wahlberg. Or listen to an Iggy Azalea song, then imagine the voice she uses when she gets pulled over by cops. Em and I were both high-pitched, exaggerated enunciators who referenced pop culture, which might start to bleed into the next reason.

(2) We were shaped by the same influences. Growing up as white dudes battling for credibility in a style of music we both respected, it made sense we would gravitate toward the same sound. I compare us to two baseball players mentored by the same coach. It's inevitable that you'll see a very similar style based on their teachings, but deviations will exist, and, in our case, those differences rested in our subject matter and upbringings. I thoroughly enjoyed Eminem's first Interscope album, connecting with his point of view and postmodern sense of humor because, well, it sounded a lot like what I had been doing for years. I can't say I heard the likeness in our voices back then as much as I do today, and that's probably because I've since distanced myself from my work. But taking a step back now, I clearly hear how you could mistake us for each other.

That said, it still irritates me to hear people think I was "biting," or copying, anything Marshall Mathers did. My voice, tone, and inflection hadn't changed since the night I performed with Rickye Kidd at Club Spice. At twelve years old I had rapped about shooting Another Bad Creation and taking a lovely young girl named Iesha to Denny's so I could hook up with her. I had been constant and unchanged, dealing in shock or ironic ultra-violence in my regular voice since before I had pubes, while Eminem's early tapes actually sounded like Nas or AZ. Believe it or not, I sounded like Eminem before Eminem did.

All this went through my head the night Jimmy Iovine's receptionist called, so I knew to keep my enthusiasm at bay. Interscope was the most elite record label in the world, the New York Yankees of music, even selling five million copies of a record from that shitty rock/rap group the Bloodhound Gang, and they were the fucking worst. But I also knew Interscope was heavily invested in the rapper I was most frequently compared to. He was the *real* great white hope. It felt weird, and even slightly suspicious, that Interscope would want us both on the same roster.

I heard rumors that Jimmy was also interested in a bunch of other Caucasian MCs, including gifted Connecticut lyricist Apathy; Atlanta's next export, Bubba Sparxxx; and a country boy out of Nashville named Haystak. The CEO appeared to be hoarding us, hoping to gain a monopoly on the profitable fair-skinned rapper trend, or to clear the way for his, and Dr. Dre's, Golden Boy by shelving any competition. The latter seemed crazy and paranoid, especially since Jimmy would be spending a large amount of money on signing any of us. Despite the fact that our contracts would essentially be a tax write-off for someone that rich, it seemed like a lot of work to stifle someone's career. But it was still something I needed to investigate before sitting down with Jimmy. I didn't really have anyone in the industry who I trusted enough to give me an unbiased opinion, but when it came to getting a whole bunch of money in a situation that could be, excuse the pun, shady, I fortunately knew one expert.

When I reached out to Mack 10 a few days before my big Interscope meeting, it was the first time I had spoken to him since he left my parents' house carrying $50,000 of unclaimed cash in his briefcase. I didn't really know where we stood professionally, but somehow I knew I could count on him to be a caring mentor and friend (no matter how rough and rugged his lyrics were). When I told him I needed some advice, he invited me to his studio so we could talk in person. When I arrived, not only was Mack recording a song, but he was there with one of my heroes, MC Eiht, a West Coast legend who had spent years in the pioneering group Compton's Most Wanted. Being a fan, I was exhilarated to meet him. We briefly talked, and by "we briefly talked" I mean I yelled questions at him about his music and he politely placated me with information, assuming I was there to meet Mack 10 because I'd won a charity auction or something. I was an annoying fly buzzing around the recording studio, lacking any of the swagger I should've had as a rapper about to sign a lucrative label deal.

So, either for more privacy or to get me away from MC Eiht, Mack took me into a nearby empty studio, where we sat down and he lit a cigar. As I predicted, he was happy to see me and interested in hearing what had happened since we last talked. I told him about my meetings with The Firm and Jimmy Iovine, and although he admitted his disappointment that I hadn't given his offer more consideration, he congratulated me on what looked to be a career moving in the right direction. I conveyed my concerns about Jimmy signing me to take me out of the marketplace for Eminem, and he understood my worry.

"Listen," he said calmly in between drags of his cigar, "Jimmy got deep pockets. I get that it looks dope to you. But would Steve Young have played for the 49ers if they still had Joe Montana?"

It was a genius metaphor, something I could easily translate and connect with, even if I wasn't happy with the question. Why would a team let an up-and-coming prospect take the field, no matter how talented he was, if their all-star MVP was still slotted in that position with a long-term contract? I felt much more comfortable moving forward because now I knew exactly what I needed to address when I met with Jimmy.

Mack let me hang out in his studio for a while and even asked me to suggest lyrics to Eiht, who finally learned why I was there and couldn't believe it. He called me "Wall Street," which, looking back, was without a doubt a better name than Hot Karl. I'm almost sure the song they were working on never saw the light of day, but if Mack 10 ever rapped, "Two glocks locked on my side, that's truth / Shoot through your car, now you gotta sunroof," a Jewish kid who's never shot a gun wrote that.

Back at Jimmy's, I took a deep breath, readying a question I had rehearsed over a dozen times in my head. I don't remember how it was *supposed* to come out, but when it was time to speak, I nervously blurted out, "Are you going to fuck me over?"

Here we are in a serious business meeting, with a man ready to make my dreams come true, and I'm talking like a seventeen-year-old girl cautiously getting back together with her ex. Jimmy laughed and asked what I meant.

"Well, I'm just wondering where I fit in with Eminem around. And I have people warning me that you would spend all this money just to shelve me."

Jimmy looked disgusted. "Why would I do that?"

I shyly pretended to come up with an idea off the cuff. "Um, so he doesn't have any competition, I guess."

Jimmy assured me that this just wasn't the case. He explained that although we were both white rappers, that's where our similarities ended. He pointed out the drastic differences in our content and explained that, if marketed correctly, he saw little to no overlap between us. He went as far as saying that what Eminem was to inner-city Detroit, Hot Karl would be for the suburbs. If he could have dozens of similar rock groups on his roster, he asked, why would two white rappers be a problem? Jimmy must've gathered that my concerns were put to rest, because he quickly changed the subject.

He exposed a slight smile underneath his curved brim.

"So, are you contemplating any other labels?"

I started to say yes, knowing that if I expected Jimmy to be honest about his intentions, I had to do the same. But before I could get my answer out, a butler walked in, escorting someone new into the room. At first I didn't recognize him, probably because it was the last place on earth that I expected to see Jeff Kwatinetz. He was now entering our meeting without warning, unable to hide his shock when he saw me on the couch.

"Hey, Jeff, you know Hot Karl?" Jimmy asked, well aware of the answer.

I shot DJ a look, completely confused by the turn of events. I quickly put two and two together. In what can only be described as a business move colder than anything in *Glengarry Glen Ross*, Jimmy Iovine, knowing The Firm was my other major label option, had invited its owner over to his house in the middle of the night, without telling him I'd be there—only to prove to me he could do something like that. It felt like the quickest checkmate in the history of the music industry. I learned that Jimmy was the Godfather and that everyone else was basically Amerigo Bonasera. Do you want to sign with the guy who gets people to come to his house at 10:00 p.m. for a meeting, or with the guy who drives across town for a 10:00 p.m. meeting at that other guy's house? It seemed like an easy answer, and I couldn't believe Jimmy was asking the question without saying a word. The man had other CEOs on call twenty-four hours a day, like they were his receptionist. "Sure, I know him," said Jeff, walking over to shake my hand. Then the two left the room to have their planned business meeting, Jimmy instructing us to start the movie without him. And just like that, they disappeared.

I didn't know where to start with DJ as he walked me to the theater. I had a million questions as we passed a concession stand on the way into a screening space that could comfortably seat a football team. I was so flustered, I hardly even noticed a magical hand from behind the counter immediately replace the Snapple and Reese's Pieces I took. (Later I would wonder just how many people worked at Jimmy Iovine's house.) Jamie rejoined us, taking a seat in the back of the theater, as I leaned toward DJ to whisper, "Why was Jeff here? Did you know he was coming?" He chuckled, and Jimmy's projectionist (another employee!) yelled, almost perfectly timed to mute any clarification of what I'd just witnessed, "OK, starting the movie!"

We watched a film called *The Yards*, set to be released nationally a few weeks later, starring interview-voice Mark Wahlberg, the first white rapper Jimmy sent into superstardom. I don't remember anything from the film, mostly because I wasn't watching it. I was so preoccupied with what had happened in the other room, and with what was now happening in their meeting, that I couldn't focus on the screen. About an hour into the movie, Jimmy rejoined us, mostly checking his two-way pager throughout the final half. When the lights came up, we all walked outside, and Jimmy asked if we could wrap up in his backyard.

Jimmy reiterated his enthusiasm for signing me. He revealed he'd be ready to send the final paperwork to my lawyer as soon as I left, again proving that time meant nothing to this tiny man. I concealed my concern with this statement perfectly, even though—because everything was moving at such a fast pace—I didn't have a lawyer yet. I nodded and pretended this was all expected. Jimmy finally acknowledged his earlier display of power by quickly throwing in, near the end of his pitch, almost under his breath, "And The Firm isn't even competition." Then he dropped it forever. Proving his point, I never spoke to Jeff Kwatinetz again.

"I can walk you over to the Playboy Mansion if you'd like. They're having their biggest party of the year," Jimmy said, further cementing his title as the closest thing America has to a real-life Willy Wonka.

I told him that wouldn't be necessary, knowing I had a lot of things to contemplate over the next few hours and that seeing Pauly Shore fondle some girl who'd just moved here from Kalamazoo wouldn't help my fears of being taken advantage of. I said good-bye, got in my car, and attempted to leave. But instead of turning the key, I found myself sitting in his monstrous driveway, motionless, thinking back on what had just happened. Since that night I've spoken to maybe a dozen other artists who signed with Jimmy Iovine at some point in their careers, and each has the same story. Most also visited his home for the pitch; others were flown to exotic locations; one was even given a car as a signing bonus that night. But each experience involved a sit-down conversation where the founder laid it out and confidently told them that, without a doubt, they'd be signing to Interscope Records. And he was always right. The man hardly ever lost. He orchestrated these types of sales pitches because he knew they worked, especially on starry-eyed kids ready to be introduced on MTV. You don't get that successful without understanding how to seal every deal.

I finally mustered the stability, fighting through an uncontrollable wave of excitement, to start my car and drive back to my dorm. On the way home I heard an alert from my two-way pager, a luxury I had recently invested in, knowing it was essential for doing business in the music industry back in the early 2000s. The message was from DJ and it read, "We're offering you a deal in the morning. Is there anything you want to reveal to me now? You can be honest." I pulled the car over and thought about it. I knew my answer. I wrote back, "Yeah, the salmon was undercooked."

9

MY MOM OPENED FOR SNOOP

I woke up the next day guessing the prior night had been a figment of my imagination, and I assumed Jeff Kwatinetz hoped for the same thing. I spent most of my morning talking to prospective lawyers (right after a call from my parents asking for every detail), knowing I'd need legal advice as I inspected this incoming deal memo from Interscope. I eventually landed on Fred Davis, an industry bulldog who grew up in the business as the son of musical genius Clive Davis. Fred was widely regarded as the go-to guy for these large-scale "one offer and done" type of deals, fielding dozens of them for musicians every year and cutting out the back-and-forth bullshit. He was the type of lawyer who had a picture of Ja Rule on his desk that read, *Thanks for getting me that cheddar,* with a signature scribbled underneath it. At the time, just a phone call with the guy would cost a few hundred dollars, something I learned the hard way when he charged me for a brief discussion we had around December 24, when I called to wish him and his family happy holidays. Yes, my lawyer charged me for wishing him a Merry Christmas. He eventually refunded me and laughed when I brought it to his attention, but I never found it funny. He's since opened his own extremely successful investment bank after helping Spotify and Shazam get off the ground; hopefully his new clients just mail him a Christmas card.

I officially hired Fred off just a phone call, since the speed with which my life was escalating didn't allow for much else. My only other option was a lawyer who seemed just as proficient, but he admitted he knew of me because his colleague was R. Kelly's lawyer, so my decision was basically made for me. And just like that, within a few hours of Fred joining my makeshift team, Jimmy Iovine made an official offer to sign Hot Karl.

I remember sitting in my journalism class and feeling the vibration of a page from Fred's office. I walked out into the hall, mid-lecture, to call him, hoping for good news. What I ended up hearing was beyond anything I could have expected. Jimmy Iovine had offered me $750,000, with $300,000 ending up directly in my pocket as a "recoupable advance," a term given to what is essentially an upfront loan from the label, paid off through eventual album sales. Fred thought he could get the total up over $800,000, once he added his fees and got me a non-recoupable $3,500 stipend for living expenses, every month, for eighteen months.

"Good luck shelving something this expensive," Fred joked.

He explained those numbers casually, like he was reading his order off a menu at a neighborhood restaurant, and all I could do was pretend I didn't want to run around USC singing, *"The hills are alive . . ."* I asked him to repeat everything, mostly so I didn't miss a detail in translation, but also because it was incredibly hard to believe. I had sat on my twin-size mattress earlier that morning, eating Top Ramen for breakfast and studying for a midterm, and now, hours later, I was worth six figures because I could rhyme words easily. Although a majority of the money would be used toward the production and recording of the album, as I learned was the case with all record deals, I was still pocketing a large chunk of cash. I was about to land a huge record deal, and I'd gotten there without changing my perspective or losing my self-respect. It was the perfect situation, and I was ready to sign on the dotted line.

Fred called it "a remarkable preemptive strike," considering there was no active bidding war or any other significant offers on the table. He advised me to sign it, since shopping around was unlikely to find us a higher bidder. He also warned me that using these numbers to create a bidding war might piss Jimmy off, forcing him to rescind his offer, since the meeting at his house basically ended with a handshake deal. I was ready to agree to the terms, but remembered one last request I wanted to submit.

Growing up in Los Angeles as a die-hard fan of the NBA, I found myself in a pretty serious pickle. Being a two-team city had its advantages, but growing up middle class and somewhat strapped for cash left one of our team's home games impossible to attend. With the storied history of the Los Angeles Lakers, and the Showtime run of the '80s, ticket prices were, and still are, unreasonably high. I only knew one kid whose parents had Lakers season tickets. They also had a tennis court and a Porsche.

His father never fully explained what he did for a living, until one day we found closets full of porn tapes and figured out what "home video distribution" really meant.

On the other end of the spectrum, I found myself clinging to the Clippers, a team with a completely different history (one of defeat) but affordable tickets. In the Los Angeles basketball landscape, the Lakers were the way cooler older brother. If the Lakers were John Belushi, we were his shitty sibling, Jim. Even when the Clippers racked up the second-worst regular season record ever in 1987, I never complained about my favorite team, attending numerous games with my dad like we were in an adorable bank commercial. The Clippers have since gone on to become one of the premier teams in the league, finishing well above the Lakers for the past few seasons, but I endured decades of misery before they finally became a championship threat.

But one thing I did remember from years of watching the Lakers on TV was that Jimmy Iovine always had prime seats for their games. So prime, in fact, that I could see him during fast breaks as I watched like a cold, poor, and hungry Russian boy looking into a bakery where diplomats laughed and ate bread. No matter how adamant I was about solely being a supporter of the Clippers, I was curious about what a new life of wealth would be like, and I was willing to start with Lakers tickets.

I asked Fred to somehow include Jimmy's courtside seats in the equation, a request that made even the seasoned lawyer snicker. But after a few minutes of convincing, he indulged my stupid idea and added seven future home games to the counter-offer, hoping for the best but acknowledging there wasn't really much of a precedent for the addendum. We got ready to wrap up the conversation, and I gave Fred my final approval.

"It looks like Jimmy wins again," Fred cheerfully yelled. He then turned serious for one last question before I hung up. "Are you sure you don't want to shop this? I know I told you Jimmy will be pissed, but this is your future. And if you're really scared about the Eminem thing, we can dig deeper."

I assured Fred I had carefully weighed the pros and cons of this decision every way possible. I hung up the phone as a new man, ready to rejoin my ordinary life as a student for the time being. I told myself that no NFL metaphor Mack 10 could muster up at this point would break my stride. But no matter how hard I tried to silence the doubt, right before I walked back into the lecture hall, my initial instincts about Interscope—my fear about something feeling weird—came rushing back. For just a few passing moments, I regretted what I had just agreed to. My gut felt uneasy, but I'm also Jewish, and anxiety-ridden fear is ingrained in my DNA, so it was difficult to distinguish between healthy analysis and just plain neurosis. I thought about calling Fred back and putting a momentary halt on the deal, but instead decided to stop questioning the decision from that point on and walked into class. There was no looking back.

I kept my newfound wealth a secret at school, even from Sancho, since I had always been taught to keep my finances to myself, advice that intrinsically went against everything rap music had taught me growing up. When Fred called me that night to let me know that Jimmy had agreed to almost everything in the counteroffer, I was ecstatic. I had spent most of my childhood rapping along to my favorite songs, practicing poses and moves for the day that I'd be able to perform my own music in front of large audiences, and now that was a real possibility.

I had become a member of the Interscope Records family, as had Bubba Sparxxx, who apparently signed his contract months before I did, though that news was only revealed to me the same day I agreed to mine. That night I got my first tattoos: an *H* on one wrist and a *K* on the other. I always joked that if for some reason Hot Karl didn't pan out, they were also my mother's initials. DJ also called me to celebrate the occasion and let me know how excited he was to get started, but the most surprising call actually came the next day.

At this point, now months since my Roll Call streak, Los Angeles radio was still keeping my name on the airwaves. I was a frequent guest on the two most popular urban stations in LA and had been asked to create intros for shows like *Big Boy's Neighborhood*, the most listened-to morning show in the city, and *The B-Side*, a drive-time program hosted by DJ Eric Cubeechee and La La, who would later go on to marry Carmelo Anthony and become the world's most famous basketball wife. Two hosts who weren't welcoming Hot Karl with open arms were the Baka Boyz, who had lost their show in LA soon after the Roll Call championship and were no longer talking to me regularly, a treatment that has since turned into an all-out silence over the past decade, without any real explanation. I assume they're unhappy with how little I incorporated them into my meetings—and my eventual Interscope deal—but I'm surprised they expected me to navigate through that whirlwind at such a young age.

For *Big Boy* and *The B-Side*, though, I would create these short musical introductions promoting the show and, at the same time, promoting myself. They'd air these promos for a few weeks, and then I'd come back to the studio a couple of months later to deliver a new custom jam. This way I always had a song in rotation at the station, even if it was just a glorified commercial. Because of these intros and appearances, my voice was becoming a daily fixture on both stations, something almost impossible for artists to get without a healthy radio budget. It was a far cry from the days of getting hotline busy signals, but no matter how comfortable I was on-air, nothing could've prepared me for the next call I'd receive from KKBT, 100.3 The Beat, asking me to perform at their Summer Jam.

Summer Jam is an annual all-day concert, held on both coasts by LA and NYC's top hip-hop stations, where the biggest acts of the year come together to perform for somewhere between ten and twenty thousand fans. The list of past performers reads like a who's who of hip-hop, including the Notorious B.I.G., Aaliyah, Wu-Tang Clan, DMX, LL Cool J, Jay Z, and Lil Wayne. Performing on that stage seemed like a dream so unattainable that I had to pinch myself when I heard the program director's offer, even if it was for the "Up & Comers Stage," a side space near the parking lot that drew a few hundred people per performance. It was a new concept for the event, where emerging artists not yet famous enough for the main stage could play in between headliners. Since I was discovered on the station's Roll Call, they figured it was only right to include me in their biggest day of the year, and for that I was thankful. I knew joining this show's lineup would be a big step for Hot Karl, so I needed to beef up my stage show, not only by having Sancho DJ behind me, but by asking my mom to join us onstage once again.

To the existing trio of me, Sancho, and my mom, I decided to make another addition. I had also been introduced to Matthew Robinson, a writer who moonlighted as Matty Boom in the Trilambs, a humorous rap group that had been garnering attention throughout LA with their over-the-top skewering of hip-hop culture. The comedy-focused group was made up of about a dozen members, including some music royalty—ranging from Quincy Jones's grandson to Ry Cooder's son—who had little to no history in rap. They would sample songs that had zero chance at eventual clearance, stealing elements from the Beatles and Simon and Garfunkel, while employing ridiculous lyrics lightly influenced by the stream-of-consciousness style of Ghostface Killah but mostly just mentioning how they were rich enough to own a camel or reminiscing about the year that homeless people went crazy. It made little to no sense and was just farcical enough to be beautiful. It was almost performance art, actually. After Matty and I became fast friends, I asked him to be my official hypeman, marking him the first Sarah Lawrence literature graduate to claim that position. As if I didn't stand out enough, I added another goofy white guy to the stage.

The radio station was nice enough to send a limo to transport the group, and my family, to the Verizon Wireless Amphitheater in Irvine, about an hour and a half away from my parents' place. We were scheduled to hit the stage around 2:00 p.m., a time admittedly too early for real action, since headliners Nelly and Ja Rule wouldn't perform until well into the night. But I was happy with *any* inclusion, especially since, because of a prior engagement, Snoop Dogg had to perform on the main stage at 1:30. We'd be able to catch some of the audience coming and going from his set, and hopefully pick up some new fans along the way. We decided to make the best of what we were given and perform our tracks like all fourteen thousand people were watching. It wasn't until we got there that we realized all fourteen thousand people *would* be watching.

As soon as the limo pulled up, DJ Eric Cubeechee, who was my most vocal supporter at the station, ran up to ask how long it would take to set up our show. Considering we only needed Sancho to plug in his headphones and my mom to dress up like an idiot, I answered, "Few minutes tops." Eric excitedly informed us that Snoop was running late (which would seem like something you plan for in advance) and that we'd be filling the gap before he arrived on the main stage. YES, ON THE MAIN STAGE. My first instinct was to say no, since I had been in a side-stage mind-set all week while rehearsing; imagining a performance in front of that many people, without notice, was daunting. Before I could say anything, though, Sancho beat me to the punch, agreeing to the new plan before I could express any uncertainty. My nerves quickly set in, bringing up every ounce of hidden self-doubt. But before I knew it, we were ushered backstage too quickly to give my anxiety any weight.

Matty removed his sweatshirt to reveal a shirt that read FREE SLICK RICK, referring to the legendary rapper who had found himself in jail for attempted murder and was facing deportation. I removed my button-up to reveal a shirt that read DON'T FREE R. KELLY, a joke more suited to a few hundred people than a packed amphitheater. Despite the raging fear, once I knew my mom was ready to roll, I motioned for Sancho to start the music, knowing any more time alone would throw me into a real spiral of self-sabotage. I quickly glanced at the audience and noticed that the crowd went on for as far as the eye could see. That was the last time I would look farther than the first three rows, knowing my heart would sink to my crotch if I peeked any further. My father was a few feet away, taking photos once again from stage right, in almost the exact same spot as when I was twelve years old at Club Spice. At both concerts I could hear him yelling "Go get 'em!" from the sidelines, and that meant a lot. And much like that night with X-tra Large, I was focused on making very little seem like a whole lot, knowing I would never forget this moment as long as I lived, no matter the outcome. So why not just have fun with it?

We reused the Lionel Richie "All Night Long" beat from my Roxy show, and I freestyled for the first few minutes, throwing in specific rhymes about the day, highlighted by the line, "Now I'm onstage, even though you expected another / Only white guy at Summer Jam like Jim Carrey—*In Living Color*." That got a huge response. So did a Tyrese diss I found a way to crowbar in. I roamed the gigantic stage, taking full advantage of the amphitheater's real estate, asking, "Summer Jam, are you with me?" like that type of question was second nature. I performed a few songs and got mostly positive reactions—remember, most of the audience was expecting Snoop Dogg, so I was cool with some blank stares—but I wasn't surprised when our final stunt fell a bit flat.

Fourteen thousand people probably look back and assume they saw Rachel Maddow in a hat rap at Summer Jam.

I announced to the audience that, in order for all of us to feel more comfortable with an unknown white kid taking the Summer Jam stage, I had convinced "someone *I* am very comfortable with" to dress up as "someone *you* are very comfortable with." And right after saying, "Here goes nothing," I introduced my mother to fourteen thousand rap and R&B fans, with "Country Grammar" blasting in the background. With that, she danced onstage and participated in what is the most embarrassing thing I've ever asked her to do.

I had somehow convinced her to dress up as Nelly, wearing

a backwards basketball jersey, a St. Louis Cardinals cap, and a Band-Aid on her face, all the while carrying around two Nike boxes, a reference to his most recent song about having "two pairs" of every shoe. I started my final track, as confident as I could be knowing that this last reveal was basically the most Spinal-Tap-tiny-Stonehenge moment in Summer Jam history. Halfway through the song, I looked back to see my mom, just to get a final laugh from her dancing with us, and realized she was *gone.* We wrapped up the set, and I looked out at the stacks and stacks of bleachers filled with concertgoers, finally allowing the number of people in the stands to sink in. I took it in one last time and said into the microphone, "Thank you so much, Summer Jam. Next up, Snoop Doggy Dogg," a sentence I had practiced in my room for years but never thought I'd be able to say. Then Steve Harvey, who walked out to officially introduce Snoop Dogg, looked offstage, confused, and said into his mic, "So what in the *hell* was that?"

I ran backstage to find my mom disheveled, looking nervous. She apologized profusely for leaving before the song's end, but admitted she was uncontrollably embarrassed and couldn't stand another minute as Nelly. "Imagine how Nelly feels," I joked.

Funny enough, that year Summer Jam ended abruptly after a fight broke out in the stands, causing a riot and leaving most of the headliners without any stage time. It makes me laugh knowing that the only Nelly the audience saw that night was my fifty-year-old mother.

Hours before police ended the show, we all walked around the venue, trying to understand what just went down. I was still on an emotional high from verbally committing to Interscope earlier that week, and now I had accomplished a completely different, but just as impressive, goal. We decided to unwind by performing at our set time on the side stage, now in front of maybe forty people. And they were only watching because they were stuck in a long line at a nearby pretzel stand. Matty, Sancho, and I performed loosely, like we were playing in a local pickup game after winning the NBA championship. I actually fell off the stage at one point and performed sitting down. Sancho played the wrong track accidentally. Matty did the Running Man. None of us cared. We had just fulfilled a dream. And this time, my mom stayed onstage for an entire song.

It might not be the Nelly Summer Jam wanted, but it was the Nelly Summer Jam got.

Not long after Summer Jam I got the physical Interscope contract in the mail. It was dense and tedious with jargon about detailed payment plans and regional breakdowns and licensing agreements—all things that made Fred's enormous fee seem worth it. I held the heavy stack of papers in my hands and smiled. I had trained tirelessly, from my third-grade talent show to the hundreds of battles I had participated in since, and at each stop I'd been told I couldn't do it. I wanted to Xerox every page, highlight the grand total, and mail it to that quarterback in high school who'd told me to quit. I remembered being booed offstage in eighth grade. I remembered my disappointment when Donald D stopped calling. I remembered staying vigilant, even when at any time I could've just given up and settled for a surefire mid-level TV writing gig that I would've hated. I felt proud. As I went to sign the final page, something caught my attention.

Scanning the text, I noticed the words *Lakers tickets*. I had totally forgotten about my last-minute request, so its inclusion, though a pleasant surprise, caught me off guard. I looked closer and quickly realized that, instead of getting two tickets to seven games like I'd requested, I was given one ticket for one game against the Houston Rockets, a mediocre team at best that season. I double-checked the wording just to make sure I hadn't missed anything, as I now envisioned myself sitting alone courtside, like a creep. I knew one was better than none, so I signed the contract and officially became a professional rapper. In the end, I would excitedly attend that one Lakers game alone and see it as another reward for sticking with Hot Karl. But don't worry—I wore a Clippers jersey.

10

RZA LOVES HAPPY DAYS, BUT PINK HATES ME

ONCE I officially signed the contract, Interscope wasted no time in getting me back in the lab. Where my daily routine once involved rebooting the Great Gazoo and Barney Rubble, I was now splitting time between early-morning college classes and nighttime sessions with guys like One Eye, a producer just coming off tremendous success with Ice Cube's platinum smash "You Can Do It (Put Your Ass Into It)." He was an incredibly jolly family man who got his name after losing an eye in a freak accident years prior, although you probably assumed that. He also grew a shit ton of weed in his garage, well before that kind of activity was a viable thing to do. Who could blame him? He had one eye, asshole.

The first song I recorded with One Eye was called "Bounce," a dance song that, if anything, showed I was energetic and excited for this new phase of my career. Where I used to look for the easiest way to ridicule my opponent, I was now hoping to connect with fans through relatable lyrics, not just disparage their dirty T-shirts and shit teeth. I preached to listeners that they "only live once" way before YOLO was a thing, and spit lyrics like "Partying ain't bad for me, what's it gonna do to me / I'mma change it up like Bow Wow's voice after puberty" and "When you diss this, I return vicious / Make you feel left out like Jewish kids on Christmas." The immediate reaction to this song, and the other few I quickly made with One Eye right off the bat, was outstanding. Weirdly, right after we recorded a handful of songs together, One Eye completely disappeared without a trace or warning. It was total radio silence for years. Then in 2014, his Facebook friend request popped up, so I accepted it and was happy to see he was doing well, now living comfortably in Texas. Although I haven't asked, I think I can safely assume the move had something to do with what was in his garage. Which is messed up because, again, he had one eye, asshole. But whether I played this first song for Sancho, Matty, Paige, or DJ, everyone seemed to think I was finding my stride and setting up what would make a great album.

Only two months into the process, a few of my tracks found their way into the hands of MTV VJ Matt Pinfield, who in turn listed me as an "artist to watch" in *Playboy* magazine, my first real mention in mainstream press. I also started getting my monthly checks, and the production budget for my album was now readily available, so my life, now usually introduced with the phrase "Interscope recording artist Hot Karl," quickly changed. With this new influx of money at such a young age, I had to be careful not to become just another story of bankruptcy. Although I tried to be somewhat cautious, I immediately purchased a Ford Expedition and a $4,000 diamond TechnoMarine watch and spent $1,200 getting a mint-condition *Tapper* arcade game—an obsession from my childhood—delivered directly to my house from Canada. It wasn't quite Nic Cage, but he'd probably see it as "a start." I was a perfect cross between your typical reckless rapper and the kid from *Big* when he became an adult.

No matter how much the music business has changed since 2000, an "open budget" will still make you a very popular person in the industry. It's much easier to get a meeting with the Neptunes—or pretty much any producer or musician—with a few hundred thousand dollars in your budget than by attempting to work with them on pure merit. So when Interscope asked me who my dream producer would be, knowing the price didn't matter, I didn't have to think long before I answered, "RZA."

Considered one of the most legendary figures in hip-hop history, RZA helped create and mold the Wu-Tang Clan, crafting a handful of my favorite songs while bridging the gap between rap and alternative audiences like never before. He was also a founding member of Gravediggaz, an obscure side project in the late '90s, whose debut, *6 Feet Deep,* is still my favorite rap album of all time. Since he was the mastermind behind two of the groups that had influenced me most, I decided I had nothing to lose in mentioning him for the album. I would've never guessed that within twenty-four hours of my request, I'd actually be on the phone with RZA, ready to talk about my project.

When I was sixteen years old, my first car had a custom front license plate with the Wu-Tang logo airbrushed on it, so I tried my hardest to act cool once I realized who had just called asking for "Karl." He said he had heard good things about my music and apologized in advance for needing to take breaks while chatting, since he was recording vocals for a new album by his alter ego, Bobby Digital, at the same time. I wanted to tell him how important his work had been in my life but figured he was sick of hearing that from dorky kids in glasses, so I held it in. We went over my history, detailing my early success and the newly signed record deal. An occasional "bong bong" from RZA was the only thing that broke up the story, a term he still seems to use in interviews to express respect.

Before I could throw around any concepts, he asked if he could put me on hold. I obliged, telling him to take his time. He placed his phone on what I assumed was a nearby stool, and for the next five minutes, I sat and listened to RZA perform ad-libs for a new song, where he would just make beeping noises or yell "Lasers!" at the top of his lungs every few seconds. One time he commanded the engineer to "bring it back," then just repeated the same high-pitched robot sounds he'd been making since he started. It was like if Johnny Five from *Short Circuit* rapped. It was surreal, and, had I not known what he was doing, I would have figured it was the weirdest case of Tourette's syndrome ever documented. I sat with my mouth agape, seeing this as the coolest fan moment ever, akin to having Michael Jordan dunk on you over and over again in practice. Eventually the song ended, and he picked the phone back up like nothing strange had just happened.

"Sorry about that. So, let me get this straight, you're like the Richie Cunningham of hip-hop?" RZA asked, trying to figure out exactly who he was talking to.

"Uh, sort of," I responded. "I'm actually not THAT big of a nerd, though."

"Oh, cool. So you're more like the Fonz."

I sort of understood RZA's logic, but shrugged my shoulders at this analogy, too.

"Well, that actually may be *too* cool. I think I'm just trying to be myself more than anything."

"OK, well then you're Potsie," RZA quickly responded.

"I'm not sure why we're sticking to a *Happy Days* theme, but sure, I guess I'm more like a Potsie," I conceded, assuming I could now pick RZA's favorite TV show with one guess. I always liked to think he did the same thing with other rappers and maybe once told Inspectah Deck he was "a real Chachi."

We talked for a few more minutes about song concepts, including my passion for the idea of him sampling Christopher Cross's "Ride Like the Wind," a song he immediately recognized by saying, "Yeah, yeah, I know that shit," which is the response you hope for when you ask RZA if he knows a yacht-rock classic. I wished him luck on the new record and we hung up, never following up to work on a song together. Honestly, though, I never really pushed to make it happen with RZA, possibly because of nerves and also because I thought I could never top that phone call. Either way, I was wrong.

As painful as this is to admit, about four years ago our paths crossed again when I found myself at a party thrown by one of the Real Housewives of Beverly Hills for their grating reality TV show. A friend involved in organizing the event had asked me to come support his efforts, promising a gaudy extravaganza, and I had obliged. He did not disappoint.

There were semi-nude models painted green and hiding in trees, simulating an orgy; a large ivy garden where mysterious arms would pop out and hand you mixed drinks; and enough C-list celebrities to make a VH1 casting agent salivate a tsunami. To cope with these bonkers surroundings, I decided to quickly down a few cocktails and silence the echo of "What the fuck are you doing here?" that dominated my brain. Right when I figured I couldn't take it anymore, I noticed RZA on the other side of the party. I had never seen him in a casual social setting, and with our one brief phone interaction, mixed with the added confidence of the alcohol served to me by weirdo ghost hands, I figured we had something to talk about. So I approached RZA, who seemed to be having as hard of a time at this shit show as I was, and said hello. He was cordial when I told him that Wu-Tang "changed my life," a statement I was smart enough to withhold as Hot Karl, but now was shameless (and buzzed) enough to blurt out in my thirties. This is the moment when I should've adhered to a set of social standards and walked away, but restraint was not fitting me well that evening.

"We talked on the phone once," I said to RZA, like we had an undeniable connection we could never forget.

RZA looked at me, understandably confused.

"I was a rapper named Hot Karl, and you were making

noises . . . I mean, you were recording. We were going to work together," I managed to explain, terribly.

"We worked together?" RZA asked me with an actual excitement to connect.

"Well, no. We almost did. Maybe. I don't know. They woulda paid you a lot. But we talked about *Happy Days*."

RZA stared at me.

"You like *Happy Days*, right?" I asked, happily reaching for anything he could relate to.

"The TV show? I guess," he responded indifferently.

We had hit a dead end. This cul-de-sac of hero worship had nowhere else to go. I was now a random fan who was entering Creepy Zone. To break the silence, I blurted out, without any explanation, "Well, I'm a Potsie," and walked away. I never told anyone about this humiliating exchange, knowing that if I couldn't explain it to the RZA, I couldn't explain it to anyone else. I do know, however, that when my half-a-million-dollar budget was still open, RZA had been a real big *Happy Days* fan.

———

In addition to scheduling phone calls with my idols, DJ was also setting up recording sessions with up-and-coming local producers, hoping to get tracks strong enough to make an eventual album. My focus had shifted from signing a record deal to creating a full release ready for the Interscope schedule. And one of the producers responsible for getting this done went by the name of Damon Elliott. The son of Dionne Warwick, Elliott had worked with Destiny's Child and was impressed enough with my first few songs that he wanted to take a shot at working with me. The industry was extremely high on Elliott that year, since he was one of the producers credited with the "Lady Marmalade" reboot with Christina Aguilera, Mýa, Pink, and Lil' Kim. Because he now had a number-one hit under his belt, collaborating with him would be considered a coup, and I was excited at the prospect.

Damon was a lovable teddy bear. Overweight, bouncy, and extremely unpredictable, if he wasn't treated for ADHD as a kid, his pediatricians should have their licenses revoked. He could never say "Hot Karl" in just a calm, regular tone. He would scream it loudly, no matter how close I was, adding a James Brown funk to the end. His high-pitched name-check became a constant during our sessions together, as he'd just yell it sporadically at random times without warning. One time, as I walked into his studio, ready to record, he jumped off his couch, visibly excited, yelling my name and handing me a phone.

"Hot Karl! Hot Karl! Hot Karl! You gotta hear this!"

I assumed it was a great song he was hearing for the first time, so I excitedly pushed my ear against the receiver, hoping to share his reaction. I soon realized, however, that I wasn't listening to a song at all. I was listening to a voice mail that Pink (née Alecia Moore) had left for Damon earlier that day.

"Damon, it's Alecia . . . fuck that piece of shit, Hot Karl or whatever his name is . . ."

She sounded tired and really angry (maybe even drunk).

"If I ever see that motherfucker, I swear to God I'm gonna knock him out."

Damon quickly snatched the phone from my ear and hung it up. He ran over to his console to start playing me beats, as if nothing was wrong. I didn't know much about Damon Elliott, but I did know that Pink was very muscular and, without a shadow of a doubt, could beat the shit out of me. I panicked. He started turning knobs.

"You like this one, dude?" he asked, looking at me for approval as an instrumental blasted over the speakers.

"Sure," I yelled, focused on something much less melodic. "But why does Pink want to beat me up, man?"

Damon turned the music down and explained that he had been listening to my song "Bounce" while she was in the studio a few nights before and a line had caught her attention. Like the detective piecing together Kevin Spacey's fake story at the end of *The Usual Suspects*, everything fell into place for me. I remembered that in that song I jokingly rapped, "My flow is sick, people get scared away / It's like partaking in a threesome with Pink and Macy Gray." Although it was a ridiculous joke to me—and so over the top that I found it weird that anyone would take it seriously, much like my prior experience with Tyrese—my target didn't seem to agree. Damon said she asked for my phone number immediately, but he was smart enough to keep that information to himself. He went on to reveal that she'd left similar messages, like the one I'd just heard, a few times. He told me not to worry, though; she'd forget about it soon. But he added, "I'd love to see y'all fight. Would be fun. HOT KARL!" I vehemently disagreed. Luckily, this "beef" never took shape beyond this instance, but to be honest, even over a decade later, I still worry about Pink every so often.

This was just a random fan who jumped onstage and exposed her breasts. We later found out she was in Los Angeles studying at NASA for the summer and has since become a leading expert in heat–shield research. Naw, I'm joking. I have no idea who that was.

"BOUNCE" LYRICS, 1999
(20 years old)

(intro)

Now you rolling with the Hotness (Hot Karl),
So let's make no mistakes here.

Well, it's the H-O-T, man I hope you hearing this,
Open the bar tab, take a shot, get ridiculous,
Let your hair down tonight, shit why not shave it off?

Make it all bald, get really fucking tossed,[1]
Take this night off, come on, don't act hard,
It's like Coyote Ugly baby, dance up on the bar,
You're a rock star, it'll probably make you stronger,
Drink Red Bull and vodka till you can't talk no longer,
'Cause this is for the clubs, but without a catchy jingle,
'Cause that style sounds faggy like that one Shaggy single
    (It wasn't me),[2]
Fact is, I could do this backwards,
Like Puff and Biggie on the freeway, now give me some leeway,
'Cause partying ain't bad for me, what's it gonna do to me,
I'mma change it up like Bow Wow's voice after puberty,
And when you diss this, I return vicious,
Make you feel left out like Jewish kids on Christmas.

(hook)

With the bounce (c'mon), bounce (c'mon),
Bounce with the uh, the uh, the uh, uh,
With the bounce (c'mon), bounce (c'mon),
You rolling with the H, the O, the T, for sheeze,
(C'mon) bounce (c'mon), bounce (c'mon),
Bounce with the uh, the uh, the uh, uh,
With the bounce (c'mon), bounce (c'mon),
What up, get drunk, get fucked now.

My flow is sick, people get scared away,
It's like partaking in a threesome with Pink and Macy Gray,[3]
Or Latifah in lingerie, it's gross,

---

1   I always rapped about what I knew, and I was right in the middle of
    a college social scene, about to turn twenty-one, so I was quick to rap
    about drinking and partying. I thought it sounded cool. Listening to it
    now, I sound like a NARC.
2   UGH, another cameo from homophobia. I still hate Shaggy, though.
3   And there you have it . . .

My visuals make you vomit when you close,
'Cause me keeping it real is so much different than you,
If I talked about guns, then it wouldn't be true,
So I stick to what I see and to shit I believe,
Never faking I'm a thug just to sell CDs,
There's still rules to kill and haters to prove malicious,
Make them see the light like Hammer when he went religious,
And shit that comes out? It don't move me,
They should never play in real theaters, like Ice-T movies,[4]
So wannabes, I'm no longer having it,
I keep it real while you fake like Madonna's British accent,
So keep drinking till you're almost dead,
Then when you're finished throwing up, go ahead and tap
    another keg . . .

(hook)

With the bounce (c'mon), bounce (c'mon),
Bounce with the uh, the uh, the uh, uh,
With the bounce (c'mon), bounce (c'mon),
You rolling with the H, the O, the T, for sheeze,
(C'mon) bounce (c'mon), bounce (c'mon),
Bounce with the uh, the uh, the uh, uh,
With the bounce (c'mon), bounce (c'mon),
What up, get drunk, get fucked now.

There's a million MCs doing a song about bouncing,
But with the verses that I kick I make it original sounding,
So put your hands up, move 'em side to side,
Damn it, start freaking out like you're all justified,
Take it all in, it won't happen again,

---

4 I figured one small jab at Ice-T for my abandoned childhood rap career
   would make us even. Joke's on me, though, since no one ever heard this
   song, and Ice-T has been making Dick Wolf money for two decades.

A hip-hop MC who looks just like you and your friends,[5]
And dudes check your attitudes, even crack a smile,
And, hoes, lift up your shirts like it's *Girls Gone Wild*,
I want you to bounce (come on), shake it, fuck it,
Get trashy like NASCAR or white kids with mullets,
The club is jumping, so guys get your brains,
Ain't no way you're going home alone tonight, so spit game,
And hoes, for one night act dumber,
Shake your ass, tease guys, and give 'em fake phone numbers,
'Cause you only live once, that's as far as we know,
So enjoy the show, pop your collar, let yourselves go.

(hook)

With the bounce (c'mon), bounce (c'mon),
Bounce with the uh, the uh, the uh, uh,
With the bounce (c'mon), bounce (c'mon),
You rolling with the H, the O, the T, for sheeze,
(C'mon) bounce (c'mon), bounce (c'mon),
Bounce with the uh, the uh, the uh, uh,
With the bounce (c'mon), bounce (c'mon),
What up, get drunk, get fucked now.[6]

---

5 Little did I know, come 2016, most every rapper would end up looking
   like they play beach volleyball.
6 I genuinely thought this could be a catchy hook for a hot song. Reading it back now, it sounds like I'm having a stroke.

11

SISQÓ'S XXX COLLECTION

DESPITE the off-putting start, Damon Elliott and I ended up recording a track together called "His Hotness," predominantly using the weird way he yelled "Hot Karl" in the beat. As my first guest feature, Damon had Mýa come in and sing the hook for a fee negotiated between her lawyers and the label: $15,000 and a coproduction credit, though she never touched the actual backing track. That's like being called the chef for an entrée you only put parsley on. I did get to meet her while she was half asleep on a couch after cutting her vocals, though. We talked about quesadillas and I never saw her again. I basically paid her $15,000 to shake my hand, sing for an hour, take a nap, and then talk to me about a specific Mexican delicacy she loves. Highway robbery aside, she did sound great on the song, and my mom was superimpressed that I met her. And with the added pressure of having a platinum artist on the hook now, I wanted the verses to double as an introduction to Hot Karl—something that could establish who I was if someone was only listening because of Mýa. Eminem was releasing more and more music, and our voices were becoming more and more inseparable. I saw this as a perfect opportunity to differentiate myself, thinking Interscope's investment in the song would guarantee it a place in the marketplace.

However, if you ask me, the main reason Mýa's contribution sounded dope was my cowriter on the track: a guy named Marquis "Da Kidd" Collins, one of the geniuses behind Sisqó's "Thong Song," a track that was nominated for four Grammys (which coincidentally is four more than *any* Bob Marley song. I'm going to keep doing this when needed). The results weren't quite "God Only Knows" by the Beach Boys—we rhymed "bum bum" and "dum dum"—but we worked so well together that he immediately invited me to another writing session, this time not for Hot Karl but for Sisqó's new album. How I fit into Sisqó's creative team was something I couldn't yet grasp, but I knew I wasn't gonna question it, especially after I found out that the writing session would take place in Sisqó's San Fernando Valley mansion. As an avid Dru Hill fan, nothing in the world could stop me from taking this gig.

My college suitemates were impressed with this new development in my career and became obsessed with telling me their theories, largely fueled by online rumors, about how Sisqó was gay. It was all opinion or thirdhand gossip, but they were adamant about their speculation and made me promise I'd share every detail when I got home.

"You should hook up with him," my fratty friend suggested.

Sisqó's house was enormous, surrounded by columns and grounded in expensive marble. The recording studio was outside, in a shed next to the impressive swimming pool, hidden like a doomsday prepper's gun arsenal. Da Kidd and I worked in the studio for most of the day, with Sisqó coming in to say hello a few times over the course of the afternoon. He couldn't have been nicer, even complimenting "His Hotness," which Da Kidd had played for him earlier that week. He thanked me for working on his music and then excused himself to run some errands. In other words, Sisqó and I were homies.

Since the studio was in the backyard, when I had to go to the bathroom a few hours later, Da Kidd informed me that I'd have to go back into the main house. He explained that the restroom would be easy to find, mentioning stairs and Sisqó's room, then a sharp right. As I made my way through the house, reciting the directions in my head, I realized that I had stepped foot into Sisqó's bedroom. It wasn't quite the sexy master lair you'd expect from the man who once sang "Unleash the Dragon," clearly not referencing his love for the novels of George R. R. Martin. It actually looked like any room you'd find in my college dorm. Every item reeked of IKEA. The bed sat on the floor like he couldn't afford a frame. Dirty laundry was scattered everywhere. Sisqó may have sung about taking a girl home with him from the club, but I couldn't imagine she stayed long.

I laughed it off and continued walking to where I saw the nearby toilet. On my final step, I noticed stacks and stacks of DVDs flanking the sides of Sisqó's big-screen television, and as a movie buff myself, my interest was piqued. It looked like he was cataloguing movies the same way the ghost librarian from the beginning of *Ghostbusters* catalogued books. As I got closer, I was shocked to see that they were all pornos, maybe over fifty titles. Although it felt like a violation, I knew that if I told my college friends I'd had an opportunity to see what type of porn Sisqó watched, apparently in bulk, and hadn't investigated, they would haze me until graduation. So I slowly tiptoed to the stacks, picked up a handful from the top, and focused on the pictures.

The pornos were heterosexual. Straight as an arrow. Then I squinted my eyes and noticed a detail I almost missed. Each movie was actually a gangbang. I relentlessly checked every DVD, frantic like Claire Danes figuring out a terrorist plot on *Homeland*, and realized that almost *all* of the movies around me were flicks where dozens to hundreds of men were having sex with one woman. Yes, they were heterosexual porn movies, but they also contained a ton of dick. Like a 100-to-1 dick-to-vagina ratio. What was I to do? I knew too much.

I quickly went to the bathroom and tried to understand what this odd collection of smut meant with regard to my roommates' gossip. There I was, standing in an Encino bathroom, at a mansion that was furnished like a messy model home, contemplating the meaning of gangbang porn found in Sisqó's bedroom. I heard a loud noise from downstairs, which I quickly thought to be a garage door opening. Terrified that the R&B crooner had returned home, I successfully ran downstairs to rejoin Da Kidd for work without bumping into anyone, all the while attempting to forget what I'd just seen. But before I made my way back into the studio, I took a few souvenirs.

When I got back to school, my friends hounded me for juicy gossip. I told them Sisqó was polite and hospitable and that sadly we didn't come up with a song that had even the slightest chance of making his album. I also let them know that I saw stacks and stacks of pornos, but that each was heterosexual, proving their assumptions wrong. They seemed disappointed as I left the room. Over the next month, I would quietly leave gangbang DVDs stolen from Sisqó's house in each of their rooms when they weren't home and wait to hear anything about their discoveries. They never said a word. Funny thing is, they'll never know those pornos were from Sisqó's personal collection—discs I had to hide in my waistband, now finding their way into a college dude's masturbation rotation. No matter the nature of Sisqó's sexuality, my tough-guy roommates sure seemed to like jerking off to the same stuff.

I distinctly remember the day I went in to write for Sisqó because it was my last day as Paige's boyfriend (also because I stole pornos from Sisqó's house, and I feel like that's a life milestone). Between homework and the album, I was feverishly working all day and night, unable to see my family, let alone go on dates, so I decided the most sensible thing to do was break up. We had grown apart, especially with her world still revolving around sorority socials and midterms and mine now taking place inside recording studios and R&B stars' mansions. And I'd be lying if I didn't admit that the grass did seem much greener on this side of the road to rap superstardom. Even though I genuinely liked Paige and she had adored me before "record deal" was even in my vocabulary, I knew there was no possible way I could stay faithful with this type of temptation in my early twenties. I tried my hardest to stay committed, but I was starting to feel like a newly converted vegan working at a butcher shop. She obviously didn't quite see it as cut-and-dried as I did, and it broke her heart, and mine, that she had become a cliché: girlfriend left in the dust. But I was just too nervous about having regrets at any point of this fun-filled journey. I was ready to take advantage of the newfound attention, and College Jensen was fading further and further away in the rearview mirror.

12

BLIND ITEM

I'LL never truly know what my life would've been like had I not called in to the radio station to battle that day, but I can assume I would've had fewer interactions with celebrities. Throughout my entire time as Hot Karl, I found myself in some pretty crazy situations with household names. For example, Justin Timberlake once invited me to his private birthday party at Dublin's after attending one of my shows. That night we talked at length about how Xbox got him a stand-up *Halo* arcade for his house and how LA didn't have any great barbecue spots. I was also the first rapper to mention Paris and Nicky Hilton in a song ("I'mma hit that shit like I was Roger Maris / Then fuck Nicky Hilton just to leave Paris embarrassed"), a distinction revealed to me by Nicky herself. And in what may have been the coolest moment of my career, Janet Jackson once watched me perform and gave me the thumbs-up when I saw her later near the bar. In all honesty, I never felt truly comfortable among these types, at least out of the studio, but I tried my hardest to fit in and live up the once-in-a-lifetime opportunities I was having. So when one A-list celebrity asked me if I wanted to fuck her, I imagined I should probably say yes.

I don't plan on revealing her name, not because I'm concerned with keeping her reputation intact or because I'm ashamed, but purely because it feels douchey to just come out and say it. Listen, Tyrese gets pedicures. Sisqó has porn. Those things you know now. But nothing makes me feel more like an asshole main character on *Entourage* than rattling off the names of people I've hooked up with. You're on your own for this one.

I had known of her work for years and unexpectedly found myself frequently around her because of a mutual friend I'd first met during my time as Hot Karl. I wouldn't say I had a "crush," but like most young men during that era, I saw her as an unattainable sex symbol, a fact I even joked about with a lyric on my demo. She was polite and funny, and surprisingly down-to-earth at times, despite being on TV every day. We'd hug hello and good-bye, and I'd actually have said we were becoming pals. Whether because of her fame or our purely platonic conversations, I never really imagined her as much more than a friend, and a surreal one at that.

It wasn't until one dinner, when I thought I saw her winking at me from across the room, that I allowed myself to imagine it could be anything different. When I did think of the possibility, I quickly brought myself back to reality, laughing it off as just rapid-fire blinking on her part. Who even winks at someone in the twenty-first century? I called one of my friends the next morning and relayed the story. I admitted she could've been joking around, but the more I thought about it, I was almost sure she was coming on to me. My friend was skeptical and, to be honest, so was I. After our talk, I convinced myself that I had made it all up in my head and went back to understanding that, although I had been lucky to date out of my league a few times, I wasn't about to hook up with a girl who's been on every magazine cover. But to my surprise, after this winking incident that may or may not have happened, I noticed that we started kissing on the lips whenever we'd greet each other. It was shocking at first, but European in nature, and despite the fact that she was born in the United States, I thought it might be par for the celebrity course. Because how could it be anything else?

One night, she had a party at her house to screen her new TV show, and I was happy to attend. After we watched it in a big group, I was one of the last viewers to walk up and congratulate her. I was impressed by the scope of the project and made sure to tell her she should be proud of the final product. She thanked me for the kind words and went in for the hug. To my utter surprise, she stayed in that position for a little too long, and I followed her lead. And just as I started to question whether I was misreading signs again, she started lightly moaning and grinding up against me. I started to believe that maybe the winks weren't a nervous tic after all. She tilted her head over to peck my neck, and with a handful of people surrounding us, she started making out with me. As much as I wanted to yell "Holy shit!" and send an e-mail to every girl who ever rejected me, I could taste the alcohol and, even though I was buzzed myself, I immediately felt uncomfortable. When she whispered in my ear, asking if I could stay over, a million thoughts went through my head. As badly as I wanted to just scream "Yes, ma'am!" and run to her bedroom with pants around my ankles, gentlemanly instincts took over and I politely replied, "Let's wait until you're sober. We can do this another time." I grabbed a nearby pen and paper and wrote down my phone number to stick on her refrigerator. "You'll call me and we'll do this whole thing again next week."

As if I hadn't just suggested a dose of common sense, we started kissing again.

"I don't know if this is a good idea," I repeated.

With that, she pulled away and said something along the lines of "Don't you want to know what this feels like," and pointed toward her crotch.

As much as her question sounded like something you'd find on a frat guy's T-shirt during spring break in the '80s, I knew my answer was yes. I said good-bye to our mutual friend who had driven me to her house earlier that night and informed him I'd be staying over. He laughed and wished me luck. Looking back, I recognize that these words of encouragement were both genuine and a friendly warning of what was to come. I walked back into the house, noticing that the hundred or so guests who had been there earlier for the premiere had now disappeared. We immediately started kissing again in the kitchen. She interrupted this second session to lead me back into her screening room, where I assumed we would disrobe and start hooking up.

As she walked in the direction of the cable box, I realized she wasn't leading me there to get cozier; we had reentered the room to watch her show's debut episode again. Frustrated, I sat there as she went over every scene and supplied me with pieces of trivia I can't imagine will ever come in handy. It was my very own cockblocking director's commentary.

We got through the show again, now sobering up, and she asked if I wanted to go to her bedroom. With the type of excitement usually only seen when a second-grade nerd raises his hand after the teacher asks if anyone wants to read aloud, I jumped off the couch and shouted "Yes!" Finally, I imagined, things were going to fall into place. After a few minutes of making out in her bed, she took her shirt off and I unhooked her bra. I had just called it off with the easygoing water-polo-playing Paige, but our relationship couldn't have felt further in the distance now that I found myself fondling the gigantic breasts of a girl who a few of my college friends had plastered on their walls. If anything had felt completely unbelievable during my time of being an accidental rapping top prospect, it was this moment in particular. As it got hot and heavy, she began to unzip my pants. Content with where things were leading, I couldn't help but smile a little. That's the moment I heard the bedroom door swing open.

Startled, I jumped out of bed, ready to attack whichever member of the Bling Ring had just barged in to rob us. My kissing partner was unaffected, showing no signs of concern with the spontaneous entrance. Still topless, the celebrity looked up and introduced me to her publicist, a pretty girl who casually sat at the edge of the bed and got comfortable. I had been convinced we were alone in the house but now came to the conclusion that I probably didn't know everything that was going on, or was about to unfold. I assume most of you think this is going to turn into a lurid tale of a Hollywood threesome, involving a megastar and her attractive publicist, but now I need you to imagine the *exact* opposite of that scenario—and then get ready for that.

The publicist started complaining about her longtime boyfriend and how her feet were uncharacteristically swollen, all while my onetime horny partner put her clothes slowly back on. My erection dissipated as the celeb dug deep into her friend's current relationship predicament, and foot problem, to dole out advice. And after they addressed those problems, they started talking about the TV show again, noting things that could change for future episodes and elements they thought really worked moving forward. Even Daniel Day-Lewis would've been like, "This is too much prep." Eventually, after about an hour, the publicist stopped talking in order to lie down directly in between us, almost pushing her way in as a barrier. The celebrity also got comfortable, now pulling the sheets over her body to signal sleep time, leaving me on the outside, completely ignored.

As they both dozed off, cuddling each other, I asked if I could borrow a toothbrush, since it's always been difficult for me to sleep without brushing my teeth. She mumbled, now understandably half asleep at 3:00 a.m., "I don't have any." Learning that she didn't have a *single toothbrush* in her house, I now sat motionless in her bed, almost hanging off the side and being pushed even farther every second by the dynamic duo. I was without my car, and my cell phone had died hours ago, leaving me no way to retrieve numbers from it. The only digits I could readily recall were my parents', and I wasn't sure how I'd explain this predicament to my mom. A fatal shooting in Van Nuys seemed easier to explain. I knew I would never find a phone charger in this dark mansion, so instead I tried to cut my losses by closing my eyes and trying to fall asleep. Problem is, anxiety kicked in, keeping me wide awake and forcing me to constantly worry about how I'd eventually get home. I began to think the *Amityville Horror* family had it easy. For the next five hours, I waited for the sun to come up, giving me just enough light to find a charger in a downstairs drawer and beg the first person who picked up my call to save me. I left her house and never went back.

It took me a full day to even comprehend what had happened that night, so when I saw our mutual friend and he asked how it went, I shook my head and kept walking. It was a night I didn't plan on recounting to anyone, and I was content with it forever being my little secret failure. Sadly, my embarrassment wasn't the only thing bothering me. In addition to the shame, I woke up with a nagging sensation in both of my eyes. It was more of an annoyance than an actual pain, but I couldn't ignore the feeling as I tried to go about my day. My eyes felt heavy and tired, but I chalked it up to lack of sleep and assumed everything would go back to normal after some well-deserved rest. So when I woke up the next morning with both eyes sealed shut and uncontrollable pus oozing from my sockets, I realized this was probably more serious than I had thought. I had a friend rush me to a doctor, who immediately put on surgical gloves and went to work opening my eyes, which were still completely closed from crust. The physician took a sample of the discharge and returned a few minutes later with a bit of a puzzled look on his face.

"This is one of two things," the doctor told me as he looked down at some notes. "You either have one of the worst sinus infections I've ever seen, or you had sex with a cheap Vietnamese hooker."

Until that moment, I never thought the situation with my eyes had anything to do with my most recent hookup, especially since we basically stopped at first base. I assumed you had to at least slide headfirst into third to catch any sort of STD. I told the whole story to my doctor, who explained, perfectly hiding any secondhand humiliation he had, that if the person you're touching is unhygienic in any matter, you can catch every sickness under the sun. Before he even finished the sentence, I remembered the fact that there wasn't even one toothbrush in her house or soap in her bathroom, something I had noticed when I tried to wash my hands in the morning. And just like that, one of the most famous women in the world, who had the personal upkeep of Pigpen from *Peanuts*, had almost certainly given me a crippling eye disease. As a result, I was put on medication and reevaluated twice over the next three weeks, racking up doctors' bills of around $1,200. I would see the famous girl a few more times over the next year at get-togethers and events, but I'd avoid hugs and wave from afar. She eventually got married, and our paths no longer crossed.

I found myself in some pretty outlandish situations over the years because of rapping, but none as disgusting as this romantic encounter. When I finally realized that her original winking probably wasn't flirting after all, but most likely an eye disease that she would eventually pass on to me, it was the worst possible M. Night Shyamalan ending our hookup could've had.

Am I the only rapper who has Photoshopped himself into the cast of Beverly Hills, 90210 *on a show flyer? Sure. But I'm also the only rapper to have ever worn that red sweat suit in a unironic fashion, so it evens out.*

"HIS HOTNESS" LYRICS, 1999

(20 years old)

Nowadays the rap game's got me furious,
I'm curious, why all these rappers act so serious,
Cool out, chill man, stop acting so mad,
Or I'm kicking you out your group like I was Beyoncé's dad
   (Say my name, say my name),
His Hotness is bringing new views,
'Cause I'm sick that college dudes only feel Dave Matthews,
Well, I've been influenced from Run-D.M.C. to Mötley Crüe,
While y'all act ignorant like white people in FUBU,
It's a brand-new thing, no violence, no bling bling,

I just love the fun in hip-hop, so that's the style that I bring,
So go and leave the anger and stress at work or at school,
'Cause that rules, it's time for hip-hoppers to act cool,
And if you were real gangsters, you wouldn't talk on it,
Y'all are liars, except for Mobb Deep, they seem honest,[1]
It's my time, so Mýa come sing after this line,
I'm gonna go run through the suburbs yelling out "Free Shyne!"

(hook)[2]

Suburbanite, rhymes tight, blazes mics,
No mention of gunfights or platinum ice, future's bright like
  Maglites,
You got me and DE, we make it all love and nice,
A black-and-white team like Crockett and Tubbs, *Miami Vice*,
I'm not claiming a gang, I'm just screaming my name
  (Hot Karl!),
At the top of my lungs like I'm insane,
I'm recording tracks in between all of my college classes,
Spiky hair, studded belt, black-rimmed glasses,
So I'm considered too pretty to flow dirty and gritty,
Stereotyped 'cause I'm from the suburbs and not the city,
Visually I'm like cable 'cause only half of you get me,
But then you heard the music and you turned half of a 360,
I'm trying to keep it real and still stay funny,

---

1 For some reason, I always assumed that Queensbridge's own Mobb
Deep was being honest when they threatened to kill you on record. A
few years later, Jay Z would expose a picture of Prodigy, one half of the
group, dressed as a ballerina for childhood dance lessons. That's when
I realized everyone was full of shit and God isn't real.

2 As I said, I didn't write this hook, and I'm not about to get all Carmen
Sandiego trying to figure out if I can publish the lyrics fifteen years
later. Let's just agree, sight unseen, that it's probably the most important stanza recorded for public consumption since Bone Thugs said
they miss their Uncle Charles.

Influenced by hip-hop when I was younger so I studied,
And made songs on four-tracks in high school with my buddies,
Never thinking one day I'd spend all of Interscope's money.

(hook)

I want the fun back in rap like it's 1985,
Like Biz Markie or the Fat Boys, when they were all alive,
You would think in the rap game we would all be one and equal,
Come on, I thought this was America, people,
But I still get weird looks, like I should leave the scene,
'Cause I'm a bit clean cut and I smile in magazines,
And I'm not really that mean, unless you fucking with my team,
Wipe your eyes a couple times to realize what you are seeing,
And I'm poking fun at people, so you might want to fight me,
Be happy you're a celebrity and take this shit lightly,[3]
Fuck, I'm like the Dirk Nowitzki of the rap game,
While y'all are lame, like Puff Daddy changing his name,
So this is the manifesto to prove that I'm for real,
Not some Johnny-come-lately who found himself a record deal,
But for now you act bitter and you make me annoyed,
'Cause truth is, I'm not acting like Tyrese in *Baby Boy*.[4]

(hook)

---

3 Pink was obviously still on my mind, even hours later while writing
   this song. I was a REAL tough rapper.
4 Never forget where you came from.

13

MY NIGHT WITH GERARDO

NEWLY single and off to a weird start, when I did have a rare night off from recording, I started to frequent trendy Hollywood nightclubs, now able to skip any line because of the record deal hoopla. The news had reached hotshot promoters like Brent Bolthouse and Amanda Demme, who ruled LA's celebrity social scene with events at spots like Joseph's, The Lounge, and Club AD. These were places where people would line up outside for two hours, only to be told they couldn't get in when they finally got to the front. I had experienced that disappointment a few times and sworn I would never do it again. But now I was being invited as a VIP, and being back on the market, I figured clubbing would be a lot more fun.

One night I found myself at Drew Barrymore's house for an after-hours party that started with Jell-O shots and ended with skinny-dipping. And a year later, I watched a recently broken-up

Justin Timberlake and Britney Spears have a surreal dance-off in the middle of the floor, an event that has since become pop-culture legend. I was partying alongside people like Heather Graham, Tobey Maguire, and Kirsten Dunst. But no matter who, or what, I saw at these events, I was no longer meeting college girls who wore pearls and talked about marriage. I started hooking up with Playboy Playmates and runway models, who seemed just as interested in my open budget as hip-hop producers were.

The first girl I hooked up with after my breakup introduced me to fake breasts, while another girl's dad owned a helicopter because he'd invented the electronic ear pick. The connection with my ex-girlfriend revolved around miniature-golf dates and rented movies. Now I was drunkenly bringing WB guest stars and music-video dancers back to my dorm room, participating in the first one-night stands of my life. Despite being signed for almost six months at this point, it wasn't until 2001, when my love life drastically changed, that I finally started to feel like a rap star.

In addition to the girls at clubs, my record label was also starting to pay more attention to me. I'd walk through the halls of the Santa Monica Interscope office and employees would come out to greet me at every stop. Word of my priority at the label, and of the positive early response to my new music, was traveling fast. DJ may have had Jimmy's ear thanks to a family tree, but he was also very good at getting the word out throughout the company. Everyone was interested in meeting the new white rapper Jimmy signed, especially one '90s icon who had recently made the transition from artist to executive.

At one time Gerardo was the hunky one-hit wonder who repeatedly said "Rico Suave" in a sexy voice—earning Interscope's first number-one single—but he had since become a well-respected A&R at the company, most notably signing Enrique Iglesias to his first American record deal. I had poked fun at both of them on "Caliente Karlito," a song now so highly regarded at the label that many of its employees would sing the hook back at me when I'd meet them. Gerardo explained that he had been pushing Interscope to sign me from the minute he heard the fake Latino track and had made sure Enrique heard it immediately, which was a fact I would later verify when I met the singer and he couldn't stop laughing and quoting lyrics.

Even cooler than that, a year or so after this initial meeting, Gerardo would ask me to write the sequel to "Rico Suave" for a possible midlife comeback, a writing gig I still think may be the strangest coup of my career. I penned the ridiculous song "Es Gerardo" from start to finish in thirty minutes, bragging in his voice that he could still steal your girl and that "Rico Suave" is where "most of you kids learned to speak Spanish from." We became fast friends, and he couldn't have been a better dude. As if writing the track wasn't enough to fulfill my need for kitsch, Gerardo asked me to perform as his hypeman at the House of Blues in Los Angeles, in what would be the first time he'd perform "Es Gerardo" live, and his first show at all in years. I couldn't say yes fast enough.

When I arrived at the House of Blues, I was pleasantly surprised to see a completely sold-out venue, comprised mostly of music-executive friends and nostalgic fans ready to have fun with the dated heartthrob. After his initial success, Gerardo, most recently seen on his own VH1 reality show, always relied on his undeniable likability and self-effacing honesty. He knew that releasing another album as Gerardo wasn't going to put him back on the Billboard Hot 100, but he was offered the opportunity by an independent Latin music label and figured it could at least be a fun adventure. And luckily, the audience shared that excitement, seeing him as more than an ironic curiosity to laugh at or a chance to act like a real-life YouTube comments section. Right after he asked me to join him onstage, I disclosed that I had a ridiculous idea on how to start his show, but I assumed there was no way he'd ever give it a shot. After telling me I was crazy a few dozen times, Gerardo admitted that my idea was the best possible introduction he could pull off.

I walked onto the empty stage to the announcer begrudgingly introducing me as "the next Latino American hip-hop superstar . . . Hot Karl," a prologue I had written for myself, ignoring the look of disgust the sound guy gave me when I had asked him to read it during soundcheck. The spotlight followed me to center stage as I heard a few friendly cheers from the audience, one even yelling "Roll Call!" like he was forced to blurt out the only way anyone in the room might know me. I spoke in the most serious tone I could muster, thanking each and every person in the audience for attending tonight's triumphant return, and then yelled over their applause to warn them about what they were about to experience.

"I know a lot of you came to see Gerardo of 'Rico Suave' fame, but I have bad news for you; that man is NOT here tonight," I revealed to a smattering of confused boos. I went on, "If you bought a ticket to see a grown man with shoulder-length perfect hair, tight jeans, a bandana, and a leather jacket with zippers strategically placed everywhere, then there's the door!" I pointed to the exits while the boos got louder and harder to ignore. "He is a grown man now. He has children! He's moved on and so should you," I started to lecture, with the ease of Nikolai Volkoff infuriating WWF crowds in the '80s.

"Let the man evolve and grow. He's not here to live in the past for *you*. He's here to play his new music and show the mature side of Gerardo," I chastised the entire House of Blues audience, which was now expressing its utter disappointment back at me. I basked in the anger, taking in each and every hiss, waiting for a tomato to be thrown. And just when the fever pitch of anger hit critical mass, the first note of "Rico Suave" unexpectedly hit the speakers—loud.

"Ladies and gentlemen, Gerardo . . ."

Just like that, Gerardo emerged from backstage, dressed in the *exact* outfit he had worn a decade earlier in his frequently lampooned music video. At my request, he'd searched through storage units to find every piece of the ensemble, even contacting a Hard Rock Cafe to borrow the genuine "Latin Till I Die" leather jacket, which was now on display near a table where you could order Tupelo Chicken Tenders (and see Fred Durst's hat). I even convinced him to sport hair extensions to cover his current buzzcut 'do. The crowd went bananas. I screamed, "Oh, you thought we were gonna act too cool for *this* shit?" I couldn't hide my elation, jumping around the stage like Tom Cruise on Oprah's couch.

I assisted Gerardo through both "Rico Suave" and our song, "Es Gerardo," pumping up the crowd between his verses, emphasizing his lines, and even helping him disrobe from his ridiculous costume. Gerardo thanked me as we finished the second track and I held up his "Latin Till I Die" jacket like I was Anthony Michael Hall proudly holding up Molly Ringwald's underwear in *Sixteen Candles*. Selling out my first real show at the Roxy, or even opening for Snoop Dogg at Summer Jam, couldn't compete with the smile permanently frozen on my face that night. It brought me back to the era when I had started rapping.

Gerardo obviously wasn't Rakim, Phife Dawg, Kool G Rap, or any other MC I'd idolized as a kid and would later open for, but as a pop-culture aficionado, this was just too cool. When I was a middle-schooler in Calabasas, only Top 40 rap artists ever made their way into our school's lexicon, and here I was onstage with one of the few who got spun at our school dances. I had my own underground legends to worship, but I knew if I could go back in time, even my old idiot classmates would acknowledge this achievement. I stayed through the show, proud of my friend and waiting to get my original "Rico Suave" cassette single signed once he came back to the dressing room. As he scribbled his name on my artifact, he looked up with a smile and said, "One day I'll be getting your autograph as you walk offstage," and although his sentiment was sweet, I was too happy to even hear it.

I hope my children appreciate heirlooms.

In addition to fulfilling one of my boyhood dreams, Gerardo was also responsible for signing Bubba Sparxxx, a weird coincidence that I hadn't really addressed yet. His recent addition to Interscope's roster had further fueled the rumors that Jimmy was constructing an army of buzzworthy white MCs only to shelve them in the name of Eminem's world dominance. It continued to sound like a cumbersome plan to me, but Bubba's presence was the first shred of evidence. Still, it didn't stop me from loving the guy when I met him.

I first met Bubba at his birthday dinner, a function I was invited to by the label in hopes that we would get along and work together, especially since Bubba's mentor was Timbaland, a man whose name was still being thrown around for a "Caliente Karlito" reboot. Bubba was an extremely gentle guy, and, at first sight, just as stark of a contrast from your typical rapper as I was. He was a pale, baby-faced, corn-fed hick who strictly wore bright Polo button-ups and khaki shorts. He seemed like he'd be more comfortable on a farm than in a recording studio, despite his undeniable skills, which helped guide his first hit single, "Ugly"— and the accompanying video, which had him wrangling pigs and riding tractors while rapping—to the top of the charts. At the dinner, Bubba and I talked about the "Ugly" clip—something he had just shot and had high hopes for, especially since Missy Elliott made a cameo appearance (I made sure to tell him I "hadn't met her yet")—and we chatted about the transition from making music with your friends to making music for a living. He was bright-eyed and enthusiastic, a demeanor I was happy to see we shared.

However, a few drinks in, when we were more relaxed, we started to talk about the elephant in the room. We never wanted to publicly address the rumors, but as a team we could approach them with confidence. We both admitted we had heard warnings that Jimmy was securing our deals to shelve us, but both disregarded it as hearsay and were happy with our decisions. But underneath the casual downplay, you could sense that both of us questioned the other's role at the label and, more important, our own. The optimism we both conveyed at this dinner would no longer exist the next time we hung out, but we enjoyed it while it lasted, getting drunk and eating steaks on the label's corporate card.

14

WILL.I.AIN'T

ONE rapper who wasn't quite getting access to Interscope's funds like Bubba and I were at that time was will.i.am. I had known of the Black Eyed Peas front man for most of my childhood, as he was a pioneer of sorts in the West Coast hip-hop scene, especially in the fields of dancing and battling. Way before selling out and rapping about lovely lady lumps or becoming a hologram on CNN, he was a scene gatekeeper of sorts, judging everyone on how "real" they were to hip-hop culture. Nowadays it's laughable, but I was always terrified to rap in cyphers with Will 1X (what he went by back then), let alone attempt to talk to the guy.

After many years as an undisputable legend at LA hip-hop clubs like Radiotron and Balistyx, where he successfully battled other pre-fame MCs like Xzibit, Will caught Jimmy Iovine's eye with the Peas, an incarnation of Atban Klann, his prior group that experienced a failed record deal at Eazy-E's Ruthless Records. Interscope released the Black Eyed Peas' debut album, *Behind the Front*, while I was a freshman in college, and not only was I happy to see someone I recognized release a major-label CD—I loved the music too. The album and its first single, "Joints and Jam," were successful enough for Interscope to renew their contract and approach a follow-up, one that would find the group hoping to expand their audience into the mainstream with a more conscious effort toward pop music. But the transition wasn't quite as easy as you'd think.

When I signed to Interscope, Will and the Black Eyed Peas (who did not yet have a female member) had just released that sophomore record, which they called *Bridging the Gap*, a reference to their attempt at capturing the pop audience with a polar-opposite combination of big hooks and underground backpack influences. The album was a tremendous failure. Even though the group used a rough draft of what would eventually become their formula for making millions, something was missing. While everyone at Interscope knew Will was an incredibly talented musician on the cusp of something big, the future of the Black Eyed Peas was in jeopardy. DJ had confided in me that Jimmy was looking to drop the Peas from the label and possibly sign Will as a solo artist, which seemed to make some sense, because I'm still not 100 percent sure what the other two guys in the group do. It was this type of desperation that I believe forced will.i.am to become friends with me.

Will would later admit in an interview that he was "jealous of the Hot Karl project." He had ideas for the Black Eyed Peas' third album, which would eventually catapult them into another stratosphere, but Jimmy and DJ had moved on to other artists and were no longer returning his calls. The budget for *Bridging the Gap* had gone above and beyond what the label felt comfortable spending, especially in hindsight, once it failed, and now Will and his group of "What do you do, anyway?" counterparts were one step from total industry exile. He had played me demos for hit songs like "Let's Get Retarded" (before it got its PC remake into "Let's Get It Started") and "Where Is the Love?" but couldn't schedule a meeting with Jimmy to show them off. Strapped for cash, Will even started walking into LA recording studios he had worked at in the past, pretending he was still recording there just to get the free food in the kitchen. You can say a lot of things about will.i.am, but that he's a quitter isn't one of them.

I knew Will didn't like my music, and I assumed that when he heard Jimmy was spending an exorbitant amount of money to sign me, it made him even more frustrated. The first few times we were introduced, Will would basically brush me off and act like I was a fan, and luckily for him, I was. A few months after I signed with Interscope, though, at a taping of *Farmclub.com*—a live music TV show that Jimmy Iovine and another music executive, Doug Morris, created for the USA Network—Will surprisingly walked up to me and started politely asking about my background in hip-hop. He wasn't being condescending or rude; it actually seemed like he was genuinely interested to learn more about the artist who was stealing the attention, and available budget, he needed. We exchanged phone numbers and just like that, after years of intimidation, I was pals with one of my favorite rappers.

At the same time I had started working with DJ Homicide, another name with a storied past in underground hip-hop, who had since found his calling as the "turntablist" for the pop group Sugar Ray. Best known as the guy who says "Shut the door, baby, don't say a word" on the song "Every Morning," Homicide wanted to return to his roots and start making rap music again.

A few weeks into working together, he played me a bouncy guitar track that was originally supposed to be on Sugar Ray's last album but didn't quite make the cut. He explained that they had worked with DJ Quik on the song, and the West Coast legend had added his own drums, which truthfully was the best part. I placed my verses into the song, focusing on strong punch lines ("As far as being just another rapper, that's over / I'm the Jewish Jay Z, the Hebrew Hova") and introspective anxiety ("If Hot Karl doesn't blow up, I'mma be pissed / 'Cause then I'm stuck with an *H* and a *K* tatted on my wrists"), knowing I was onto something big. Homicide loved what I had done with it, but we both were at a loss for what to do on the hook. Will had recently played me a song called "Ev Rebahdee," a funk-inspired jam he did with another neglected Interscope signee named Planet Asia, and it caught my attention. It wasn't the beat or Planet Asia's rap that really stuck out; it was the hook that Will half sang, half rapped. To me, it shined a spotlight on a new talent he could exploit in the pop world, specifically on my song with Sugar Ray and Quik.

Unfortunately, DJ didn't seem to share my enthusiasm. He

explained that Will might not even be part of the Interscope family in a few weeks—and that there was no buzz around him or the group—so it might be best to steer clear of including him on the album. I told him I didn't care about the label's politics and that I knew what was best for the song. With that, I drove the track over to Will's studio, and two hours later, I not only had proof that this song could be my first single, but evidence that will.i.am still showed signs of life for Interscope. For as much posturing as Will did during his days as the "keep it real" monitor, he wholeheartedly loved the track and even dropped by one of my shows a week or two later just to perform it live with me.

Will's eventual success had nothing to do with my song—trust me, I know that. But at the time, DJ admitted that his inclusion on my track, now titled "Sump'n Changed," did help Jimmy and the A&R division understand where the Black Eyed Peas could still go. For a few months after we recorded together, Will would call me about once a week, asking if I was with DJ, hoping I would pass the phone over. He knew that was the only way he could pin him down to talk about new BEP songs. Sometimes it would work out, while other times DJ motioned to say he wasn't there. I knew Will was using me for my position within the label, but I was fine with that because I truly believed in his talent.

The night we recorded "Sump'n Changed," Will admitted to feeling low, giving me a rare look into his insecurity and vulnerability. He mentioned that he was most afraid because he had just bought his mother a house and wasn't sure he could afford to help her with the mortgage like he had promised. He admitted that he had heard the rumors the group was about to get dropped and worried about the future of his bandmates. I explained that including him on my song was the least I could do to try to get the label to notice him again. He thanked me. That's why his behavior, once he blew up, would be so shocking.

Once the third Black Eyed Peas album, *Elephunk*, was released, there was no stopping the group, which now found the perfect combination of pop and rap in the form of a new member named Fergie. No matter how close they came to being released from Interscope, or how you feel about the change they made in their music to stay alive, with over 76 million records sold, they've become one of the world's best-selling groups of all time. They've won six Grammys (popping back up here: Guns N' Roses never won a Grammy) and become one of only eleven artists to simultaneously hold both the #1 and #2 spots on the Billboard Hot 100, owning the top spot for a record twenty-six consecutive weeks. Any regrets Will may have had about ditching his credible underground past were obliterated a long time ago by his bank account. Years after ignoring his phone calls, Jimmy Iovine would even recognize Will's significant contribution to the Interscope empire by making him an equity partner in Beats by Dre, allegedly giving him 5 percent of the company, and in turn around $125 million in its sale to Apple. He may have made his mom move from that house after all, but it was only to buy her a much bigger one.

Will and I did keep in touch for a bit after he went mainstream, and we'd laugh about the 180 degrees that DJ and Jimmy turned since the days of "Sump'n Changed." He now solely referred to me as "Hairy Potter," both to my face and to others, a cute moniker he still uses to refer to my resemblance to the literary wizard and my Armenian background. And a few years into his career resurgence, he called me to collaborate on an idea for a movie he wanted to release alongside a solo record he was prepping. He hired me to sit in the studio with him for two weeks and knock out a script based on the songs he was recording. I agreed to do it, especially since he had promised me $3,500 no matter what came of the script. And so I sat in his studio, as he worked with Common, Nas, and Fergie, just listening to the music and the way he talked. I eventually crafted a script, inspired by his new material, and he seemed very excited by the results. But once it made its way to Interscope, they weren't quite as excited. The concept was killed before it ever left the ground. In an ironic twist, from that point on, Will and his manager stopped taking *my* calls and I was never paid the $3,500 I was promised.

About two years later, Will called me in the midst of what some might assume was a manic episode. But those who knew him well understood that this was just his way of being creative. He apologized for what had happened with the movie script, saying he always disagreed with Interscope's notes and wished he'd stood up to them, especially since the solo record tanked, an unpredictable result based on his hot streak at the time. He was talking so fast that his words were difficult to decipher. From what I could make out, he wanted to bring me back into the studio to write a Broadway musical he envisioned, based on the Slick Rick song "Children's Story." He rapped parts of the classic track to me and explained his vision for how it would play out onstage. He wanted to meet as soon as possible to go over a possible partnership and asked about my schedule. I remember being somewhat flattered that Will would still think of me for an idea, but also burned over the money he owed me. As much as I wanted to say yes as a fan of will.i.am (and, more important, Will 1X), I declined. Surprised by my answer, he asked, "What's Hairy Potter got going instead?"

I calmly said, "Trying to buy my mom a house."

Matty Boom and me in 2001, taking a break from that rap life, to meet celebrity dog Mr. Winkle.

"SUMP'N CHANGED" LYRICS, 2000

(20 years old)

(hook)

Things don't seem the same, things is rearranged,
  something's changed,
I said who done fucked it up,
Who done fucked it up,
Things don't seem the same, things is rearranged,
  something's changed,
I said who done fucked it up,
Hot Karl gonna switch it back up.

Something's changed, let's go toe for toe,
'Cause no nobody's watching you, like Queen Latifah's
    talk show,[1]
And as far as being just another rapper, that's over,
I'm the Jewish Jay Z, the Hebrew Hova,
A college graduate, yo, I'm not here to fight,
(I don't get it—a white rapper who acts white?),
But when I grab the mic, with the style that I bring,
Nerdy white kids line up like it was *Lord of the Rings*,
It's changed—try to front and play the high post,
But admit that if we battle, then you ain't coming close,
It's a joke, you musta thought I'd amount to zero,
'Cause I list Suge Knight and Woody Allen as my heroes,
Why's that kid on MTV with a sombrero?[2]
The man, while you just The Fan like Bob De Niro,
But if I'm found dead, laying in a gutter,
Make a poetry CD and tell Meadow that I love her.

(hook)

Things don't seem the same, things is rearranged,
    something's changed,
I said who done fucked it up,
Who done fucked it up,

---

1   Queen Latifah was a frequent target in my songs, mentioned almost
    as often as Tyrese, for no reason other than I thought her career trajec-
    tory was so random. I'm actually a huge fan of her early songs. This
    joke about her talk show would work twice, separated by a decade,
    since she's had two daytime runs and both times she delivered less than
    Marshawn Lynch at a press conference.
2   I had assumed that by this point audiences would've heard "Caliente
    Karlito" and the video would've had me in a complete Mariachi outfit.
    Instead, it just sounds like I want to be on MTV wearing a festive
    ethnic hat.

Things don't seem the same, things is rearranged,
  something's changed,
I said who done fucked it up,
Who's the motherfucker that fucked it up.

If Hot Karl doesn't blow up, I'mma be pissed,
'Cause then I'm stuck with an *H* and a *K* tatted on my wrists,
With a college education that didn't mean shit.
'Cause I had the opportunity but couldn't make a hit,[3]
Oh well, I won't be surprised if that happens,
We live in a world where O-Town goes platinum,
It's hard to tell, exactly what'll sell,
I really miss Aaliyah 'cause I'm stuck with Blu Cantrell,
What the fuck?
I mean, every rock-rap group sounds exactly the same and
  still blows up,
So now I'm pissed, on some West Coast shit,
So you know I had to make a call to DJ Quik,[4]
'Cause to tell my story, it had to be bumping,
To prove the suburbs could flow just like Compton,

---

3 My dad used to complain when I'd prophesize my eventual music-industry failure, saying it was a jinx. Maybe he's right, but also he was the Jewish parent, so if anyone is to blame for my negative outlook on life, it's him.

4 Eventually I did have to contact DJ Quik to clear the song. Photographer Jonathan Mannion would introduce us by driving me to his house one weekend. Quik, an eccentric man in every sense of the word, was a bit jumpy that night, despite giving me full permission to work on, and release, the track. After an hour of casually hanging out and playing video games, his mood changed abruptly. He told us to leave because something scary was about to go down, implying that he had just been told someone was coming to his house. Jonathan and I proceeded to run out of his place at full speed, never knowing what he was referring to and never really wanting to find out.

Here's a rap lesson for kids who act shook,
Here's the sixteenth bar (breath), now here's the hook.

(hook)

Things don't seem the same, things is rearranged,
    something's changed,
I said who done fucked it up,
Who done fucked it up,
Things don't seem the same, things is rearranged,
    something's changed,
I said who done fucked it up,
Who's the motherfucker that fucked it up.

I grew up with white kids that lived suburban lives,
Who graduated college just to work a nine to five,
To satisfy the parents that they secretly despise,
And when it's all exposed people act like they surprised,
I got dissed for rapping, ain't that silly,
'Cause now they the ones going "uh-ohhh" with Nelly,
It went mainstream and it caught mass appeal,
Hey, that ain't bad, shit, that's why I got a deal,
But no matter what I'mma just be me,
Go triple platinum by myself and bang Alicia Keys,
I'm here to make sure all those kids know the truth,
That fake rappers hide in they trunks like Rae Carruth,
And I make fun of people so I'm genuinely hoping
That cats in the game understand I'm only joking,
But it's my time, HK gonna do it,
Make three million kids scream out "Keep it Jewish."

(hook)

Things don't seem the same, things is rearranged,
    something's changed,

I said who done fucked it up,
Who done fucked it up,
Things don't seem the same, things is rearranged,
  something's changed,
I said who done fucked it up,
Who's the motherfucker that fucked it up.[5]

---

5 During the outro to the song, I shout out Will, the producers of the
   song, and even the Sugar Ray guitarist who plays on the track. I also
   ask DJ AM to bump the song at Las Palmas. He did throw it into the
   mix days after I recorded it, mostly because it was the first time anyone
   had ever said his name on a rap song, something he reminded me of
   just days before he passed away.

15

BIG CHECKS AND VERY LITTLE BALANCE

AFTER a year of recording and a few possible singles under my belt, Interscope began to book sessions in New York City, the place where DJ had started his music career and thus had more established hip-hop connections. I had just graduated college, a feat Jimmy Iovine had promised would happen during my development and recording process, and I was happy to prove him right. It was mid-2001, and although there was still no set date to release the album, the positive feedback I was constantly getting—and the label's readiness to spend large amounts of money on travel, producers, and guest features—made it difficult to find anything in my life worth a complaint.

However, days before my first musical trip to the East Coast, my parents informed me they'd be divorcing, which hit me like a ton of suburban only-child bricks. Their marriage, and individual well-beings, had disintegrated so quickly, it was jarring.

The two people who were so supportive and positive throughout my entire life had grown apart—and into a negative, preoccupied disaster. My father had fallen into a heavy depression, a pattern learned from his own father, disconnecting through sleep during the rare hours he wasn't selling cars, a job he had grown to despise. Once one of my biggest fans, he was now leaving the room when I'd ask if he wanted to hear my newest song. My mother, the woman who at one time laughed and danced onstage beside me, had also disengaged, holed up in her office playing endless games of Minesweeper. She began to look astonishingly unhappy and became so stressed, she was hospitalized for debilitating acid reflux, an incident I missed while in New York attending MTV VMA after-parties. Communication between them had become almost nonexistent, each living in sadness triggered by personal disappointment. A family that had once exhibited the harmony of *Full House* had quickly turned into the Fishers from *Six Feet Under.*

I'd finally run into the first roadblock on my seemingly flawless journey into a new profession, which was painful mostly because I knew I should've paid more attention. It's like on Splash Mountain at Disneyland, where the first ten minutes are full of birds chirping and tiny animals singing songs about happiness and shit, but then, right near the end, the music turns macabre and there's a rabbit with a black eye crying about the epidemic of child abuse. Then there's a drop out of nowhere.

Their separation also led me back to therapy, something I had frequented as a preteen and now figured couldn't hurt. Since childhood, I had wrestled with what would later be diagnosed as obsessive thoughts disorder, a condition where negative visions repeat in my head to a point where it's impossible to function on an everyday basis. It started as constantly seeing the tombstones of my still living grandparents when trying to fall sleep at eleven years old and hasn't really let up since. Sounds super chill, right? The disorder had taken a backseat during the Hot Karl excitement, but the divorce, which was the most painful experience of my life up until that point, reminded me exactly how rough I could be on myself. OTD is harder to control during times of stress or pain, since the floodgates of self-doubt are then opened and my brain basically becomes a Woody Allen monologue.

But my mom and dad's decision to uncouple came way before I developed methods of coping with OTD, and I couldn't avoid constant thoughts of both my parents breaking down and dying alone. I would be lucky to get three or four uninterrupted hours of sleep or thirty minutes a day without an obsessive run of thoughts. Depressing thoughts like *"Your dad is unemployed and always alone"* would constantly replay in my head, which made writing funny lyrics like "Yo, you don't want no bad blood in between us / Like we're standing right next to Magic Johnson's intravenous" quite a contrast in my life. It's not like I wanted to be the next Maya Angelou, but the cognitive dissonance I was now experiencing was immense. No matter how hard I tried to remove myself from my parents' rough patch, their situation was the only thing I could think about.

Making matters worse, someone at Interscope had secretly leaked me a few songs from Eminem's third album, *The Eminem Show*, during his recording process, thinking it would help me understand what direction he was going in. Instead, it threw me deeper into a hole of anxiety. I heard "Cleanin' Out My Closet" and "My Dad's Gone Crazy," both still in demo form, but both also absolutely brilliant and surefire signs he wasn't going anywhere but up. Eminem was getting significantly better, and I couldn't get out of my head.

But almost like the music industry had its own version of antidepressants, right when things got unpleasant, more money found its way into my bank account, allowing me to stifle any real feelings of discomfort for the time being.

———

When people talk about the record industry nowadays, the conversation is usually dominated by talk of the financial struggles that musicians, even successful ones, have to endure. Since the transition to the digital era, their only regular income comes from touring, merchandising, and corporate endorsements/sponsorships, leaving record sales—and to an extent publishing—rather disappointing for the wallet. "Selling out" is no longer a term. We're living in a climate where Bob Dylan's "I Want You" was used in a Chobani yogurt commercial and nobody gave a shit. So imagine how difficult it is for an emerging musician to live comfortably while building a name and fan base in 2016. But in 2001, the fury to sign new artists was still in full effect, so when I got a call from a prominent publishing company, it couldn't have come at a better time.

An executive at the company had been tipped off by some

Interscope employees that Jimmy was poised to make Hot Karl the next Eminem, so he wanted to make an offer on the copyright of my words before a bidding war happened down the road. So, in simpler terms, they would become a partner in managing my lyrics and intellectual property in situations where they could be used in media. They'd join my team, collecting royalties on my behalf and actively searching for films, TV projects, and yogurt commercials to license my music for.

The catch here was that, in return for this partnership, they'd need to pay me a large advance against possible future earnings, creating a bit of a dice roll in case I never actually recouped that upfront payment. The publishing company would be betting my advance against my ability to eventually pay it back and then start making them profits. So, you really only had two options as publisher: (1) you sign a tremendous success story who quickly repays the upfront loan and makes you look like a psychic, or (2) you throw a shit ton of money into a fire. It's these kind of odds that might make it a little easier to understand why the music industry has been in a steady financial decline over the past twenty years.

Adding fuel to the fire, another publishing company reached out after Timbaland brought my name up in a meeting as someone he'd be working with soon. I now had two large conglomerates jockeying to give me ungodly amounts of cash with a bet that even Pete Rose would say was "too risky." When the dust cleared, I had signed a publishing deal worth $500,000. It would be broken up into two payments—$250,000 upon signing and $250,000 with the release of my major-label debut—and I didn't have to record anything new, or even lift a finger, to fulfill the agreement. Keep in mind, no Hot Karl album, or even a single for that matter, had a set release date, but they were willing to make that bet. Who was I to say no?

I had read enough depressing Motown biographies to know that giving away your publishing was an easy way to find yourself eventually living in an abandoned car wash, but I also knew that the opportunity to earn that kind of guaranteed money could not be ignored. After I asked my lawyer, Fred, the same question maybe fifteen times, he assured me that a publishing company, just like a record label, has never gone after an artist who didn't recoup their initial advance, as long as the musician didn't act like a real asshole and change their name and move to Mexico the day after they got the check. Feeling safe, I quickly signed the paperwork they sent me, hoping to get it to them before they changed their minds, and planned to pick up my check from Fred's office during my upcoming New York trip.

However, before my trip to become USC's richest recent undergrad, I wanted to finish a new song I had been working on called "The 'Burbs," a track where, only a few years out of high school, I chronicled the most disturbing parts of growing up among spoiled classmates in the San Fernando Valley. In early versions, I included my own experiences in the lyrics, like mentioning the varsity point guard who secretly videotaped unsuspecting girls during sex or the honor roll students who implemented complex cheating systems just to keep their grades impressive. As the song got more attention at the label, I got less specific about my high-school issues and tried to relate to frustrations that all lower- to middle-class kids might have had when comparing themselves to peers born with silver spoons in their mouths.

Looking back, it's the song that makes me cringe the most, purely because it reeks of white privilege and whining. I make myself feel better about it by acknowledging that I was the first to address this specific suburban angst through rap, something regularly addressed by 2016 MCs with names like Hoodie Allen, Lil Dicky, and Mac Miller. And in truth, whether "The 'Burbs" worked or it didn't (it didn't), I always tried my hardest to deliver the song's lyrics in a tongue-in-cheek manner, joking during live shows that the track sampled the world's smallest violin.

"The 'Burbs" included lines like "From the outside, they pretend it's sweet home / Where little eight-year-old kids have their own cell phones" and "If girls have problems, Daddy buys them bigger breasts / Like every answer to the test is resting in your daughter's chest." As I was recording the song, I would regularly hear the term "second single" from DJ, meaning we could follow up a more humorous pop debut with something a little deeper and emotionally revealing.

The plan was to get a special feature from a well-known singer for the hook, since what I had written for the chorus had the feel of a big rock ballad. The label immediately suggested Fred Durst, which theoretically felt right and would only strengthen my standing within Interscope; I'd be using one of its own stars. Despite our rocky history, Fred expressed interest after hearing the track—and finding out that he could make a whopping $50,000 for the appearance—so we quickly booked a mutually agreed-upon studio time for him to record. As is the case with almost everything described as "mutually agreed upon," one of the parties didn't show up, and once again I was on the receiving end of Fred Durst's true douchebaggery. He would later explain that he "lost track of time" and now wasn't sure he was a good fit for the song anyway. I didn't allow his fickleness or erratic behavior to affect me this time, however, and decided to dust myself off and just find someone else.

Since I was still working with Sugar Ray's DJ Homicide on a few tracks, he suggested that the lead singer of his band, Mark McGrath, take a shot. I had never really been a fan of Sugar Ray per se, and even if I were, I wouldn't admit that in a book that will last forever. Despite this fact, I saw how his inclusion on a song about the suburbs made perfect sense, since most of his success was surrounded, and validated, by those exact white people I was rapping about. I agreed with Homicide's opinion, giving me the chance to now write a sentence so based in the 2000s that I might as well post it on MySpace: I had a song with Mark McGrath.

Mark became famous for a reason: his impeccable singing. No, I'm fucking with you. He can't sing. He's famous because he's insanely likable (and the first to admit his strengths and weaknesses). When the time came to record vocals for "The 'Burbs," he made sure none of us were in the studio when he sang his parts because, as he put it, "Then you'd find out I can't carry a tune." He always knew—and still knows—his role in pop music, employing a self-effacing approach that makes it nearly impossible to hate the guy. In the end, no matter who he recorded in front of, Mark sounded great on the record, even if the background vocals, once just a reference track sung by the producer, were still loud enough to be the leads. And when we finished the song, he sent me a very pleasant message via two-way pager suggesting I leave space on my mantel for a Grammy. I knew he was bullshitting me (and if Hot Karl had won a Grammy, I'd obviously make a joke here about how Nas has never taken one home). Nonetheless, it's obvious that Mark McGrath, in another life, would've made a great politician.

*Sugar Ray? Jurassic 5? Phantom Planet? All we
needed was Elián González on a Razor scooter and
this would've been the most Y2K shit of all time.*

A few weeks later, still high off our collaboration, Mark texted me after finding out that my birthday was coming up. He asked what my plans were for the big night, and I answered him with the truth: "I'm having pizza with my divorcing parents." Mark, realizing that I'd somehow found a way to make pizza sad, informed me that he had reservations for a table at Las Palmas, the city's most exclusive nightclub at the time, and would love for me to join him. He planned on turning this birthday into something I'd never forget. I accepted the gesture and braced myself for another strange Hot Karl experience.

It's difficult to remember the details of a night so clouded by alcohol that one falls asleep in the bushes outside his friend's house, but I'll try my hardest. Even to this day I'm not much of a drinker, so when Mark kept ordering bottles of Cristal for our table—and I kept drinking direct from them like I was Damon Dash on a yacht in an old Jay Z video—I shouldn't have been surprised when I blacked out. I do remember sitting in a booth next to Hugh Hefner and an accompanying group of fifteen Playmates, only to eventually do the Running Man for one centerfold who I would later kiss because Mark told us to. I also remember telling one of the members of Crazy Town, inexplicably named Squirrel, about my parents' divorce, then escaping to the bathroom to cry in a locked stall. And I remember eventually getting kicked out of the club for falling asleep in someone else's booth (OK, I don't actually remember that; it's what people told me the next day). The last thing I vaguely recall is getting in a taxi, only to wake up in a planter, holding an empty bottle of Cristal close to my face like a baby with a security blanket. I somehow managed to make it back to my place, nap all day, and still attend that night's pizza party with my splitting parents, which at times was more painful than the hangover.

On my way to hang out with my mom and dad, I finally heard from Mark via text. I was excited to recall what we did the night before, but more important, to get filled in on what I didn't remember. I was about to tell him about waking up next to azaleas when he easily one-upped me. He revealed that he woke up with a Virgin Mary tattoo on his neck and didn't remember getting it. He seemed genuinely shocked by this discovery, especially the immense size of the body art, considering he wasn't religious. He admitted he'd somehow still had a great night, but was "never drinking again." I went on to thank him for the birthday hospitality. He jokingly told me to pray for him. He had the tattoo removed shortly thereafter.

A few weeks later, in the middle of the night, Mark paged, inviting me to come hang out with him and Jay Gordon, the lead singer of Orgy, as they "built a BattleBot." I asked if he was kidding and he responded in feverish detail about the remote-controlled machine's arsenal of weapons and precision. I began to think maybe he wasn't serious about the "never drinking again" thing. I politely declined his invitation, never finding out if that night also ended at a tattoo parlor, but honestly, I've never had another birthday as exciting as the one Mark McGrath threw me when I was almost famous and turning twenty-one.

Finally of legal drinking age, I checked into my New York hotel, drank a celebratory beer, and arranged to stop by Fred Davis's office to pick up the first half of my publishing payment. In the year since I had signed with Interscope, I had realized that most of the money from that outlandish deal would go toward my production budget. This newfound wealth from publishing, on the other hand, would go directly into my pocket. I walked the ten blocks to his building, almost skipping the entire way, assuming there'd be fanfare at the office, like a photo opportunity of me holding a gigantic novelty check like it was the state lottery. I walked into Fred's lavish Manhattan office and braced myself for noisemakers.

Slightly more calmly than I expected, I informed the receptionist that I was "Hot Karl, here to see Fred Davis." She looked up from her computer, gave me an irritated look, and mumbled something about me being early. I apologized and coyly admitted I was excited, but before I even finished my sentence, she handed me an envelope that had the name *Carl* written across the front. I was surprised by the quickness of our interaction and lack of balloons or blaring horns, so I sort of just stood there, waiting for her to congratulate me or bring out a cake. She looked up, annoyed, and asked if that was all I needed. When I inquired about seeing Fred, she informed me he'd be in meetings all day but sent his best. I said thank you and walked out as she jumped onto a new phone call, which I could only assume was Ja Rule calling to wish Fred a Merry Christmas.

I sat in the lobby, staring at the misspelled envelope. Maybe the celebration I had hoped for was nonexistent, but seeing my name attached to a check with that many zeroes was unbelievable. I'd been given a rap career in the same way John Goodman was given royalty in *King Ralph*. I kept thinking someone was going to abruptly show up at one of my recording sessions, tell me it was all a misunderstanding, and ask me for the money back. But instead, all I ever heard was that I was "the next big thing" and one of the most talented up-and-coming MCs in the game. And people were just throwing money at me.

With nearly $1 million invested in my rap career, I was in the Big Apple now, the birthplace of hip-hop, ready to meet and work with a whole new set of producers and rappers in an attempt to round out my album and get it primed for release. The label promised to connect me with some of the hottest names in the industry while I was in New York, and I was ready to take full advantage of those resources. Among them was a new producer named Kanye West, who had just begun his roller-coaster ride toward fame. At the same time, mine was getting closer and closer to the free-fall drop that would eventually define my career forever.

While performing songs with titles like "The 'Burbs,"
I started to notice an audience whiter than
Birkenstock's corporate holiday party.

"THE 'BURBS" LYRICS, 2000/01

(20 & 21 years old)[1]

---

1   I went back and forth about including these lyrics in the book, mostly because the song hasn't aged well (and truthfully never sounded the exact way I had imagined). It's by far the most embarrassing song from the Hot Karl library, since without any context it feels very corny and reeks of the dated 2000s teen aggression that dominated the charts. BUT, I'll say this: movies like *American Beauty* and *Alpha Dog* (which is also inspired by a true story from my high school) would visit similar subjects soon thereafter, and that white-kid angst became the cornerstone for most of pop punk, so maybe the lyrics were just ahead of their time. Or maybe this song just sucks and I'm making excuses.

I was raised in a suburb that was hardly healthy,
Grew up in the middle of the most affluent and wealthy,
'Cause most people assume happiness within the 'burbs,
But please hear my words, that lifestyle is absurd,
Remember *Clueless*? See, that's my hood but more ruthless,
The method on how they call it, depends on your wallet,
From the outside, they pretend it's sweet home,
Where little eight-year-old kids have their own cell phones,[2]
It's the 'burbs, where money's the only need,
'Cause millionaires survive on principles of lust and greed,
See, we talk about a place where middle class is second rate,
Ridiculed at an early age for not having a guarded gate,
And in this case, parents try to buy their kids' love,
How do you think most of these kids can afford all of these
    drugs?
But we sit back and act like it's the best place on earth,
Without admitting the worst shit happens right in our
    suburbs.

(hook)

When you're on top of the world it's lonely,
When you have everything it's empty,
And the ones you call friends are your enemies,
But that's the way that it goes when you live in the 'burbs.

The 'burbs, the 'burbs, the the 'burbs,
Where it looks like a dream but it's never how it seems.

It's so sick, my high school was like a fashion show,
A runway for expensive clothes and cash flow,
At such a vital age, puberty can't run its course,

---

2 This is sort of the norm now, right?

Kids are dissed for looking different and 'cause they can't play
    sports,
No surprise, when we'd come back from Christmas break,
To see most of the girls' noses molded into pretty shapes,[3]
And if girls have problems, Daddy buys them bigger breasts,
Like every answer to the test is resting in your daughter's chest,
There's so much plastic surgery, people look obscene,
Girls following images that can't humanly be achieved,
It's a vicious cycle, reality is distorted,
Why do you think all of these girls develop eating disorders?
'Cause girls who weigh more get called ugly and fat,
And we expect these kids to keep levelheaded through all that?
Yeah, we look happy, but what's it all worth,
'Cause you lose your identity living in suburbs.

(hook)

When you're on top of the world it's lonely,
When you have everything it's empty,
And the ones you call friends are your enemies,
But that's the way that it goes when you live in the 'burbs.

The 'burbs, the 'burbs, the the 'burbs,
It's all about the salary and nothing 'bout reality.

I'm sure there's places like this wherever you call home,
Same fucked-up suburb just with a different zip code,
Where spoiled brats live in a fake reality,
Where the student parking lot has better cars than the
    faculty's,
And the sickest shit? The richer, the quicker they are to fight,
Despite all of this cash they live like it's Thug Life,

---

3   No matter what I think of the song now, I still really like this line.

With a bunch of racist kids trying to be tougher than the next,
It's like they're obsessed with *American History X*,
But in due time, these problems will show,
Why do you think these high school shootings don't happen in
  ghettos?
So next time you see a student driving a Porsche,
Throwing cash like Jermaine Dupri, living like Brandon Walsh,
Imagine their classmate, who ain't got shit,
Can't find his place in Utopia, although he's supposed to live
  in it,
And getting picked on for years eventually hurts,
But then again it's just another day up in these suburbs, huh?

(hook)

When you're on top of the world it's lonely,
When you have everything it's empty,
And the ones you call friends are your enemies,
But that's the way that it goes when you live in the 'burbs.

The 'burbs, the 'burbs, the the 'burbs,
Where all the kids are rich, but the good life's a bitch.

(Shit's fucked up in) the 'burbs, the 'burbs, the the 'burbs,
Where adults are corrupt, yo I'm telling you straight up.

The 'burbs, the 'burbs, the the 'burbs,
It's not the inner city but suburbia is shitty.

The 'burbs, the 'burbs, the the 'burbs,
If you wanna compete, your morals take a backseat.

The 'burbs, the 'burbs, the the 'burbs,
It proves that success don't equal happiness.

The 'burbs, the 'burbs, the the 'burbs,
The all-American dream isn't exactly how it seems,
Look closer.[4]

---

4   Once a year someone still tells me about how much this song meant to
    him or her in high school, and that always feels weird. The song was
    heavily downloaded on file-sharing sites like Napster and allegedly
    ended up quoted by some kid in a manifesto in which he threatened
    to shoot up his school. Truthfully, that tainted the song forever, and I
    haven't been able to listen to it since.

16

KANYE WEST OWES ME $300

THE day after I became the most unlikely hundred-thousandaire in hip-hop, I began working at Baseline, a now defunct multiroom studio where, at the time, Jay Z was recording *The Blueprint* next door. No matter what time of day it was, you could see any of the biggest rappers in the world working or just walking room to room to say hello. Baseline would be the epicenter of Roc-A-Fella Records in its heyday, the birthplace of most of the label's biggest hits. Hov, Beanie Sigel, Young Gunz, and Freeway all recorded songs there, and I like to think I was the only white rapper to have done the same, a theory I dreamed up after Memphis Bleek once asked me for a soda in the kitchen area, assuming I was a studio intern. I regularly joked that my recording sessions there looked like the opposite of Hootie and the Blowfish.

I first heard of Kanye West, an eventual Baseline frequenter, through beats given to me by my manager at the time. In anticipation of my first NYC trip, he passed me the snippet CD that read in Sharpie *K. West*, hoping we could find someone new (and cheap) to include in our itinerary. Kanye was being touted as an emerging producer and had yet to really take off since recently moving from Chicago, but I was told that a handful of rappers were currently writing to his stuff. Also, two of Roc-A-Fella's main consiglieres managed him, so I assumed he was at least producing a few songs for the dudes who held Jay Z's weed.

At this point in rap history, the "beat CD" was the industry-standard vehicle for producers to introduce their work to rappers. Think of it as a business card of sorts. Producers would submit instrumentals to labels, managers, and artists, in hopes of getting rappers to flow on their music and getting a check for the release. I had heard *every* beat CD making the rounds at the time, and everything started to sound alike. All I kept doing was bugging the label to connect me with Just Blaze.

It was nearly impossible to avoid a Just Blaze track when listening to urban radio in the early 2000s, and his rise to dominance is important to note when discussing Kanye's origins. Just Blaze's signature sped-up, chipmunk-sounding soul samples are an essential part of the era's legacy, and I was a huge fan. So when my team told me I was being directed toward Kanye (who shared a manager with Just Blaze) instead of my pick, I insisted that we just keep bugging them for their top dog. I felt cheated, like I had asked a DJ to play a Michael Jackson song and he instead played Alien Ant Farm's cover of "Smooth Criminal." Eventually Interscope informed me that Just was too busy to take on new work, and I was told something that, for better or worse, would stick with Kanye for the first year of his production career: "When you can't afford Just Blaze, you get Kanye West."

This theory was echoed by their shared management and somewhat validated by Kanye's similar dependence on soul and pitched-up samples. For as unique as Kanye West has become, his origins lacked the inventiveness he now displays on every new release. When I became friends with Just Blaze years later, I told him about this anecdote and he shrugged it off with class, explaining, "Everyone starts somewhere," and that he had never heard the saying about Kanye before. For the record, I think he's being a nice guy and knows exactly what I'm talking about.

But even though he had a reputation as a plan B, I wanted to give this "K. West" CD a listen. After only a few seconds of the first song, I called my manager and told him to set up a time for Kanye and me to chat. After listening to the rest of his music,

I fell in love with a later instrumental track that sampled Laura Nyro's "Woman's Blues," and I knew it would fit perfectly on my album. Jay Z would later turn that first beat I heard into "Izzo (H.O.V.A.)," so I sleep better at night knowing that even though I had the chance to make that Jackson 5 sample my own, Shawn Carter did more with it than I ever could have. On the resulting conference call with our managers, Kanye was polite and accommodating, excited to be making what would be, at the time, the most money he'd ever made from music: somewhere between $5,000 and $7,500. But that all took a quick turn when he heard which track I selected. The vision and stubborn determination we're now accustomed to seeing from Kanye suddenly cropped up out of nowhere.

"But that's the one I made for Ghostface," Kanye explained.

One of his managers, Gee, reminded him that Ghostface had heard it and passed.

"Yeah, but I gotta talk to him. Pick another one."

I said excitedly, "Oh, you know Ghostface?" Even after my personal experience with RZA, I still wasn't cool enough to hide my enthusiasm whenever Wu-Tang was mentioned.

"No," Kanye said abruptly.

Gee quickly changed the subject, knowing they had a bird in the hand from Hot Karl and that Ghostface had no intention of working with Kanye. We compromised by agreeing that I would write to the beat, and if Ghostface were to change his mind in the next two weeks, we'd pick another one and go from there. But no matter the resolution, Kanye didn't say another word to me for the rest of the phone call.

I was never late for a session. I was raised with a strong work ethic, and while I'd sometimes have to wait five or six hours for a rapper to arrive, or to get stood up by Fred Durst, I treated this job like it involved the government. So when I got to Baseline Studios for my first day with Kanye a few minutes before our session was supposed to begin, I was surprised to see him already at work. I was also pretty taken aback by what "K. West" looked like. The swagger you see in the megastar now was entirely absent. His Enyce tracksuit jacket and baggy pants were about two sizes bigger than anything a rapper would wear, even in 2001. He was sporting an outfit that a fifty-year-old woman in a wardrobe department would put together if a "rapper" was mentioned in your script. We were more than a decade away from rappers mentioning Tom Ford and Marc Jacobs in songs—or from Kanye debuting his own weirdo high-end clothing line during Fashion Week—but the guy just looked plain goofy. And the gold chains and Jesus piece that would eventually appear around his neck were replaced by the only bling he had at the time: adult braces. I vividly remember saying "This guy looks like Bowfinger" to my manager, who would whisper "Urkel" in my ear over and over.

Coincidentally, K. West seemed just as shocked to see what H. Karl looked like, and not just because I wasn't Ghostface Killah. He took one look at my vintage rock shirt and ripped jeans and seemed instantly relieved. While most rappers would've just assumed I was there to play bass on the song, he found my appearance comforting.

"Aw, man! I would've dressed like myself. I do this for rappers," Kanye explained, pointing to his outfit, which was so baggy, it could've doubled as a Jesse Pinkman Halloween costume. And on our second day of recording, he transformed just like he promised. The future icon ditched his Juggalo-esque threads for a Jim Morrison T-shirt and rock-inspired jeans. Don't get me wrong, though, he still looked nerdy as fuck.

And in turn, Kanye was treated like the ugly stepchild of Baseline Studios. He was too eager and too dorky, lacking the restraint and tough-guy persona that ruled rap music and, more specifically, New York City, for decades. When he heard me rhyme the *Karlito*-inspired line "Me and Kanye made this real *picante* and *grande* / While you suckers act—Armand Assante" on our song together, he visibly displayed excitement, saying no one outside of his friends had said his name on a track yet. Traditionally, he would've pretended he didn't even hear it, trying not to look so fervent. He talked too fast and altogether too much, a tendency we now know is something he can't change as fast as his wardrobe. On that first day of recording, we found ourselves alone in the room together, and that's when he let me in on a secret.

"You know, I rhyme too," Kanye nervously divulged, making sure no one else heard him.

I was caught off guard. No one had even mentioned that he was more than a producer. Not even in passing was he called a rapper.

"I'm actually keeping a lot of the best beats for my own shit," Kanye said confidently, seeming to forget I'd just paid something like $7,000 for a beat he didn't think was his best shit. "I'm just doing this to rap."

But the way Kanye said it, that first time we met, it felt like he was telling me something he wasn't supposed to share—something someone constantly reminded him not to bring up in sessions. I'd learn quickly that no one at Baseline considered Kanye a rapper. They'd get annoyed whenever he'd talk about it. Even his managers rolled their eyes when he mentioned his rap career. Everyone knew he was a talented producer—with only that one complaint, that he sounded like an affordable Just Blaze—but popular opinion was that he didn't have the skill, or look, to take the stage himself.

I remember one day while recording, Kanye played an early version of "Jesus Walks," several years before its release, to a room that included myself, some A&Rs, some assorted industry types, DJ Clue, rapper Fabolous, and engineer Duro. As the song played, Kanye acted out and mouthed his lyrics, something he always did while his own music played, and I assume still does. He acted as if a music video was always being filmed around him, displaying yet another example of the unaware enthusiasm (and egotism) that would make him the butt of almost every joke at Baseline. The song ended, some people shared some positive (but subdued) comments, and Kanye left for the kitchen. A few seconds passed before the entire room erupted in laughter. A few people even mocked him, mimicking his rap voice and making fun of his over-the-top zeal. One major producer in the room even asked his assistant to make sure Kanye never performed like that again. Lucky for him he didn't have to, because three years later, "Jesus Walks" would win a Grammy for Best Rap Song. (No joke here. He deserved it.)

Let's be straight, though. I too was "a hater," and just as guilty of underestimating Kanye, when, in reality, I should've understood being underestimated more than any rapper in the game. You see, when I first met Redman, who I recorded a track with on this trip and paid way too much for, we sat and talked for twenty minutes about what would become of our joint effort. I played him the track, with my raps already recorded onto it, and smiled ear to ear when I saw him bobbing his head along to my words. We threw around ideas for his part and talked about his philosophy on writing lyrics. About an hour into the session, after I thought we had a real creative connection, he politely asked when I thought the rapper would arrive. Confused, I told him I *was* the rapper. I was also the guy he had been collaborating with for the past hour and the dude paying him to be on the song. He admitted that he thought I was just the studio assistant, leading me to wonder just how much musical credit Redman is giving studio assistants. Right then I promised myself I would only feature rappers who were actually my friends. For example, I wanted to have an underground remix of the Redman song featuring up-and-coming MCs like myself, not just dudes we paid $15,000 to pretend they were my friends. So I asked my pal Mr. Eon from the High & Mighty to participate, and Redman suggested—slash demanded—that we use his buddy Ikarus. I obliged because "at least he's *someone's* friend."

I called Kanye to see if he wanted to hang out at Baseline that day, and he showed up early once again. At some point during the day, Kanye asked my manager if he could also jump on the remix, and I still kick myself to this day about my response. Now, in my defense, my opinion about his rapping ability at the time was shared by most of us around him. And people who hear his early demos still agree: he just wasn't very good. He sounded like a crappy Ma$e and was so breathy that sometimes I couldn't even understand his punch lines. I remember he played me one new track over the phone where he used only movie titles as lyrics. I could understand maybe five of them tops. He sounded more excited by what he was saying than any listener would be. So when my manager asked what I thought about adding him to the remix, I laughed. I told him to say it was already too long and suggested that he could be one of the many voices that yelled the hook. So, if you're keeping score at home, I said no to Kanye West rapping, but yes to two rappers you've never heard of, and paid another to mistake me for a studio employee, just so a soon-to-be rap superstar could be one of the seven voices yelling one word during the hook (which he is). Also, why are you keeping score of a book?

After recording our song, Kanye would come to LA frequently to record with rappers and meet with labels about his own career. I would hear behind-the-scenes talk that labels like Interscope, Capitol, and Atlantic were also unimpressed with his rapping aspirations, but were eager to work with him as a producer, so they'd take the meeting. One radio DJ I knew called to tell me that one of my friends from New York had visited their weekly station meeting, played his song unbearably loud, and jumped on the conference table to sing along. He didn't have to tell me who it was. I knew.

Kanye started to get buzz for his continuous work with Jay Z and Beanie Sigel and was developing an R&B guy, who also worked with will.i.am, named John Legend. Since we kept in touch, we would also try to hang out during his visits to the West Coast. We weirdly saw the movie *Master and Commander* together, which Kanye loved and I fell asleep during. We went to Las Palmas together, where he would pay DJ AM $50 to scratch the part of "Guess Who's Back" where Jay Z said his name. And one of our meals together was at the Mel's Drive-In off Hollywood Boulevard. (Funny enough, I would stand outside that exact Mel's location as Kanye's face was projected on its sidewall to debut a new song in 2013.) I paid for that lunch, and that wasn't the only time I paid for something Kanye needed, a concept that now makes me laugh harder than a bunch of rap dudes at Baseline hearing "Jesus Walks" for the first time.

After one of our late recording sessions, I wanted to finish up the song and knew we had about an hour left of work. Kanye was living with his mother in New Jersey, feverishly working on beats (and, secretly, lyrics) at the time—a period of his life he commonly talks about to this day. He didn't own a car and would take the train into the city whenever he worked, which is impressive when you take into consideration that he was also always early. He said he wanted to keep working that night, but in an hour he'd miss the last train home. I assured him not to worry, as I could easily just call a car service. He explained how far and expensive that would be, but since I thought the song was really coming together and I actually liked hanging out with Kanye, I let him know I'd pick up the bill. He insisted that if I did, he would need to pay me back one day. I said sure, not really paying attention, but he repeated himself numerous times, making me promise I'd actually take his money. The car cost me a little under $300, so it wouldn't break the bank, but I assured him I'd have no problem taking it back. For the next year or so, he reminded me via two-way pager about this loan a few times, making sure I never forgot about it, somewhat kidding but mostly serious. I never *really* cared about the money, but since he was making a big deal out of it, I started to keep track. For his recent *Yeezus* tour I spent about $300 on mid-level seats. He never paid me back. I don't miss the irony.

After our song together, the team around me continued to work with Kanye. My manager actually did believe in his rap career and unsuccessfully tried to help get him signed to a major label. Weirdly, Kanye had always seen Roc-A-Fella as his back-up plan, since he knew that his managers could pull a favor and get him a deal if everyone else passed. In the end, everyone did pass, and he obviously signed to the Roc, despite hearing at the time that even they didn't really want him. Around that same time, an Interscope A&R hired him to work on a rock-hybrid act he was developing, which was actually the session Kanye had just left when he got into the car crash that would spark it all: his rap career, his presence in the fashion industry, and his decision to run for president. Quite a chain of events. At this point I doubt he still loves that piece-of-shit Russell Crowe ship movie.

Kanye and I would talk consistently when we were both carving out what would be, or wouldn't be, our rap careers. We conversed mostly over pager, where he would frequently ask me what to rent when he was at Blockbuster. I would suggest a movie I figured he had never seen and he'd immediately pick it up. So if he ever says *Ghost World* is his favorite movie, I can finally say I see my influence in his work. And in what can only be seen now as psychic ability—or just plain insanity—his signature for every message sent through his two-way listed the title of each album he planned on releasing over the next decade, in order. He didn't even have a record deal yet. Weirder? He actually followed this checklist perfectly until *808s & Heartbreak*, leaving *Good Ass Job* as the only unused album title on the list, but picking up a slew of awards and acclaim for the ones he chose, and announced, before his managers would even acknowledge he was a rapper.

Did I see the egomaniacal madness behind his nerdy unassuming exterior? Absolutely. He'd randomly ask waitresses taking his order if they wanted to hear him rap. When they'd say no, he'd just spit a verse anyway. Even after being advised not to, he forced himself onto the red carpet at Jay Z's bowling birthday party—where he was kind enough to make me his plus-one—so he could throw up the Roc sign for the first time for photographers. He was annoying, but he knew what he wanted, and looking back now, I don't think he was going to stop until he got where he is today.

We talked briefly while he was in the hospital after the crash. I joked that having his mouth wired shut and not being able to rap for strangers seemed like his personal *Twilight Zone*, and I don't remember if he laughed. But I do remember he had the last laugh because he made a hit song in that condition. We had a few light conversations right after "Through the Wire" hit LA radio, but after that, we lost touch completely. You can easily say that I failed and Kanye blew up, and that he ditched me because of that. But the truth is, I never really gave him the opportunity to ignore me. I was thrilled for him but didn't really know what to say as he became rap's biggest sensation. I was so excited to see this passionate friend—someone I had seen ridiculed and undervalued—achieve his dreams, but I also knew he was headed for the type of universe where he would rant about leather jogging pants for two hours. For the record, he also simply became a better rapper. He doesn't sound like he just ran a marathon anymore. I would've put all my money against the little dweeb in braces and his attempt to make it big rapping. He showed me, and everyone else around him, that he was a mad genius.

When I say that I was no longer in touch with Kanye West after 2002, that doesn't mean we haven't seen each other since then. In 2009, I helped out 88-Keys, another rapper/producer I maintained a friendship with way past my days as Hot Karl, with a music video. 88-Keys was also a close friend of Kanye's, and at the time doubled as an advisor of sorts during his meteoric rise to the top. Since then, 88-Keys has found himself with production credits on two of Kanye's most critically acclaimed albums, *My Beautiful Dark Twisted Fantasy* and *Yeezus*, but back then he was releasing his own solo project on an indie label. He secured Kanye to be the album's executive producer and to rap on the first single, "Stay Up! (Viagra)." 88-Keys reached out to me, hoping I could convince my friend Pete Wentz from Fall Out Boy to appear in the music video they were scheduled to shoot in LA. Pete was a big fan of 88, and obviously of Kanye, so it wasn't hard to make the connection. The next thing you know, without much information at all, we were told to meet the crew on Hollywood Boulevard at 4:00 p.m.

When we arrived, we didn't see 88-Keys or Kanye mouthing the words to the songs, but rather two old black men, arm in arm with two scantily clad video vixens, looking like they'd just escaped a retirement home. We realized quickly that they were actually Kanye and 88-Keys in disguise, *Bad Grandpa* style, causing havoc on one of LA's trashiest blocks. Oddly enough, they stayed completely in character to cast and crew, even when the cameras stopped rolling, which is just the right type of crazy for Kanye West. Besides us, there wasn't a person in Los Angeles who knew the true identity behind Kanye's elderly disguise. If they did, he'd have been swarmed. Pete filmed his cameo—which took place in a sex shop—quickly, as the whole video was being shot without permits. As Pete wrapped, both old-man 88-Keys and old-man Kanye walked up to say good-bye to us. Both, still deep in method acting, complained about back pain and endlessly thanked Pete for hanging out with two "old geezers like us." Kanye kept joking, almost like he was a community college improv student, talking endlessly in an excited and ancient tone, until his eyes met mine. At that moment, he stopped talking immediately.

KANYE WEST OWES ME $300

He may have remembered the months of convincing me he was going to be the biggest rapper in the world while still living in his mother's house. Or maybe he heard those rappers and producers laughing behind his back when he left the room at Baseline. He might have recalled the nights at LA clubs, when no girl would talk to him or believe he produced for Jay Z, or the baggy Enyce sweatshirt or the braces. He may have even remembered the remix I wouldn't let him rap on. Or maybe he didn't recognize me at all. Either way, he abruptly stopped riffing, turned, and walked outside. He disappeared into a car and was immediately on his way to the next location. As we watched the car drive away, an intrigued girl who worked at the sex shop asked, "So, who was that guy anyway?"

I turned to her and said, "I don't know anymore, but he owes me $300."

Here we are: Hot Karl and the biggest
Master & Commander *fan in the world.*

"ARMAND ASSANTE" LYRICS, 2000/01
(20 & 21 years old)[1]

The game's on, Hot Karl dominates y'all ears,
I'm makin' suckers disappear like Amil's career,
I'm just joking but you having trouble coping,

---

1   One night, while recording at Baseline, I had eaten dinner with Kanye
    at the nearby Pan-Asian restaurant Ruby Foo's, still located in the heart
    of Times Square. I had fearlessly eaten sushi, and paid for it later with
    explosive diarrhea that interrupted our session numerous times. I con-
    templated calling our song "To Ruby Foo's, Thanks for the Poisoning,"
    but DJ convinced me not to. I instead picked my mom's favorite charac-
    ter actor and made sure to include his name randomly in the lyrics.

'Cause you beating me is like Def Leppard's drummer jump
  roping,
'Cause me and Kanye made this real *picante* and *grande*,
While you suckers act—Armand Assante,
Suburban strangler, able to rip a stranger,
With lyrics so hard I'd even make Mystikal say "Danger!"
And right here's an MC that you should fear,
Underground like snuff films, throwin' bows like Laimbeer,
Crushing the rest, till there ain't nobody left,
And if I don't go double platinum then I'm blaming Wyclef,[2]
So rhyme for rhyme, line for line, let's get it done,
None other will do when my crew is out there having fun,
Punch lines like landmines, Bensonhurst to Anaheim,
I'm dropping dimes, while y'all suckers silent like pantomime,
  what?

Don't let me,
Run off at the mouth.

I'm always into something, got everybody running,
It's my year, dog, warn Tyrese that I'm coming,
Fucking up the scene, take away your self-esteem,
The Jewish Jay Z, call me William Hollastein (Hova),
I keep attacking, and send your crew packing,
Nobody's feeling you, like Kobe Bryant rapping,
So keep on yapping, it's obvious you hate me,
Real racy, expose myself like I was KC,
Now I'm bringing new views to the table,
Able to bring in more kids than Jermaine Dupri's label (So def),
Take you out and watch you flow come to an end,
Able to go three the hard way without Puffy's friends (Let's get it),

---

2 This is a very specific joke for very specific hip-hop nerds about a battle
   rapper named Canibus who blamed his album's dismal response on his
   mentor, Wyclef Jean. If you were one of the seven specific people who
   got it, we should be friends.

Changed the game before one song was finished,
Spent so much cash made Farmclub go out of business,
You ain't touching the Baldwins at all,[3]
It's a family, dog, drink babies and suck balls, like what.

Don't let me,
Run off at the mouth.

Can't wait until I'm platinum and drowning in wealth,
So I can talk about my cash and sound like everyone else,
Wrecking this, more infectious than asbestos,
Making heads bob up and down like motherfucking Pez dispensers,
I'll take your wig and part it in the middle,
'Cause any one of your mizzles ain't fuckin' with Hot Kizzle,
And that for shizzle, obvious, and of course,
Dangerous like sporting ice to the next Source Awards,
The shit I kick is on a unique level,
And we call up Rebel when we got some fights that we want
    settled,
Beating 'em, till they can't hear like Halle Berry,
You try hard but still fuck up like Darryl Strawberry,
Rip you apart, so baby don't start,
Driving down Mulholland in a Hummer go-kart,
This is lyric shit, tough shit, never soft,
Hot Karl dot com, log on, fuck off (fuck off).

Don't let me,
Run off at the mouth.

---

3 People always asked me if I had "a crew." Em had D12. Nelly had the
   St. Lunatics. So, I made one up just so I didn't feel left out. We called
   ourselves the Baldwin Brothers, and it was a posse consisting of myself, Matty, and two incredible rappers I grew up near: Abnormal and
   Ryu. I have many regrets from my time as Hot Karl, but very few as
   genuine as wishing I could see rap fans wearing merch that said "The
   Baldwin Brothers."

17

GOING HAM

AFTER finishing my session with Kanye, I stayed in New York City for another week recording a DJ Clue–produced song with Fabolous, who had just released his first single, "Can't Deny It." Before that song blew up, my manager and I randomly met the lyricist standing in line at a Popeyes, which is where all great rap songs should come together. We kept in touch with him, and next thing you know, right when his career was taking off, he became another big name to officially appear on a Hot Karl song. As was the case with every new development regarding my project, there was no negotiation or pushback from Interscope when they found out Fabolous wanted somewhere near $15,000. Cost still never seemed to be an issue.

During my time in the industry, musicians were still recording together in the same studio, rather than just e-mailing parts back and forth, which is now the most common practice in hip-hop. During our session, Fabolous was an incredibly humble and delightful guy. After hearing what I had written for the track, he seemed surprised by how much he enjoyed it, which also caught me off guard, since I'd included an obscure *Simpsons* reference ("Just point 'em out and I'm down to go get 'em / 'Cause most rappers say stupider lines than Ralph Wiggum"), a shout-out I didn't expect much praise for. But Fabolous kindly admitted he dug it, an uncommon disclosure from one competitive MC to another, and decided to throw out the lyrics he'd brought to the studio in order to match my intensity. I took his willingness to start over as a compliment and sign of respect, even when he included a subliminal diss to me in his new bars. When he rapped "I'm constant hated, listen to the nonsense stated / But n*ggas can't shit on me like they constipated," I definitely understood he was talking about me and that I'd never have to explain to him what a "Hot Karl" was.

Not everyone was as quick to catch on to the true meaning of my moniker, though. A majority of people I met during the years I was signed to Interscope called me "Karl," as if it were my birth name. And most actually believed it was. Some probably still do. Even my hypeman, Matty, called me Karl until only a few years ago—and I was in his wedding. My mom always seemed offended by people's tendency to use the nickname off-stage (something that rarely happens now), mostly because she'd worked so hard to find a unique name like Jensen that would stand out. And I had also happened to adopt one of the most popular German names of all time, which, for a different reason, offended my Jewish father.

I always loved learning who did, and didn't, know what the other meaning of my professional handle was. I remember Jimmy Iovine being confused, and somewhat grossed out, when I finally had to tell him that the origin involved feces. On the other end of the spectrum, one night in 2001 I was introduced to Christina Aguilera. Her assistant at the time was dating an avid Hot Karl fan—and had played her my music—so in the middle of a crowded nightclub the assistant decided to make sure I met Xtina, secretly hoping we could make music together. Christina was just about to reshape her image, ditching her initial bubblegum pop persona for more provocative songs like "Dirrty," which had a music video that you could basically catch HPV from watching. The music in the club that night seemed louder than usual, so Christina's assistant had to yell our intros.

"THIS IS CHRISTINA!" the assistant screamed as I reached out to shake her hand. Christina smiled politely.

"THIS IS HOT KARL," the assistant followed up, leaning in and yelling to reach Christina's ears.

"WAIT, Hot Karl? Your name is HOT KARL?" a surprised Christina yelled even louder, unable to tell if we were joking.

I nodded yes. Her assistant, who believed my real name was Karl and that I had added the "Hot" just to brag about how good I was at rapping, seemed confused.

Christina howled with laughter, unable to keep her composure. She was like an audience member at Def Comedy Jam in the '90s, jumping and cackling down the aisles after a Martin Lawrence punch line. She tried to mutter "Nice to meet you," but struggled as she caught her breath in between laughs. As awkward as the exchange was, I walked away happy to assume that Christina Aguilera knew the slang term for shitting on someone's chest.

Urbandictionary.com lists the definition of "Hot Karl" as "The act of leaving feces on your partner's stomach, chest [or] mouth area while engaging in sexual activity." But to this day, the site also includes an alternate definition: "A rapper from the San Fernando Valley." It's not necessarily the legacy I expected to leave behind, but I'll take what I can get.

—

With a Fabolous song now in the can and positive feedback from my East Coast encounters, I was picking up a good deal of momentum and getting more and more industry attention. Another heavyweight who became interested in Hot Karl was Steve Schnur, an executive hired by EA Sports to curate music in their popular sports games like *Madden NFL* and *FIFA Soccer* as part of an initiative called EA Trax. He had reached out to my management, hoping to tap me for a song to include in the newest installment of my favorite game series, *NBA Live*. I jumped at the opportunity, even before I knew the game would feature every musician as a hidden character in the game, a benefit so cool that I envision it being inscribed on my tombstone.

They digitally scanned my face and took my measurements, using the data to create an unlockable player by typing "CALI-

FORNIA" into a menu screen. The producers picked that code after I asked them to please use "JEWISH" and was ignored. To announce EA Trax, I was summoned to a posh hotel near my house where I'd meet with press and talk about my excitement. My enthusiasm escalated when I found out that the other rappers who would be heard, and seen, in the game included Just Blaze, Fat Joe, Snoop Dogg, Joe Budden, and one of my favorite rappers of all time, Busta Rhymes. Most of the other participants were stationed in New York, so I was their only sure bet to attend, until they got word that Busta would also be in town for the event.

I wasn't expecting much from my entrance into the hotel room that now doubled as an EA media hub, considering I was the least famous of the bunch, but there seemed to be something stealing the employees' attention as I walked in unnoticed. There was an overall sense of urgency everywhere I turned, with a dozen or so people in EA shirts whispering to each other and unsuccessfully trying to hide the outright panic on their faces. And then, out of nowhere, a man barged into the room and yelled, "REMOVE ALL THE HAM! EVERY PIECE OF HAM!"

With that, everyone scurried to different corners of the space, removing pieces of ham from platters that were scattered throughout for snacking. Everyone moved at an almost comical speed, searching high and low for slices of deli meat like a businessman fifteen minutes late for a meeting trying to find his car keys. The concerned EA supervisor looked at his watch and sternly said, "He will be here soon, and I need to make sure there are NO pieces of ham anywhere in the vicinity for Busta

Rhymes!" I had no idea what was happening, but I couldn't have been more intrigued.

Then, as if I'd just seen something I wasn't supposed to see, someone grabbed me by the arm and hurried me into another room, where three men, introduced to me as the game's producers, were stationed around computers. I was shaken up, confused by the last few seconds of pandemonium, and depressed that I'd never get to see what happens when Busta Rhymes is around ham. It consumed my thoughts until the programmers started asking for details about my in-game custom baller, and then my attention went straight back to the video game.

I asked that my digital representation wear jersey number 88 (the year *Straight Outta Compton* was released), protective goggles, and vintage John Stockton short shorts, all demands that were respected and seen in the final product. They also inquired about my skills rating—a way gamers could choose the ballers they wanted to play with—on a scale of 1 to 100. Calculated by averaging out scores assigned to players based on attributes like speed, ability to dribble, and field goal percentage, this ranking decided how well you played in the game. For example, Shaquille O'Neal, playing in his prime back in early 2000s, was a 92, making him an unstoppable force and someone you looked forward to dominating with. The developers explained that as a celebrity addition I could pick *any* rating I wanted. They revealed that the other rappers selected numbers in the 90s, with DJ Clue picking 92 and Baltimore rapper B. Rich, being slightly less modest, selecting a 99. As they got ready to jot down my rating, I had a bit of a dilemma. My entire rap career had been based on authenticity. I never wanted to represent something I wasn't, and based on my hardly impressive freshman basketball stat line of 3.6 points per game, I knew I wasn't a 99. I thought it over and said confidently, "Seventy-five."

The producers looked at me in disbelief. They made me repeat my answer again, reminding me that I could pick *any* number I wanted and that people would decide whether or not to play with me based on this ranking. I was like a boy who found a genie in a lamp and when asked for his first wish, he said, "A haircut." But I was positive I wanted to stick with 75, understanding that if I were to be graded as a basketball player, I'd actually be thrilled with a steady C. And just like that I was the lowest-rated celebrity player in *NBA Live*, on par with other mid-level athletes like Brent Barry, Keith Van Horn, and Robert Horry. When the game was released, my mediocrity was painfully obvious, especially for kids who excitedly stumbled upon

Looks like the kid who got picked last in gym finally got his revenge.

the code to unlock me, only to realize that I was a glorified benchwarmer.

Being included in *NBA Live* was an accomplishment I still consider one of the coolest of my career, especially since they sold over a million copies of the game and, in turn, the CD of our music that came with it. Sometimes, still, when people realize I'm Hot Karl, they bring up the *NBA Live* song immediately, claiming they remember every word from their hours and hours of game-play. As a basketball fanatic, the ability to rap lines like "When I throw another dream, it's gonna fall of course / I'm wearing the goggles that Kurt Rambis used to sport" and "You coming up short like Spud Webb, gets to walking / I'll pull a Mutombo and let my finger do the talking" meant the world to me. There was no option to create your own soundtrack, so, honestly, players' ears were held captive. I too played the game religiously, often online against competition from around the world. I was testing the product in the field, wearing a headset to talk to opponents randomly selected by the server—something I couldn't imagine DJ Clue doing between yelling on mixtapes. My song, a basketball-focused reworking of my track with Fabolous, would frequently play on the game's main menu while you were waiting for an online game to start.

During the game's entry screen, not only could you hear my song, but you could also converse with the person you were about to face, a human you only knew by their gamer ID. I had selected my gamer ID around the same time EA Sports contacted me, and at the time, the idea that HotKarlMC would mean anything to anyone on my PlayStation never really crossed my mind. Even now that I was on the soundtrack, if anyone ever tried to talk to me, I would usually just ignore them, making me question why I even wore the headset in the first place. One day, while listening to my song on the headset as I waited for a game to start, my opponent, JEFFGOLD12, surprised me by speaking.

"Hey, man. Good luck," he said, hardly audible over my jam but still clear enough to sound like he was maybe eleven years old.

"Thanks," I said meagerly, still weirded out by talking to a stranger I was trying to beat in video-game basketball.

There was a moment before he spoke again.

"Your name is HotKarlMC, like the rapper in the game."

I perked up, excited about the recognition.

"Yeah, like the rapper," I reiterated with a smile, ready to acknowledge that yes, he was about to play *NBA Live* with the *actual* celebrity in the game. But before I could get the words out, he cut me off.

"That guy is a fucking loser," the preteen announced, with a disdain in his voice that let me know his feelings about my work loud and clear.

I sat in embarrassment, no longer wanting to play the upcoming scrimmage.

"Yeah, he is," I said, then unplugged my PlayStation for the rest of the day.

Despite that teen's opinion, EA Sports would hire me again to consult on another basketball game, *NBA Street Vol. 2*. It was the sequel to their popular playground basketball game that rivaled, and ended up being more impressive than, its competition,

NBA Jam. They reached out to me, knowing I was a fan of the series and a die-hard EA customer in the midst of my climb to celebrity. They were to fly me out to Vancouver, where the company's headquarters were located, in order to test an early version of the game and give notes on possible additions and its soundtrack. I was to be joined by Just Blaze, who I would finally connect with, and another up-and-coming rapper who, after a troubled past riddled with a mythical amount of violence, was rumored to be signing a major-label deal soon. His name was 50 Cent.

After I landed at Vancouver's airport, I ran into 50 Cent and his manager in customs. As a hip-hop nerd, I knew of 50 from his prior attempt at fame—way before he encouraged Shorty on her birthday—with a song called "How to Rob." I introduced myself, we shook hands, and they both seemed like pleasant guys. 50 Cent was incredibly charismatic. I remember his smile being infectious, even if it was somewhat mangled by a recent shooting that infamously changed both his career and jawline. We stood patiently in line for permission to enter the country, a feat that proved simple for me once I revealed I was in town to work for Electronic Arts. I was waiting for a car outside, now joined by a representative from the company, when 50 Cent's manager walked up to let us know they wouldn't be able to join us on the ride to the hotel. Assuming he meant they'd lost their luggage or planned on eating at the Tim Hortons in the terminal, I shrugged it off. I figured it wasn't a big deal until he explained that 50 Cent had actually been deported.

After learning that Curtis Jackson, as 50 Cent is known by the government, had been arrested on drug charges at some point in his life, Canadian officials quickly denied his entrance. Not only was he banned from *NBA Street*, he was banned from literal Canadian streets too. Bummed, I said good-bye to his manager and got in the car. 50's criminal record works as the perfect excuse, but the government has also since stated they believe his violent content could influence and steer young men into a life of crime and mischief. And as crazy as that sounds, maybe the Mounties were onto something.

When 50 Cent *was* eventually allowed to perform in Canada in 2003, a man was shot and killed outside his concert in Toronto, and similar violence ensued at a Montreal venue after he took the stage. As a result, a member of the country's Parliament officially addressed permanently banning 50 Cent forever, making him a hilarious exception to NAFTA. But no matter how intense this immigration-based rivalry became, I can always say I was there the first time Canada treated 50 Cent like a platter of ham in Busta Rhymes's dressing room.

———

As my career progressed, so did my parents' divorce. I was put in the middle of their intense disagreements, pushing my obsessions into an even more unavoidable place. Heartbreakingly, they decided to sell my childhood home and split the money. My mother rented a small house only a few blocks away, while my father, in an attempt to get lost, packed up and moved to Las Vegas. He quickly began self-medicating and acting erratically, rarely leaving the house yet finding himself in questionable situations that I never saw coming. My mother also fell into a depression, so in between recording sessions I would try to spend as many nights as I could with her. The worst-case scenario was in full effect.

Despite being engulfed in my music, my obsessive thoughts disorder reappeared to focus on my father's unemployment and the worry that my mom would never find someone to take care of her. I wasn't sure how much more I could take. And that's when my father was first diagnosed with lung cancer. He'd been a frequent smoker during many periods of his life, but hadn't relapsed for most of my teenage years. I had assumed that during his pilgrimage to Las Vegas, smoking was one of the many vices he decided to pick back up, but I never thought the damage had already been done. He moved back to Los Angeles for his treatment, and I became a part-time rapper, part-time caregiver. This marked the beginning of the hardest time of my life.

While my dad was getting radiation and chemotherapy, I began discussing release schedules with DJ at Interscope, trying my hardest to give my career the attention it needed. Even if I had bigger issues to attend to, everything seemed on pace at Interscope, with the excitement for my album still at a fever pitch. I was still competing in battles when I found time, able to channel humor during a difficult patch, although it came from a much darker place—with lines like "Remember Corky from *Life Goes On*? / Well, you're way more retarded, so don't get me started." Sure, it's pretty offensive in retrospect—although timid for rap standards—but I was angry, and battling seemed like a safe outlet to let off steam. Meanwhile, Eminem started releasing music from *The Eminem Show* around the same time. It sold 1.3 million copies in its first week, and he eventually raised that total to over 10 million. His graphic lyrics and hateful content sparked protests and became talking points for political pundits, while critics celebrated the work, which would go on to win a Best Rap Album Grammy—and deserve it. (His 2015 win for *The Marshall Mathers LP 2*, on the other hand . . .)

Interscope also announced they were teaming up with producer Brian Grazer to make a film starring Eminem that was loosely based on his life, and it was clear that he was not only the top priority at the label—he was running the building. Any hope that he would just fade away, opening a lane for a similar artist to emerge, had dissipated long ago, leaving me to hope that the audience, as well as the label, would be able to notice the obvious differences in our content. And it seemed like there was precedent, at least in other genres. In pop music I watched 'N Sync surpass their predecessors, the Backstreet Boys, almost perfecting a formula the latter had debuted. There was room for at least two boy bands in that genre, even if you ignored groups like LFO and O-Town, who were both hot garbage. But I wasn't sure the same could be accomplished in hip-hop. I went from being described as "a white rapper" by almost everyone to being called "a rapper like Eminem." It hurt, and seemed like unnecessary pigeonholing.

Despite the undeniable success of the other white guy, DJ continually assured me that everything was copacetic with Hot Karl. When we lightly started to discuss details, I decided I would name my album *Your Housekeeper Hates You*, a statement I believed most Caucasian families I grew up around should have to come to terms with. Production costs continued to roll in and the monthly stipend had come to an end, yet Interscope extended it for four more months without flinching. My days may have been dismal as I battled my concern about my parents and watched Marshall Mathers soar, but at night I continued with late-night recording sessions and a somewhat lavish lifestyle that was still undeniably exciting.

Matty, Sancho, and I were as strong as ever, constantly performing around Los Angeles and making stops in Arizona and Reno for shows at college parties. The label continued to make big moves, now serious about getting Christina Aguilera to sing the hook on "Caliente Karlito," an idea I'd had the moment she lost her shit after hearing my name. DJ also promised me the song was still on schedule to be remade by Timbaland, who had only become more popular during the wait. But nothing proved Interscope's undying interest in Hot Karl more than its willingness to entertain my desire to include a childhood hero of mine on the album.

While talk of multiplatinum guest musicians steadily flowed, I focused on the one name that had meant the most to childhood Jensen while he rapped into a comb and danced in front of the mirror. This person wasn't well known or particularly famous, but he was the first credible white MC I ever saw, and he had given me hope that I too could be a rapper. I wanted MC Serch, from the seminal rap group 3rd Bass, on my record, and once again, I didn't hear "no."

When Serch asked for $15,000 to appear on the song, I assumed the label would balk and laugh at his request, considering he hadn't rapped on a track in over a decade, let alone had a song on the radio. He'd be making as much as Fabolous, who was quickly becoming one of New York's most promising MCs with two songs on the charts and deafening buzz in the streets. No one would be buying my album because MC Serch was on it, which was a requirement I knew had to be met for them to spend that type of money on a feature. But when DJ asked me how much Serch's involvement meant to me as a person, I was quick to state my case. I explained how he was my sole inspiration to start rapping, and that I'd always looked to him to see what was acceptable—and what wasn't—for a rapper born outside the race that invented the form. I told DJ how I'd teared up when Serch walked out to freestyle as a surprise guest during a Redman and Method Man concert at the House of Blues I had attended during college. I revealed it was my lifelong dream to collaborate with Serch, but if the price was too high and it seemed impossible to get approved, I would understand and genuinely appreciated his attempts. And after one phone call, five minutes later, I was planning a song with MC Serch.

The streak of approvals continued and the tracklist of my eventual album started to take shape. Not only would it feature producers and guest artists who made the product viable in the marketplace (Mýa, Redman, DJ Clue, Fabolous, Sugar Ray), but I would be staying true to myself in both content and spirit. I could see the finish line. As I imagined what the next year would look like, expecting to experience the fame and recognition constantly promised to me by a dozen employees and the president of the label, I never could've predicted what came next. If I had, I would've quickly started looking for another job.

18

THE WORST PHONE CALL

MONTHS after MC Serch confirmed his participation, I found myself more at ease than ever. My father's cancer was showing signs of remission after positively reacting to treatment, my mom broke out of her funk to start dating, and I moved a street away from Matty in Brentwood. My carefree days consisted of writing raps and playing video games, a job I would've killed for at twelve years old (and still would).

I had a call scheduled with a product manager to begin the process of leaking songs to college DJs and planning a music video, which would kick off a timeline that would end with the release of *Your Housekeeper Hates You*. Finally, the gears were in motion to accomplish my ultimate goal. I was ready for a life-changing call, which I did end up receiving that week; it just wasn't the call I was expecting.

That Monday I received an e-mail from DJ explaining that

the product manager call would be postponed while "they worked out some details," so I casually went back to writing over some new beats. A few days later, when an Interscope employee called me unexpectedly, I figured it was to reschedule the meeting or to go over some ideas during the wait. However, when I heard the tone of his voice dramatically change, a shift I'd experience again years later when a nurse hinted that my brain's X-ray had more blemishes than a teenage Adam Levine, I realized we were about to talk about something much more serious. But no matter how quickly my instincts picked up his somberness, I had no idea exactly how much his words would hurt.

I trusted this employee, since every encounter we'd had up until this point was straightforward and genuine—two words I couldn't use when describing most people I met in the music industry (or any industry, for that matter). He started the conversation by asking if I'd be able to keep his identity completely secret, no matter how emotional I became about what he was going to reveal. I laughed, asking if this was about his involvement in the JonBenét Ramsey case, because I'd always had my suspicions. He didn't hear me. He admitted he was taking a very big risk here and needed to feel like I understood that gamble. I promised him anonymity, something I've been able to keep for over a decade; this is truly the first time I've ever repeated the details of that call. I thought he was just going to say, "I'm fucking with you!" and then I'd return to figuring out new ways to make fun of Tyrese, but instead he told me that this new revelation was as difficult for him to understand as it would be for me to hear. With that, he told me to leave Interscope Records immediately.

I was inclined to hang up and pretend I'd never gotten this call. He began talking again, but I didn't hear the words. I stood motionless and the walls started to close in, like that camera trick they do in movies when a wife hears that her husband died overseas. He wasn't heavily involved in every aspect of my project, so I *could* just play it off as hearsay, but he was speaking directly to my fears. My anxiety took over. I had no plan B. Leaving Interscope after all the hype would not only make Hot Karl appear tainted to any other label; it would also totally break my spirit. In recent years, musicians leaving or being dropped from record labels has become more of an opening for other companies to come in and seize the opportunity, but during my run in the early 2000s, it only hurt your reputation. It made you look like you couldn't deliver. Minutes before the call, my career had been on track. Now it was a train wreck.

He informed me that everything was about to change. The blind spending would come to an end, and I would now take a backseat to basically every other artist on the label. He revealed that my biggest fear was coming true: they had decided to never put out my album. As I grasped for any possibility that he could be wrong, I felt the tears well up in my eyes. I fought every inclination to break down, unwilling to let him know just how much this was crushing me. I calmly asked if he knew why this was happening. He said that the label would be creative with their explanation, but the truth was that someone wanted the project stopped. He said it involved "a conflict" with another artist but didn't reveal which individual specifically. But by reading between the lines, I understood it came from somewhere in Marshall

Mather's direction. I couldn't think of one reason this employee would lie to me, even though I so badly wanted to find one.

We kept the talk short. I bit my lip, hoping not to reveal that I was now crying. Before he hung up, he told me how talented I was and how unfair this situation had become, which was why he'd called; he didn't want to leave me hanging. He said it was the least he could do. He hoped I wouldn't kill the messenger, but instead look for a better situation to get my album heard—a mission he thought was culturally important but understood would now be difficult. He asked me again to never reveal my source, and I thanked him. I hung up the phone, unsure of what to do next.

As I lay in bed that night, unable to sleep, I felt the OTD trickle back into my brain. I feared that everything I had done up to this point now meant nothing, and I wasn't sure I had the skills to cope with that. I hoped my source had heard it wrong or that this was some sort of cruel joke conjured up during a lunch break, but I knew that wasn't the case. I stayed awake for the entire night, anxious, knowing this would not end well. I saw the sun come up.

I tried to keep a positive attitude, knowing that everything could change at any moment, but, as predicted, my communication with DJ and the label was drastically minimized. They stopped calling me altogether and would return only about half my calls. When we did talk, I had to keep a poker face, somewhat annoyed by being ignored but not tipping anyone off to the news I had secretly received. DJ, once a fixture in my everyday life, had all but become a stranger. I knew the position well, having seen will.i.am similarly shunned the previous year. As quickly as the open budget had brought in friends, a closed one pushed them away even faster. A mutual industry pal told me that Timbaland, the star once aligned to reproduce "Caliente Karlito," was now allegedly saying that he was only going to work with me because he was "contractually obligated to" by Interscope. A future trip to New York was cancelled as the label "readjusted strategy," and studio sessions were getting harder and harder to approve. Reimbursements were becoming chores, with months passing before I'd be paid back for expenses of even $100. If Eminem was *E.T.*, I became *Mac and Me*, the copycat remake no one cared about. The anonymous caller was right: I was no longer a priority.

Things were falling apart quicker than they'd come together. Had I not been warned of the tide's turning, I would've sat around for years, blaming bad music or bad breath or anything I could fault for the label's cold feet. No matter how depressed or obsessive I was becoming, or how much I wanted to just curl up into a ball and retreat, I knew I had to act. I called Fred Davis and informed him of everything that had happened. He was confident that he could convince Jimmy to cut to the chase and avoid dragging out this holding pattern for too long, letting me attempt to salvage any career I might still have left. Leaving Interscope without releasing any music, an act I'd never imagined could actually happen, was now something I could no longer avoid.

I was devastated, but I knew if I was going to actually do this, I wanted to meet with Jimmy Iovine one last time. I wanted him to tell me exactly what had happened, why he was unable to keep the promises he'd once made. I wanted him to explain it to my face. With that, I asked Fred to hold off on any communication with Interscope lawyers as I set up my own appointment with the man who had once offered me the world. After some calls, I was scheduled to meet with Jimmy a few weeks later. It was a far cry from the instant access I used to have, but I knew I needed answers, and there wasn't a fucking salmon plate in the world that could calm me down.

As I waited for my rendezvous with Jimmy to take place, I coincidentally ran into my old friend Bubba Sparxxx. I was happy to see Bubba and hoped he could calm my nerves, especially in a time of such turmoil, but he seemed just as rattled as I was. The round and innocent rapper I'd first met had given way to a thinner, more antagonistic Bubba, now with the words NEW SOUTH aggressively tattooed on his forearms. He was knee-deep in work on his second release, *Deliverance*, an album eventually all but thrown in the trash by Interscope's marketing department, despite it being one of the most underrated hip-hop albums of the 2000s. He seemed so much angrier than when we first met, admitting that he also felt ignored by the label and didn't know how much longer he'd last.

Similarly to my situation, a different Interscope executive had privately warned him about the world's most powerful rapper, but instead of it involving his declining position at the label, it was to alert him that Eminem had dissed him on an upcoming song. Bubba was visibly angry, mentioning that he had friends back home who wouldn't appreciate that type of talk, a violent threat that I never could've imagined coming from his smiling mouth back when we were both the toast of the office in 2000. Now defeated, we understood that our blind optimism was, in reality, bullshit. The diss from Eminem never actually came to fruition, but it caused such obvious paranoia in Bubba that you'd have to assume it contributed to his demise at the label, which happened a few years later.

As much as Bubba's attitude concerned me, I knew where it came from. I shared that rage. I related to that need for revenge. I deserved answers. The talk of my project all but disappeared. Whatever buzz was left disappeared. Soon thereafter, the *Los Angeles Times* wrote an article detailing my story and issues with the label, as well as the stories of other white rappers having a hard time fitting into a post-Eminem world. They interviewed me for the piece, which wondered if another white rapper would ever find success in the industry, a question that can now only be laughed at, considering most popular MCs in 2016 look like they work at a PacSun. While other labels mentioned in the article were quick to retaliate and blame the artist for their failures, Interscope was the only company that declined to comment.

I watched what was left of my initial advance dwindle every month without any viable plan for future revenue. I traded in my Expedition for a Mercury Cougar in what the appraiser joked was the "MC Hammer Special." He laughed and laughed and laughed at that one. I didn't. I obsessed over every little decision I made, wondering if I should've just focused on my college education and forced any dream of a rap career back into the realm of fantasy where it belonged. Should I have signed with Mack 10? The Firm? Anywhere other than Interscope? Should I have changed my natural voice and immediately avoided any comparisons to Eminem? Why did I have to pick a name that involved shitting? I withdrew even further from friends and family. It all felt too painful to deal with. The optimism I'd experienced over the past year had now expired, with an entire album of songs sitting on a shelf at Interscope, collecting dust instead of royalties. These tracks represented more than just possible club bangers or #1 hits; they were also my soul. And now it was all taken away so fast.

Eventually, I was officially told that the Hot Karl record would never see the light of day. Interscope publicly cited "scheduling conflicts" for the decision, a term that actually seemed to address the internal conflict at the label yet give no details at the same time. It was as vague as they could be. I was basically retired by the company that had once touted me as the next big thing and then spent over $500,000 to produce a CD that now was more likely to be a drink coaster than a source of music. As I drove to my meeting with Jimmy, I promised I would make him pay for what he did to me.

I sat across from Jimmy Iovine for the second time in my life, this time under drastically different conditions. We were alone in his office, a condition I had requested but figured wouldn't be honored. Not surprisingly, the intensity of the situation ended up intimidating me much more than it intimidated him. The bright-eyed, optimistic college student ready to hear how famous he'd be had now given way to an unshaven—and thirty pounds heavier—poster boy for disappointment. I hadn't even talked about my rap career in a month. We stared at each other for a few seconds before talking, Jimmy once again hidden under a baseball cap and me fighting back the urge to break each of the platinum records that covered his office's walls. There was one unhung plaque on his floor for 50 Cent, a rapper who had clearly lapped me since our few minutes together in Canada. This meeting could go many ways, but I knew that, no matter what, Jimmy Iovine was going to change the course of my life once again.

The silence was broken as he began to explain the current dilemma of my project. He was indistinct yet polite, waxing poetic in his shrieking, high-pitched voice about "scheduling conflicts" and how if I stuck around for a bit, the congestion might lighten up and we could take another look at it down the road. I asked if this had anything to do with Eminem, and he laughed at the notion. "I have a ton of similar rock groups, and what they have in common doesn't stop me from releasing their music," Jimmy argued, forgetting he had also used that angle when explaining why I should sign there. When I asked how I'd be able to stick around if I wasn't making any income, he didn't have an immediate answer, but when he did try to lessen my fears, his suggestion was mind-blowing. He pulled out a stack of CDs from under his desk, each without official artwork or titles, almost looking like homemade mixtapes someone had burned on a computer. He said, "Maybe it's time to give you the Gerardo treatment." With that, his receptionist walked in with the only interruption our talk would endure, letting him know that "Axl" was "on hold."

He took the call, giving me time to look over the stack of CDs. I realized I was looking at the finished, but unreleased, albums of acts like 4th Avenue Jones, Valeria, and Bionic Jive, musicians also on the verge of being exiled from Jimmy's empire. He hung up the phone and asked if I could ever see myself as an A&R, explaining that my sensibilities and understanding of songwriting would be assets to the company, and that this would be a great way to transition from being an artist into a career that made more sense at this point. I felt my face flush with both anger and embarrassment. I was only a few months removed from being the company's future star, and now I was being encouraged to hang it all up. Jimmy asked that I take the music home with me and e-mail him my thoughts after a few listens.

As I listened to Jimmy's offer, I realized that no matter what my goals were before I walked in, truth was, I was hardly talking. He was asking me to become the very thing that had just stopped my dreams from coming true: an A&R. Not only would I be ditching my own hopes, but I'd be involved in repeating the same pattern for other artists on the brink of success. I'd become DJ, bearing bad news to musicians who'd given their all for a chance, only to learn they were sold a plan of smoke and mirrors. He wanted me to become the enemy. I wanted to scream at him for repeating the sales pitch he had driven into my head when I had shared these initial concerns over a year ago. I wanted to remind him of how he thought Eminem and I differed, since I still didn't believe his explanation that Marshall, or Marshall's management, had nothing to do with this. I wanted to show him my father's doctor's bills and explain that he deserved to see my album get a proper release after all the shit he'd been through too. And I wanted to ask what the fuck Axl Rose was calling about. I wanted to say it all, but instead, I said almost nothing.

I picked up the CDs and calmly announced, "I'm disappointed. This is really the worst-case scenario for me. I'll think it over and let you know." Jimmy shook my hand, and I walked out of his office, and the Interscope building, for the last time ever. On my way home I called Fred Davis and told him to get me out of the deal any way he could, explaining I could never become the kind of judge and jury that had just crushed my own ambitions forever. Fred understood and promised he'd get it done. As I hung up the phone, I made the decision to retire from rap. I officially severed all ties with Interscope a week later.

To go along with the track, I worked with Jonathan Mannion on a photo shoot that would play out just like a music video. I entered Serch's office as a loyal, wide-eyed, backpack rapper, eager to start recording my vision . . .

"LET'S TALK" LYRICS, 2000/01

(20 & 21 years old)[1]
Cowritten by MC Serch

---

1 While still at Interscope, I had my song with MC Serch to complete. When it came time to record with my childhood idol, there was only one thing on my mind: the downfall of my career at the label. I decided to make the song a report on my time in the industry and, more specifically, the neglect, broken promises, and misunderstanding of my project I experienced while working for Jimmy Iovine. I believed if I had just changed who I was, I would've gotten a chance. That's a notion I've grown to disregard. Who I am, or could've become, had nothing to do with it.

[In the intro, you hear a young, hopeful Hot Karl walk into a busy record-label office, asking for "VP Serch." I enter Serch's room and excitedly start to explain how he's my hero, only to be told to hold on as he finishes up a phone call. I wait patiently while he tries to connect with Dr. Dre in St. Bart's and am completely ignored. Eventually he hangs up . . .]

Serch: It's my man Hot Kizzle, take a load off, have a seat,
How you feelin', big dog?
Hot Karl: Well, good . . . I think . . . [2]
S: Listen, congratulations, I just heard you got signed.
HK: I had to stop by, you were my favorite back when you
   rhymed.
S: Well, that was a long time ago, when the rhymes were more
   slow,
KDAY was on radio, and rappers didn't make dough, but yo . . .
HK: Creatively, I really wanted to discuss—
S: Listen, I've been thinking of a formula ever since you signed
   with us.
HK: Oh, a formula—like Serch is D.O.C. (laughing).
S: Now listen, don't you get snappy with me (not laughing),
Now sit down, we gotta break it down, how to make you sound,
First we'll put some freestyles in the college underground,
Put out two white labels, then two CD singles,
Combine 3rd Bass choruses into two-line jingles,
Put you on alternative sold-out tours,
Pop your collar, triple platinum, maybe four.
HK: Wait, hold on, Serch, I'm not dissing, but are you listening,
I'm hip-hop and I thought you were too, your point I'm missing,

---

2 Almost like it was a Make-A-Wish situation, we set up the micro-
   phones facing each other so we could have an actual conversation with
   each other while recording. We allowed a little room for improv, making each take different. Considering that for most of my childhood I
   would stand in front of the mirror pretending to be Serch, and that
   now I was looking right at him, this was both creepy and a dream come
   true.

Are you taking my vision to abuse it,
I've seen this shit before on Suge Knight's *Behind the Music*,
I remember *The Cactus Album*, you were a trendsetter,
Now you've sold out you're like 2000's Jerry Heller.
S: Jerry Heller? Let me tell you something, that kid got cash . . .
HK: Sorry I'll pass, even I know Cube got stuck in the ass.
S: Yup, he got cups filled with stacks, cribs filled with plaques,
George Karl, give it a chance.[3]
HK: Who? Me in shiny pants?
Doing a dance? I can already hear those sell-out chants . . .
S: NO! Sold out, twenty thousand seats in advance.
HK: No thanks, I'll stay underground and bust a B-boy stance,
I'mma stay true, even if my idol thinks I'm a joke,
And I'mma keep it real.
S: Yeah, you're gonna keep it real alright, keep it real broke.

(hook)

HK: It's all about the art of hip-hop, no matter if it sells.
S: It's about that Carson Daly and that *TRL*.
HK: We should talk about my thoughts and ideas, give me the
   chance to.
S: We should talk about recouping that money we just
   advanced you.
HK: We should talk about the love and the history from the parks.
S: Yes, *106 & Park*, number one on their charts.
HK: Man, you got it all wrong, you see, that's not where I'm from.
S: Listen, hip-hop is a business, stupid, don't act dumb.

---

3 Serch wanted to keep forgetting my name throughout the song, getting it wrong over and over and not caring about the mistakes. We figured it would make for the biggest asshole A&R either of us could ever
   imagine. Every time he threw out a different name, I would laugh. So
   when he said "George Karl" during one take, the name of a veteran
   NBA coach, I lost my shit. The "Who?" you hear was a genuine response.

S: See, I can understand your dilemma, you're struggling to
   hold your soul,
But after all that struggling, you need to let it go,
Free your mind and the dough will flow and won't be far behind,
Just think about the platinum mountain I got Nas to climb.
I'm feeling a little hesitant.
HK: Why's that?
S: You're being obstinate, credibility or cheddar?
HK: I think I'm lactose intolerant.
Alright, Serch, I see what you see,
Just another white MC, able to be packaged into cute little CDs,
I'm not another gimmick, don't sell me off my image,
Don't assume my marketing until my material is finished,
'Cause no matter what happens, it's about my satisfaction,
And without a plan B I'll be assed out like Toni Braxton,
I'm hip-hop till death, what are you, insane?
Imagine me with all gold teeth and a huge platinum chain.
S: Hmmm, platinum chain, matching fronts,
Featuring Cash Money and Mannie Fresh, yes, Karl, anything
   you want![4]
HK: Come on, Serch, I was joking . . .
S: (cough) I'm choking off the cash I'mma clear,
Karlito, Eminem ain't got shit on you this year.[5]
HK: Awww, listen to this cat, pigeonholing me in rap,
Imagine me getting jiggy just to equal SoundScan stats,
In fact, chief, this could start some beef,

---

4   As a gift, Serch actually got me gold grills with "HOT KARL" in dia-
    monds encrusted across them. I still have them in storage, and every
    once in a while I'll blow someone's mind by putting them in and not
    saying anything until they notice.
5   I went out of my way to never mention Eminem in a song, but the plan
    was to be as honest as possible in these lyrics, hoping to tap into my
    pain through a funny and inventive concept. I knew I had to admit to
    the comparison at some point, and since I was never able to escape it in
    the end, I'm happy I did.

I'd rather quit rap than have an R&B joint with Tyrese.[6]

S: Ohhh, Hot Karl, another brilliant idea,

Quick, let me call Tony Monte and start getting the single cleared.

HK: Ohhh, dude, are you joking, what are you talking about?

It's becoming obvious why Pete Nice kicked you out.[7]

S: Don't get it twisted, I left first.

HK: Well, Mr. Big Executive needs to finally get his ego burst.

(hook)

HK: It's all about the art of hip-hop, no matter if it sells,

S: It's about that Carson Daly and that *TRL*.

HK: We should talk about my thoughts and ideas, give me the chance to.

S: We should talk about recouping that money we just advanced you.

HK: We should talk about the love and the history from the parks.

S: Yes, *106 & Park*, with Free riding your jock.

HK: Man, you got it all wrong, you see, that's not where I'm from.

S: Listen, hip-hop is a business, man, don't act dumb.

HK: So I came in here to talk, sit down and show respect,

But I haven't been able to get out one word yet.

S: Karl, you're not listeni—

HK: No, listen to me! I was able to get this far,

Able to resume my passion without being a pop star.

S: Karl, you're not—

HK: Shut up, right here I finally wanna get rid of ya,

Run up in your office like Puffy after Nas's video.

S: Sheila, get Stoute on two . . .

---

6   You can't say I wasn't determined. Leave the same way I walked in.

7   The history of 3rd Bass is littered with infighting and turmoil, so I basically forced Serch to address it in our song, convincing him it was a track where both of us had to face our complex careers.

HK: Oh, like what's he gonna do?
I'm not a thug but Hot Karl is gonna run right through.
S: Yes! Big Karl, that's what I'm talking about,
You came in an underground MC but now look how you
    walking out,
Now you understand, my boy, you're ready for the plan,
Here's your first advance, chachi, a hundred and fifty grand.

(talking)

HK: That's a hundred and fifty Gs?
S: That's a hundred and fifty thousand dollars, Karlito. A
    hundred and fifty Gs. Can we go to the club now?
HK: Yeah, let's get jiggy.

*. . . but in the end, like many other artists, I threw away my
integrity for a wad of cash and diamond teeth. No matter what was
going on behind the scenes, this photo shoot was really fun, especially
since we got to satirize a career path I knew I'd never follow.*

19

SPRING BREAKDOWN

MONTHS after my decision to walk away from Interscope, my mental state hadn't improved. Where some artists may have been motivated by doubt or determined to prove their haters wrong, I just retreated. As if I needed to be kicked while I was down, I went and saw *8 Mile* the day it was released in theaters and realized if you watched it backwards, it was basically my rap career. I went back to therapy twice a week and immediately was put on medication, testing the ability of drugs like Zoloft, Ativan, and Wellbutrin to help combat my constant depression and obsession.

As news of my exit traveled around the industry, I started to get calls from insiders, even ones I didn't know, that verified the Interscope employee's story about Eminem's camp squashing my chances. Still, I've never been able to consider it anything more than legend. But anytime anyone encountered evidence or overheard anything that could substantiate the theory, they would let me know in that same way someone tells you that your ex-girlfriend is fucking someone better-looking.

On my end, one of the first people *I* had to contact was my publisher. He obviously had a lot to lose in this predicament, but despite the now likely financial loss in his future, he seemed eerily calm. It was like contacting the captain of the *Titanic* while it was sinking and only hearing about what a gorgeous night it was. He assured me that his gamble wasn't purely dependent on my situation at Interscope and that he knew I'd be back on my feet in no time. He cited a handful of other artists he represented who blew up after complicated releases from major labels, assuring me I'd just be the next in a long line of those who deserved revenge. He suggested a few different acts I could write songs for, and I slowly became optimistic about a second chance. If the man with the most cash invested in my music was unaffected by the recent chain of events, then maybe I was overreacting. During that conversation, although it wasn't an easy task, I tried my hardest to see everything in a different, more positive, light. I remember being filled with a sense of possibility after that phone call, especially considering I expected him to declare my career dead and admit to a major misstep in handing me a lavish contract. It truly felt like I had the right team around me to survive this rough patch.

But weirdly, despite my good cheer at the time, in one of the weirdest occurrences during my run as Hot Karl, I never really spoke to the publisher again. The most correspondence we had was when I received the termination-of-my-services notice when my contract expired a few years later. Where I assumed the publisher would freak out and try every which way to recoup his steep advance of $250,000, I actually experienced quite the opposite, with him sort of just leaving me out there to die. I'd call him frequently, to try to get work, and he'd either just avoid my call or small-talk me until I figured it was time to hang up. Not shockingly, he left his position soon after and was joked about in the industry for giving out too many expensive, unsubstantiated deals during his tenure. Ironically, he's now the president of one of the largest music-publishing companies in the universe, proving none of this shit will ever make sense.

Despite the publisher's all-out avoidance and my hope of disappearing without a trace, a few labels did end up getting in touch with me to learn more about what had happened and to see what I planned on doing next. A&R Craig Kallman, who has since become CEO of Atlantic Records, actually found my mom's phone number somewhere on the Internet and left a message, saying he hoped to hear any new music I was working on and learn more about a rapper he said "was still a hero on the Web." When we did eventually talk, I admitted I wasn't even sure I wanted to keep rapping, and understandably his interest waned. Tommy Mottola's office also expressed interest on behalf of Sony after I was brought in to write lyrics for his wife, Latin superstar Thalía, who had heard my silly song with Gerardo and wanted to collaborate. Since I was mostly focused on nurturing my own shell shock at the time, most of these inquiries would go unanswered.

Whenever I would attempt to go back into the studio to record new music, I would either encounter writer's block or make music that not only lacked any commercial appeal but would actually bum people the fuck out. One sample lyric went "Spent twelve months working on a compact disc / Which seems like a lot of work for a little piece of shit." Not exactly material for "da club." I also entered a few open battles, hoping to get the creative juices flowing, but not only did I tarnish my undefeated streak, I also learned quickly that "used to be dope" rhymed a little too easily with "dropped from Interscope."

Without any money coming in, I needed to find something to do, not only for my bank account but for my morale. Feeling the lowest I had ever felt professionally, I decided to search for a real job—the type of job with scheduled hours, a steady paycheck, and no need to listen to beat CDs from grown men named Aya-tollah and Megahertz. The question "Where do rappers go to die?" may have been something I was never really ready to ask myself, but now I would be forced to find the answer.

After driving by their office's "Now Hiring" sign, I applied to be an assistant at a real estate agency near my house. I completely hid my recent musical history, only to be told I was "too outgoing" for the position and that my personality was better suited to be an agent, a career that would require a new round of schooling—something I couldn't see myself doing, yet. One meeting with a headhunter went sour when he asked what the two-year gap in my work history was all about, and I answered, "Cancer." I meant my father's bout with the sickness, which wasn't exactly true, but I ended up taking it one step too far by mistakenly implying that *I* was the one with the terminal illness just to hide my silly rap background. She responded with sympathy, and instead of correcting my mistake, I quickly changed the subject, now looking like the asshole who outright ignored her concern. In short, thanks to my straight-out-of-college rap career, I was a bit green when it came to job interviews. I also responded to a few ads on Craigslist: one for a part-time job as a nanny, which I was told within five minutes I wasn't right for, and another as part of a "marketing sales force," which ended up being a pyramid scheme. I may have been attempting to start careers in brand-new fields, but the results were starting to feel very familiar.

When I wasn't contacted after turning in an application to work as a flower deliveryman, I found myself out of options. I had spent a large chunk of my remaining advance on a new suit to help me start this chapter of my life, since the meds ballooned me to over two hundred pounds for the first, and only, time in my life. The pills weren't working, and I hit a point of depression at which I was willing to do anything to improve my situation. Even rap again. Perfectly timed, in 2002, I was contacted by an independent record label out of New York City that was interested in resurrecting Hot Karl.

In the same way that an aging bank robber will do one last heist before he calls it quits for good—only to get shot while on his run to the getaway car—I accepted an offer to once again release music. It paid me an advance of a few thousand dollars, which was a bunch of zeroes away from what I'd made during college, but I knew it would buy me a few more months. I felt absolutely dismal about the prospect of returning to the mic, and this feeling was hard to hide from everyone, including Eddie, the excited young East Coast A&R/label owner who was fronting the money to make it happen. In good faith, Interscope sold him "Let's Talk" and "Sump'n Changed" for pennies on the dollar, only to have the latter blocked by separate financial demands from DJ Homicide, who I understood owed me nothing as another name I neglected during my embarrassment of a career downgrade.

Another reason I decided I could survive a second record deal was a beat CD Eddie sent me from a guy named 9th Wonder, who at the time was earning critical acclaim for his work as the producer in the underground rap group Little Brother and who would later find success with heavyweights like Jay Z, Beyoncé, Drake, Kendrick Lamar, and J. Cole. I was impressed with what I heard, feeling for the first time since my introduction to Kanye that I was listening to a future superstar. I was finally excited again about something in hip-hop, and it helped me rekindle my desire to rap. After freestyling to almost every instrumental on the demo, I asked Eddie to make the connection.

He reached out to 9th, hoping to set up studio time for us to collaborate, only to quickly receive an astounding no as an answer. Even though I had fallen head over heels in love with his work, after hearing *my* music, 9th Wonder admitted he "wasn't feeling it." There was no way to sugarcoat his feelings; he just didn't want to be associated with any of my music. He wished me luck but, without mincing words, hard-passed on the opportunity. I couldn't help but feel the harsh sting of rejection more than ever before.

It's easy to see why I titled the eventual album *The Great Es-*

cape, and why the cover art was a photo of me running away from a gigantic popped champagne bottle, swimsuit-clad models, fancy cars, shiny jewelry, and a luminous rapping shadow lurking above the scene. Some people assumed it referred to my departure from Interscope, but its double meaning was really the only part of the creative I was sure of: I needed to escape not just that label but the entire industry. Unfortunately, I wasn't quite sure what else I could do. I became jealous of my friends from college who were now, years after graduation, comfortable with companies and careers they had set out to enter, while my experience involved more happenstance and baggy pants. I assumed I'd always have my writing ability to fall back on, but even that was now in question.

Now available at your local dollar bin!

When pen did eventually hit paper for new songs, my lyrics couldn't find a comfortable place to manifest. One minute I was recording an upbeat dance track called "After Party," urging listeners to "keep doing shots till it's too hard to think." The next, I'd be creating a two-song musical accompaniment to David Lynch's *Mulholland Drive*, unraveling the story of a young girl who moved to Hollywood, only to be left with shattered dreams and a suicide note. My metaphors were never subtle. I thought I was creating a postmodern concept album, allowing fans into the mind of a disoriented artist praying to move on yet still unable to let go of the club single. But in real life, the results would later force one of my favorite writers, Nathan Rabin, to say in his review of *The Great Escape* for *The A.V. Club*, "Karl's creative soul might not be worth the hassle." Deep down, I knew he was right.

Despite my intensely lethargic attitude toward the project, Eddie had set up a few promotional performances before the album would be released. He had produced hundreds of four-song samplers for the album and wanted me to hand them out after the concerts, hoping it would lead to album sales once the full-length was released. I knew avoiding these shows would be selfish, especially since I happily took his upfront money. I tried my hardest to put on a happy face, but my performances were riddled with mistakes as I battled copious amounts of sweat and pockets where I couldn't catch my breath because of the weight gain. As if my spiritual slump wasn't enough, now my skills were continually declining.

We were set up with a residency at the Roxy, the same venue I had sold out years prior and where I had first found out Jimmy Iovine had an interest in signing me. Except instead of performing on that same stage, this time we'd be playing once a week at the small bar above the theater, On the Rox. I accepted the offer, assuming my hometown would at least be interested in seeing how I'd reemerge as an independent artist. Much to my chagrin, we never had more than thirty people come see us, and every week the attendance decreased, until by the end of the month we were performing for a total of six people. That night Matty thanked someone in the audience for being "our biggest fan." When I excitedly asked who, he pointed to a gigantic floor fan near the stage. I deserved that. It was so demoralizing that the final night I jokingly had Sancho play Elliott Smith as I walked offstage.

Despite my lack of cooperation or any sign of fandom, the indie label continued to try to get the comeback some traction and booked me a Jamaican spring-break tour so I could perform for college kids from around the United States. I was asked to spend almost a week on the island, alongside Matty and Sancho, rapping at various bars and taking part in a multitude of different activities for the event company footing the bill. I was contractually obligated to promote the album to the best of my abilities, and if I didn't make myself available for something like this, I understood it would make me look unreasonable. I had never been to Jamaica and I figured some time out of the country might help my psyche, even if I had to participate in an activity I despised. How difficult could rapping to a bunch of drunk college kids be? And I'm a big *Cool Runnings* fan. So I accepted the offer, understanding it would probably be the last big effort I put into my rap career anyway. I would soon find out it would have to be.

When we arrived in Jamaica, we were told we'd be staying at Hedonism II, a resort that sounded like a sequel to a low-budget Cinemax movie, and for good reason. Touted as the world's top nudist resort, it was "singles and swinger-friendly," with most of the premises advertised as clothing optional. The promoters said they selected the resort because it was clear of any college kids and would be a good place for us to relax in between shows. I had assumed we'd be smack-dab in the middle of a *Playboy* shoot, looking at impressive naked bodies nonstop, but upon arrival at the resort, it didn't take long to realize that the people abandoning their swimsuits were *not* the types you'd ever want to see naked. It was more like a racy wrap party for the movie *Cocoon*. Our first encounter with the over-sixty set was near the hotel's check-in. The group's floppy penises and saggy boobs doubled as some sort of satanic hotel greeter. It was like an IRL Lemon Party. Naked senior citizens were everywhere we turned—most disturbingly in line for the all-you-can-eat buffet, where sneeze guards had never been more important. It was not the type of starting point I'd hoped for. For the entire week, we didn't see one naked person who we'd voluntarily have sex with, despite being propositioned for the task several times.

We were scheduled to perform a series of shows throughout the week at bars with names like "The Jungle" and "Risky Business," mostly jumping onstage in between DJs paid to make underage kids, drunk enough to end up sleeping on the beach or getting an awful tattoo, dance to Britney Spears remixes. With my experience at Bling Bling, I assumed I'd be an expert with this crowd, only to be blindsided once we took the stage for the first time. The DJ announced our name in an annoyed tone, like the way someone might introduce their embarrassing mom after being forced to do so with a question like "Aren't you going to introduce me to your friends?" He seemed to see us as a nuisance breaking up his killer set rather than as the headlining act, an opinion the audience apparently shared.

We started our first song to a cluster of boos, with most of the crowd immediately leaving to go get another Jäger shot or Long Island Iced Tea or whatever you drink when you're a piece-of-shit kid. We performed from a balcony, looking down on a dance floor that at one time had been packed with patrons and was now completely deserted. At the end of one song I announced, "Stick around, because Bob Marley is up next. He's alive, guys!" and I didn't see a flinch. I quickly realized that no one was listening and I was in Jamaica for no reason at all.

The second show was no better, this time with a cup of water thrown at me for good measure. The energy that at one time defined a Hot Karl performance and helped me stand out was now replaced with a lethargic complacency and a desire to cut every song short. I would finish these sets completely defeated, then return to our naked geriatric hotel just to hide in my room. While Matty and Sancho would tour the grounds for adventure and eventually see an elderly couple banging in the Jacuzzi, I was alone in my quarters pretending to play Gameboy but, in reality, totally breaking down.

My body was rejecting every attempt I made to be a rapper,

physically trying to stop me from continuing to take the stage each time. I would feel sick before, after, and during every gig. If the bedcovers weren't over my head, I was riddled with panic. This is how my body decided to deal with trauma. I had started another new antianxiety pill but was still a few weeks away from feeling its effects. I was also unable to call my therapist from abroad—the luxury of international smartphones had not arrived yet—so I was without any professional help for the time being. That night we had our first late-night show, which I dreaded even more than the day parties because I assumed the teens would be even drunker and even less receptive to rap songs that referenced obscure *Annie Hall* lines. Even though I knew the chances were slim, I genuinely prayed I'd be performing in a cage like the Blues Brothers at Bob's Country Bunker in Kokomo. I knew this night was destined for disaster.

I have some recollections of that night, mostly out of order and somewhat cloudy, but I know that once I hit the stage, I turned on an autopilot I didn't even know existed. In order to perform, I had to leave my own body and basically watch from afar, ignoring the boos, ignoring the dude who every few seconds yelled "Fuck you!" and ignoring the club's speakers, which sounded like they were occupied by small children beatboxing my tracks into a megaphone. A few feet from the stage, one drunk girl vomited in the middle of our second song, and the smell instantly circulated around the space. I audibly gagged before introducing the next track to the uninterested crowd by just asking aloud, "What the fuck are we all doing here?" Matty looked at me like I was a maniac, which made sense, because

I was. It was hands down the worst performance of my life, so much so that I forced Sancho to skip the last three songs and rush into our finale. I was nauseous and dizzy and needed to get home. And by home I didn't mean that weird episode of *Real Sex* we were staying in. I meant home as in back to Los Angeles, where I could get the help I so desperately needed.

The bright lights shined on my face as I barely mumbled out the words to our last song. Each individual drum kick shook my vision. As soon as I rapped my final word, I dropped the mic and ran outside the club for any sense of relief or fresh air. I knew I was having an intense panic attack and frantically searched for an open cab that could take me back to Hedonism II. Sancho and Matty would stay behind to drink, assuming I had a stomachache, an alibi I'd created much earlier in the day in case something like this happened. By the time I got back to the hotel, I felt seconds away from fainting. I stumbled into my room, running past grotesque nudity at every corner, and fell onto my bed. My OTD had hit a climax, with only negative thoughts now flooding into my consciousness.

"You failed."

"Your father's cancer will come back."

"You're going to run out of money."

"You've lost your skills."

"You have no plan."

"No one loves you."

"And no one will."

"I want to die."

I couldn't find a moment of solace. I turned on the television to shift my focus but couldn't stop pacing the room. I screamed as loud as I could. I searched the room for anything to help. I threw a pillow, hoping the aggression would release some tension. It didn't. I ran a shower, thinking it would calm me, but the bathroom felt so small and constricted that I couldn't spend another second standing in it. I was terrified, and while I had been experiencing panic attacks since childhood, this one felt different.

"You failed."
"Your father's cancer will come back."
"You're going to run out of money."
"You've lost your skills."
"You have no plan."
"No one loves you."
"And no one will."
"I want to die."

A few seconds later, I saw my bottle of pills on the bedside table. I needed to stop the thoughts. There was no alternative plan. I knew I couldn't survive the night feeling this kind of pain. I had taken my prescribed dosage earlier that day and was yet to feel its effects. I opened the bottle and counted eleven Ativan pills left. I knew I was making a foolish decision, especially since I had drunk a few beers at the show, but something had to be done. So to silence my thoughts, and finally have a moment of clarity, I downed the eleven pills with a glass of water. I knew there was a possibility of never waking up, or falling into a coma, and I still felt I had to do it. If this was my last night, I understood that I could no longer face this struggle. I just needed to fall asleep. If that meant dying, I had to accept that. I sat on the edge of my bed and practiced breathing deeply, trying to finally relax.

"You failed."
"Your father's cancer will come back."
"You're going to run out of money."
"You've lost your skills."
"You have no . . ."

That's the last thing I remember until I heard my door open eight hours later.

I woke up the next afternoon, laid out on the floor, with the room spinning. The resort's housekeeper had just unlocked my door to see me posing for a crime-scene chalk outline, an image that I'm sure was nowhere near the scariest she's ever walked in on. I turned on my side to ask her to come back later, only to realize I was lying next to a puddle of my own vomit. The housekeeper got the message and quickly left. My mouth was dry and my body felt like it had just gone five rounds with Tito Ortiz. I ran to the bathroom to throw up but didn't make it to the toilet, missing by just a few feet and hurling onto the floor. I looked in the mirror, stunned at the shell that now stood before me. I was bloated and pale, with a huge bruise on my shoulder from where I probably fell from the bed. I made my way back to the scene of the crime, thankful I hadn't choked on the vomit in my sleep.

I had already missed an early event I was supposed to host and knew I had one more show before we were to go home. I cleaned the mess and somehow managed to make it out of my room, each ray of sunlight stinging my skin as it was exposed. No sunglasses were dark enough to save me. I met Matty and Sancho at a bar, where we were whisked away to perform a song and judge something I don't recommend anyone having a mental breakdown sit through: a wet-T-shirt contest. As each girl doused herself with water, hoping we'd validate her with a score high enough to get her and her friends free shots, I could barely hold up the numbered signs they gave me. If I wasn't already disappointed enough in the choices I had made, being disappointed in others' choices really was the final straw. When they'd ask me for my opinion, I could hardly speak, and when I did, I asked where their parents were, like the world's biggest boner killer. I walked offstage at one point to throw up in the bushes. After crowning the victor, I sped through my one song, this time to surprisingly interested (or just horny) kids, and got back to my room as quickly as I could.

I told Matty and Sancho that I was still battling the flu, and neither suspected anything otherwise. I stayed in my room for our final night in Jamaica, recovering from the extreme distress I had put my body through over the past twenty-four hours. I drank enough Gatorade to fuel an entire World Cup and faded in and out of a deep sleep, only to wake up in the middle of the night, finally rested enough to rejoin humanity. I contemplated calling the guys to fill them in on what had happened, but there was no need to alarm them, especially because I assumed they were both busy watching a sixty-year-old fingerbang his wife for a crowd.

I was awake and thankful to have survived. After regaining my energy, I decided to pull out a pen and paper and write to one of those forbidden 9th Wonder beats, determined to finally be honest about what I was facing and answer the producer's understandable criticisms. I was no longer interested in making the listener laugh or dance or vote for my song on a countdown show. I gave up trying to be witty and just focused on honesty.

As a result, I wrote the majority of a song called "I've Heard," a track that unapologetically faces every ounce of insecurity and sadness I encountered as an MC, written at the only time in my life I was vulnerable enough to do so. It mimicked every obsessive thought that echoed through my head while I was trying to salvage a life that had gotten out of hand. Once I finished writing, I rapped the lyrics over the phone on Eddie's voice mail; he then played it for 9th Wonder. After listening to the message, 9th gave his blessing for the song, and we recorded it just in time to make the album's tracklist. As a result, I made the one song that every critic praised and fans to this day still tell me they connect with the most. It's also the only one of my tracks I can still listen to. Fittingly, it was the last song I'd ever write as Hot Karl, and that trip would mark my last professional show ever.

I remember leaving Hedonism II for the airport, still fighting off nausea and exhaustion while keeping my secret. On my walk to the shuttle, I suddenly noticed our hotel's view of the ocean, a beautiful scene I had completely taken for granted all week, too caught up in my own bullshit. As I stood there, surveying the scenery, I knew no matter what hardships I'd face moving forward or how many false starts I'd had, this was my last stand. I looked at the *H* and the *K* tattooed on my wrists and didn't feel the regret I expected, but rather the relief of letting go. The beauty of that view helped me understand there was an entire world out there for me to explore, and I was ready to start looking. Then, out of the corner of my eye, I saw some movement about a mile down the beach. I waved, thinking it was Matty and Sancho walking up to join me for our departure. It was perfect timing. I readied myself to tell them the news. Squinting, I realized it was two old people fucking. And just like that the world was terrifying again.

"I'VE HEARD" LYRICS, 2001
(22 years old)

I've heard I'm always corny and I'm only punch lines,
I tread on thin water, oceans filled with landmines,
I've heard I copy Eminem with everything I write,
But I guess there's worse rappers that a cat could sound like,[1]
I've heard I made a stupid move by leaving that place,
Ditching a CD that Redman, Fab, and Mýa laced,
I've heard I'm just a gimmick that cashes in on a fad,
Well if it's so hot, why's my career so bad?
I've heard I got a million-dollar deal based on a lie,

---

1   I knew it was time to release the resentment I had toward what may, or
    may not, have happened with Eminem or someone within his camp. I
    knew he was an incredible rapper, and at least people weren't saying I
    sounded like Tyrese or something.

I signed the contract and then ran away to hide,
I've heard my parents' divorce, it fucked with my mind,
Popping Ativan, panic attacks all the time,
I've heard that "independent" means I'm not good enough,
If it's not on MTV then my whole album must suck,
I've heard I'm either selling four million or just four,[2]
I'm that dude you love to hate but that dude you can't ignore.

I've heard my money's running out, I better find new hope,
But then I heard that Kanye West and Just Blaze still think I'm
  dope,
I've heard I wasted four years of my life on pipe dreams,
If I'm asked again what happened, then I'm gonna fucking
  scream,
I've heard my girlfriend try to convince me of my skills,
I don't think that I'm wack, I'm just sick of standing still,
I've heard that *Playboy* mag said I'm next to blow up,
But that was three years ago and now I feel I've dried up,
I've heard that Timbaland talks shit behind my back,
But I can't really tell what's just made up and what's fact,
I've heard that message boards are filled with only haters,
But still I gotta peep them out sooner or later,
I've heard in this game there's only room for one white,
Although 90 percent of all rappers are virtually alike,
I've heard I got Muhammad Ali up on my arm,[3]
To remind me to keep fighting and to always stay strong,
  is that wrong?

_____

2   This was an exact quote from Fred Davis after hearing my music for
    the first time.
3   Soon after I returned home from Jamaica, I had the image of Mu-
    hammad Ali standing over a knocked-out Sonny Liston tattooed on
    my arm. A documentary about Ali was being replayed on a Jamai-
    can sports channel the night I woke from the Ativan haze, so I al-
    ways wanted to remember the determination and strength the champ
    showed throughout his life and apply those traits as I build my own
    legacy. This is my reminder.

I've heard I can't relate because I never sold drugs,
Like every rapper out really did grow up as a thug,
Because of this divide I know my passion's slowly dying,
Only 'cause these popular MCs keep lying,
I've heard that no one likes that I'm a true throwback,
No one cares 'bout MC Lyte, Biz Markie, or G Rap,
I've heard a lot of compliments about my different style,
But I'm convinced that they're lying, so I'm nervous all
   the while,[4]
I've heard that this record might be my last chance,
But I can't find myself doing the same song and dance,
I heard it would be easy if I just gave in,
But I couldn't live with myself if I just caved in,
I've heard that I'm stuck fighting a lost cause,
At least I'm being honest, show the world I got some balls,
I've heard this is my heart and soul all on one track,
I've heard a lot of things, but all I want to do is rap.[5]

---

4   I never wrote a realer line.
5   I always romanticized the idea that the last line I ever wrote would be
    "All I want to do is rap." It's the state of mind I had as a teen, and I
    wanted it to be the edict I gave while walking away. Looking back, it
    also would've been funny to say, "All I want to do is nap."

OUTRO

OVER the next decade, I moved on, leaving Hot Karl as part of a past life that I never wanted mentioned, like I was Disney casting Tim Allen as Santa Claus and hoping kids would never find out that he was once arrested for smuggling 1.4 pounds of cocaine. If someone asked about the story or, God forbid, was a fan, I would laugh it off and quickly find a way out of the conversation. Whenever a video of me rapping would pop up on YouTube, I would immediately flag it for removal. The easiest way for me to get over the letdown was to pretend it never happened, and I needed everyone to play along. This was a mandatory step to help control my obsessive thoughts disorder, alongside years of intensive therapy, light medication, and a new dependence on my favorite hobby for spiritual growth: running. Whenever I encountered my own indignation or sadness about the demise of Hot Karl, I'd get up and run a few miles, allowing my brain to find somewhere else, somewhere safe, to go.

And when my most repetitive fear did come true and my father passed away from cancer, I stayed strong and survived. His advice to find happiness, to finally accept and celebrate what I experienced as Hot Karl, was crucial. I knew he was right, but it was like asking Bill Buckner to go play first base at Shea Stadium again: there was trauma there and I didn't know how, or when, to face it. I never expected that Howard Stern would help me make that decision.

Howard had become obsessed with the Roll Call after finding out that a member of his staff was involved in producing the contest's New York incarnation. Even though it hadn't been on either coast's airwaves in years, he found it to be ridiculous regional radio (it was) and couldn't wrap his brain around why people enjoyed it. I heard him mocking it on and off for a few months and laughed, figuring he'd soon forget about the topic and move on to something else. However, after listening to a year of Howard continually discussing it, even getting 50 Cent to participate during an appearance, I had a feeling I'd somehow get mentioned. When one of Howard's producers contacted me in 2011 to call in to the show, I almost felt like I was being pranked.

Mostly because of his demons, my father and I didn't find much to bond over late in his life. Howard was everything to our relationship, though. My father was a proud New Yorker who enjoyed explaining the postmodernism and importance of an East Coast pioneer like Howard to his young son, who rarely left LA and was happy at the time with his West Coast sense of humor. I became a superfan immediately as we laughed together, listening to the show. We even saw *Private Parts* at the first midnight screening in our neighborhood during my junior year of high school. Howard was on the radio every time I drove my father to chemotherapy. One of my father's last birthday gifts to me was a Sirius radio subscription, which helped me follow the show to satellite radio without missing a broadcast. I even vividly remember listening to Howard the day my father died. The fact that this common bond would push me to finally admit, and accept, my past—the *exact* advice my father gave me days before he left me forever—is a spiritual coincidence on par with Patrick Swayze helping you make pottery.

Howard interviewed me for almost fifteen minutes, asking about the odd events that took me from conscientious college student to lauded up-and-coming rapper then back down to regular guy. After being shown my picture, Howard lovingly observed that I looked like Woody Allen, and Robin less lovingly joked, "No wonder your career went nowhere." I tried my hardest to contain my excitement, especially when we jokingly performed a Roll Call together and Howard earnestly said, "Wow, you're good!" It was something I was thrilled to hear. Not only had it felt like a lifetime since I talked about Hot Karl; it felt just as long since I'd rapped.

I hung up the phone, once again having one of the best moments of my life on the radio, feeling like millions of pounds had been lifted off my shoulders. What was once embarrassment now felt like success. I wasn't quite chomping at the bit to get back in the studio and resurrect Hot Karl—I had found a comfortable life outside the business—but thanks to this interview, I no longer felt like a victim. So when I was diagnosed with brain tumors and facing mortality soon after, I knew that finally telling my story was the next, and last, step of acceptance. Well, almost.

A year later I was having lunch with my friend Justin, when I looked up and was stunned to see Jimmy Iovine and his children entering the restaurant. I had played out this scenario in my head hundreds of times, what I'd say to Jimmy now that I was a grown man unafraid to express his own thoughts and opinions.

But only a few feet away from him, I once again froze. My heart started to race and I felt the sweat start to build, and despite a long time passing, I felt like I was once again walking up to his house, hoping he'd change my life forever.

I had already made amends with DJ, as we occasionally texted each other, mostly about the Clippers, a team we both have season tickets for—mine in the 200 section, his courtside. We had never dug deep into Hot Karl, or ever addressed how he, and the project, just vanished, but at this point I don't really need those answers from him. Now that I was facing the *actual* decision maker, my repressed feelings of contempt and obsession came back at an alarmingly fast speed.

Justin, the friend I was having lunch with, immediately noticed my obvious discomfort and asked what was wrong. Knowing that Justin had also worked for Interscope at some point in his life, with a much less dramatic departure, I pointed out Jimmy and frowned. Justin turned around to see, and I went back to eating, of all things, a salmon plate. Acknowledging the coincidence, I started to think back on everything that had happened. I couldn't help but laugh—all this because of a bar mitzvah. I had always concentrated on the painful conclusion, yet at this moment I couldn't help but focus on the happier times: street-performing for Missy, Sisqó's porn collection, Mack 10's briefcase, Suge Knight's kindness, my phone call with RZA, my A-list eye infection, loaning money to Kanye West, forcing my poor mom to dress in numerous ridiculous costumes, and my dad yelling "Go get 'em!" from sidestage. I was a person with stories that no one else could tell. For the first time in my life, I felt pride in being that person. Filled with that newfound confidence, I looked at Justin and said, "Let's go say hello." Justin, understanding the importance of this statement, silently stood up and followed my lead.

When we got to his table, Jimmy immediately recognized Justin and greeted him, introduced his kids, and asked how he was doing. I stood by patiently, listening to the small talk, wondering how everything would go down and trying my hardest not to focus on the nicely sharpened knives on the table. After a few minutes, which felt like hours, Justin turned to me and said, "And you know Jensen."

I watched as Jimmy's mind worked overtime, trying to recognize the face and name he knew were familiar but was unable to place. I broke the silence with a sentence I hadn't said in quite some time: "I'm Hot Karl."

He looked surprised, unable to hold the poker face that has probably made him billions of dollars in infamous negotiations. His son, Jamie, who had joined our initial meeting back in the day—now in his twenties—was stunned, but tickled, by my announcement. I could tell Jimmy was also happy to see me, something that threw my plan off. He instantly started asking sincere questions about my life, and I filled him in, letting him know that I owned two art galleries in Los Angeles and was writing for a few TV shows and websites. When he asked if I still made music, I shook my head no. I noticed his son was visibly upset at this admission. Then a club DJ, Jamie reminded me that I was one of his favorite rappers, and that felt better than I would've expected. Jimmy asked if I ever thought about doing it again. I laughed and revealed that, now over thirty, I was well past my prime. I explained that I was happy falling back on my college education, something he'd actually helped pay for. Without missing a step, Jimmy cracked, "You and everyone else at this table." After the resulting laughter, Jamie asked the question I've been asked a million times, something even I'd ask myself if given the opportunity. It's the same thing you've probably wondered throughout this entire book. It was an inquiry that normally reopened the wound, something I would've gone out of my way to avoid in this encounter, but now I had to face it.

"So, what happened, man? You were so dope, and then you just disappeared. It was like the ending of *The Sopranos*," Jamie said earnestly.

I waited a second, shocked I would get to respond to this in front of the only man who actually knew the answer, and the only person I wanted to hear me. I wanted to say a million things. The anger wanted out. I opened my mouth to ruin a perfectly good lunch—and then remembered my father's advice. I had grown. I had moved on. There was no reason to revive the gloom. Despite how it ended, I was given an opportunity and I took advantage of it. I had the time of my life, and I've accepted how it ended. No matter how much I had fantasized about delivering a resentful and threatening response, I earnestly joked, "Well, it *would* be like *The Sopranos* if the actors didn't know the show was ending. I kinda didn't want to stop."

I saw Jimmy nod his head.

With that we said our good-byes. Jimmy was friendly and seemed genuinely interested in my life, which was a nice feeling considering everything I had assumed. It was the respectful, and mature, closure I knew was best. Before I left, Jimmy made a big deal out of giving me his e-mail address, saying he'd love to meet and see if there was any way he could get me back into the fold, this time far away from the microphone. He remembered my work ethic and marketing mind, saying I was ahead of my time and possibly now a professional asset. I thanked him and walked away, proud of myself and well aware of the growth I had just exhibited. "Well, that went well," Justin observed with a sense of relief.

I e-mailed Jimmy a few days later, letting him know it was great to see him after all these years and that I was happy to see his beautiful family. I told him the days I was available to meet and that I looked forward to fully catching up. I sent the message knowing this was a whole new Jensen. Hot Karl was finally just a happy memory.

Jimmy never e-mailed me back.

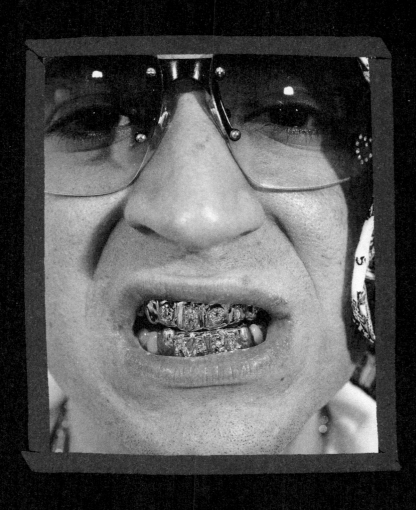

POSTSCRIPT

TO find a happier ending for Jensen, and ultimately Hot Karl, visit JensenKarp.com and see what he's been up to since Jamaica.

ACKNOWLEDGMENTS

SHOUT-OUT to my mom, my family, Matty, Sancho, Brunch, Bill, Katie and David Sutton, Justin Siegel, Matt Inman (my incredible editor, who listened to me talk about how I didn't know our deadline on my podcast and never really brought it up), Seanie Civale, Ellen Folan, Julia Elliott—and everyone at Penguin Random House/Crown—Rickye Kidd, Kyle Sanchez, Dave Holmes, Justin Siegel, Nano Tissera, Jack and Alex, Caroline, Danny & Dan, Mark Hoppus, Chris Bentz, Mike Bentz, Rachel Rusch, Oly Obst, the great Richard Abate, Paul Scheer, Sean Larkin, Sam Srinivasan and Stefani Roberts, Paige Peterson, Evan Bogart, Nova Rockafeller, John Cena, Hannibal Buress, Kevin Smith, Kay Cannon, Bun B, Seth Rogen, Evan Goldberg & everyone at Point Grey, Ben Winston, James Corden & everyone at Fulwell 73, Michael Bloom and everyone at TBS, J. J. Redick, Julian Kasten, Mazin Elsadig, Jonathan Mannion, Stephanie Hsu, Vanessa and Jonah Bayer, Adam Pally, Jessica Macomber Diaz, DJ Mormile, Bobby and Ben Hundreds, Mike and Anna Shinoda, John Mayer, Pete Wentz, MC Serch, Rone, CM Punk, Pete Davidson, and anyone who has ever tried to be creative and found a dead end. You can always make a U-turn.

PHOTOGRAPHY CREDITS

PHOTOGRAPHY CREDITS

Courtesy of the author: Pages iv, 6, 12, 18, 24, 26, 30, 35, 45, 48, 55, 80, 91, 93, 139, 141, 158, 172, 181, 191, 201, 209, 215, 229, 238, and 277.

Author's mother: Dear Abigail Guadalupe, Page 19

Jean Chudo-Corijo, Page 104

Jonathan Mahmon: Pages 255, 264, 283, 284, and 295.

Paper texture, javropan/Shutterstock: Pages 26–28, 104–108, 158–176, 172–174, 191–195, 199–213, 229–231, 254–264, 281–355.

ABOUT THE AUTHOR

MELISSA STETTEN

JENSEN KARP, formerly known as Hot Karl, is a writer, comedian, and co-owner of Gallery 1988, the nation's leading destination for pop culture–themed artwork. He hosts the *Get Up On This* podcast on the Earwolf Network, co-owns Patti Lapel pins, and has written and produced for *The Late Late Show with James Corden*, the Grammys, the MTV VMAs and Movie Awards, *Rolling Stone*, *WWE Raw*, The Hundreds, and the ESPYs. Jensen has recently appeared rapping on NFL on Fox and Comedy Central's *@midnight*, and is currently an executive producer, writer, and coach on *Drop the Mic* on TBS. He was influenced by early Tom Hanks comedies, Chino XL, and Dennis Miller (before Dennis became a real piece of shit).

KANYE WEST
OWES ME $300

ESSAYS,
READER'S GUIDES,
AND MORE

KANYE WEST
OWES ME $300

"Does Kanye Know About This?"

In the year since my book was first published, the two most-frequently asked questions from readers are: 1) "Who is the A-list celebrity that gave you dual eye infections?" and 2) the unavoidable "Did Kanye West ever pay you back?"

Well, to answer the first query, no matter how many times you tweet your guesses at me, I'll never actually disclose the name. Sorry. I'll leave that type of douchey behavior to bros who wear fedoras and vape indoors. BUT, I will give you one more clue, finally putting to rest a major rumor and maybe giving you the closure you need to move forward: It wasn't Dame Judi Dench.

And listen, as far as Kanye goes, mirroring my past fifteen years outside of the music business, I've basically encountered total silence from the man, aside from paying exorbitant amounts to attend his concerts. I was always nervous that he'd somehow find out the book's clickbait-y title in advance and quickly rush to send me a check, undermining the entire concept and destroying my ability to generate any attention, or humor, from its ridiculousness. That would've been the coolest move, at least. He could've started by mailing me the $300, maybe even in pennies, and including a letter that read, "Nice try!" or "*Master and Commander* is an incredible, Oscar-winning Peter Weir film, you idiot!" It would've blown my mind, and any momentum I thought I had. Fortunately, while he was busy tweeting that Bill Cosby is innocent or performing on a floating stage, I predictably went undetected. But that's not to say I didn't try my hardest to be really annoying.

Before the book's debut, when I was coming up with possible ways to market it, one concept in particular stood out as "genius." It was crafted by me and my publicist at the time, and it was *just* crazy enough to work. The idea was simple: we wanted to actively include readers in my journey to finally collect the $300 from Kanye West, using social media and, most important, physical engagement. So, a week before the book's release, I planned on posting a video online that would start with the quick elevator pitch of my career, followed by a brief synopsis of my early dealings with Kanye. I'd cap it all off with a mention of his recent announcement that he was $53 million in debt, a tidy coincidence with my title that could only be seen as God's apology for my Jamaica trip, since we had locked in that name months before we even knew Kanye might be financially struggling. Unlike my signing to Interscope, the timing was perfect. I'd send my condolences but admit that his recent disclosures had me slightly concerned that I'd never see a return on my loan and that no time was better than now to line up and collect, before he was bled dry by creditors.

And if you think I'm being a dick, keep in mind, Kanye isn't actually "in debt." He's just out of pocket on a lot of unrealized concepts, from his clothing line of knapsacks and *Les Misérables* costumes to a video game where you fly to see his mother in Heaven (for real) to what I can only assume is an ark made of gold sitting in his backyard. He's put tons of money into things he hasn't seen profit on, or really ANY return from. He said "debt" he's accumulated, but clearly meant "money I've spent." Because if you're selling hundreds of thousands of $60 concert tees, printed on $2 Gildan blanks, you can't really complain about "debt" without a few raised eyebrows.

And once I'd gotten to that point in the video, I'd drop *this* fucking bomb: If you can get Kanye West to give you the $300 he owes me, in person and documented on video, I will give you, as a prize . . . $10,000.

That's right. I somehow convinced two different companies to each fork over $5,000 cash in return for a mention of their names and services in the video. I even secured a cameo from actor Ryan Phillippe, who would randomly walk into the shot and ask, "Jensen, if you have ten thousand dollars cash, why do you need the three hundred?" I'd casually push him out of the way and say, "That's not the point, Ryan Phillippe. This is about principle."

We'd end the sketch with whatever rules we'd have to disclose, and then I'd immediately top the *New York Times* bestseller list and read an accompanying *AdAge* story with the headline, "Best Book Campaign Since the Bible." It seemed like such a no-brainer. I wondered why Jonathan Franzen hadn't done shit like this.

As I hired a director and film crew for my call to action, I thought, with the same nonchalance you might exhibit when you go back into your house to get an umbrella because you see just one tiny suspicious cloud, "You know what couldn't hurt? Maybe I'll call a lawyer. . . ."

I mean, I didn't really see any issues on the horizon, but I wanted to make sure I had all my bases covered. I figured the most he or she would do was structure the exact wording of the rules that would quickly flash on the screen at the end of the bit. Things like "entries from Hawaii prohibited" or "please send low-resolution videos because Jensen doesn't want to pay for a larger Dropbox account." So I got a recommendation from a friend and soon thereafter ended up on a "consultation call" with a lawyer who specialized in "sweepstakes."

"So, what's the idea?" the lawyer enthusiastically asked me after a few minutes of small talk, eager to hear the "untraditional" concept that I had alluded to in my email.

Then I hit her with the pitch. I was really selling it, doing the voices, laughing when I needed to, taking long pauses to emphasize emotion. You could hear my pride. I wrapped up, nailing the final line: "And that's the marketing plan we concocted to sell my book," sort of performing a jazz hands finale from the other side of the phone, in the same way comedians end that joke with "The Aristocrats!" In my mind I remember a few seconds of dramatic silence, but I know, based on her tone of finality and assurance, there probably wasn't even a breath between our dialogue. She abruptly responded, without having to think twice, "Absolutely not."

She broke down every aspect of the idea, point by point, explaining exactly how many laws I'd be breaking and how I left myself open not only to numerous lawsuits from Kanye, but maybe jail time. He would be constantly harassed and followed by fans and put in grave danger. I'd also be capitalizing on his name way beyond the true statement that doubled as my book's title, destroying the legal reasoning my publisher depended on to print it. In every way, this was a colossally dumb idea. She chuckled with judgment and said, "Jensen, people get *killed* for a few thousand dollars every single day. I can only imagine what you'll incite."

She had a point. I never thought of it that way. *The logical way.* For the rest of the call I attempted to find loopholes or different routes into the idea, and each time she would block my progress like a law school Dikembe Mutumbo, wagging a finger of denial at a failed rapper who just didn't see how inconsiderate his harebrained scheme was. She was trying to get off the phone quickly, not wanting to waste any more time on this silliness and likely now afraid she had become an accomplice, so I thanked her and hung up. I had no backup marketing plan. So I did what anyone who gets embarrassed by his own naïveté does . . . I kept trying.

I spoke to three more attorneys, each one more disgusted by the idea than the next. One didn't even let me finish the explanation, stopping right before the Ryan Phillippe part, which I safely assume, despite his undeniable longevity in Hollywood, doesn't change the legality of my idea. I knew defeat when I heard it, and sadly decided to ditch the attempt altogether, focusing instead on a Twitter raffle for a pair of Yeezys and a video of me rapping for the first time in ten years. It wasn't quite forcing Kanye to face his responsibilities by giving out $10,000, but I'm also not in civil court giving an old friend all of my savings while wearing handcuffs. It's a fair trade. So despite the roadblock and the more traditional release, I'm happy that word got out and the book is currently in your hands.

BUT, by this point of the book, you should know me well enough to guess this bullshit doesn't end here. My ideas don't die that easy. Ask Tyrese.

Right before the book's release, I was also developing a TV show idea with a company named Bunim-Murray, best known to me as the pioneers who created *The Real World,* but probably best known to you as the juggernaut reality-TV production house that brings you *Keeping Up with the Kardashians.* They were high on a concept I had pitched them for a music-focused reality show, so we met a few times and unsuccessfully approached a few networks together. But it was one day, very close to the on-sale date, at their offices in the San Fernando Valley, when they asked about how I planned on promoting the book. That's when things got weird and I would finally get an answer to the question *I* continued to ask myself since I got the book deal: "Does Kanye know about this?"

When they asked about the plan, I went right back into the song and dance, despite the revelations from a handful of unsupportive lawyers. I at least wanted them to hear the beauty of it. I explained the video; I acted it out; I revealed the $10,000 part in the same way a magician might release a dove into the air. I might not have had the legal grounds to perform such a stunt, but I sure did have the confidence to explain it. And when I was done breaking it down, I quickly juxtaposed it with sadness, admitting that once I thought about it, and spoke to experts, I knew it was illegal to plan and, honestly, unfair to Kanye.

One of the TV producers looked at me, still smiling from the absurd nature of what I just performed, and without any inclination of sarcasm inquired, "Wanna ask Kanye to be involved?"

What? Huh?

"Because he's right in there," the producer said, pointing to a nearby closed office door.

And, just like that, I realized I was in the same building as Kanye West for the first time in over a decade, just days away from the release of my book bearing a title that depended on our lack of interaction.

I was obviously startled and a bit shaken by the idea of running into the now superstar without any preparation. This could ruin everything, right? It felt a bit like Marty McFly running into his future self, forever changing his timeline and causing a shockwave through events that could never be repaired. What was he doing there?

"He's been sitting in on *Keeping Up with the Kardashians* editing sessions," the producer disclosed. "He's actually been looking for ways to be more involved. This storyline could be perfect."

He suggested we just barge into the edit bay and hang out, get reacquainted as friends, and pitch the idea. My mind was blown as other high-level employees around us agreed with this outrageous plan. They were all convinced that Kanye would be interested in staging the stunt and giving money away to whoever approached him first to collect the $300. It would all play out on television and Instagram as real, but I wouldn't have to worry about his consent because, well, he'd be in on it, all in spirit of their quasi-reality TV show. I hated to bring the room down, but I was still having trouble wrapping my brain around this possibility.

"You guys *actually* think Kanye would be into this idea," I asked, trying to find any moment in the man's career where self-awareness or humility had been center stage.

"For sure," the executive assured me. "He's a totally different guy now. He's chill."

It went against everything I wanted it to be, but I knew it would be my only choice at this point. And after a few more minutes of tireless convincing, they *actually* had me believing this was possible. Sure, the

Kanye I knew would *never* do this, but I hadn't spoken to the guy in fifteen years, and who knows if the madness I read online was true? I was willing to give him the benefit of the doubt, especially with Bunim-Murray's ringing endorsement. But I knew I didn't want to see Kanye so close to the book's release. As great as it would be for this story, it still felt like a bride seeing her future husband the morning of the wedding (I'm the bride).

I couldn't shake the aura of bad luck and possible disaster with a direct face-to-face approach. So instead, I wrote out the proposal on my iPhone and emailed it to everyone in the room, and to another address they made sure I included, telling me it was Kim's main production contact, who would also have to be involved in the process. Mind blown, I quickly left the office, knowing they were about to go in for the pitch. As I hightailed to the parking lot, I yelled back to them to call me when they had an answer.

I went home and freaked out. Although it was the exact opposite of the plan I had first imagined, if Kanye tweeted even once about me, my book would sell like it had the words "girl" and "train" in its title. An hour passed without contact, but I figured details were maybe being worked out. Then another hour passed. Then three more hours. Then it was nighttime. My nerves got the best of me and I called my contact at the production company just before a dinner I had planned at 8:00. He picked up after a few rings.

"So, how'd it go?" I excitedly asked.

*"DOES KANYE
KNOW
ABOUT THIS?"*

315

And like I asked him how the maiden voyage of the *Titanic* went, he somberly replied with, "Not so good, Jensen."

He said that Kanye was "happy to hear [I was] doing well," but he found the book's title and the video idea to be "opportunistic," which, yeah, NO SHIT, DUDE, THEY ARE. Coming from the guy who takes advantage of every Taylor Swift diss and stage-rushing moment he can get his hands on, this felt real kettle versus pot. Kanye said he'd pass the email along to his publicist, but not to expect much. The producer admitted I was right the whole time, and that Kanye had much less of a sense of humor about himself than he expected. I felt real stupid, so I could only imagine how the producer felt. Shaking my head, biting my tongue as not to repeat "I told you so" for an hour straight, we ended the conversation knowing this whole thing had gone terribly. I checked Kanye's Twitter account and noticed that about an hour after I left Bunim-Murray he tweeted, "Don't try to use me for advertisement or to make your proposed trend relevant." I'll never know for sure if that was about me, but I think it's safe to say it wasn't about the newest cut of his wife's shit television show.

We never heard from Kanye's publicist—or anyone from his team, for that matter—about the proposal or the title. We went back to being two guys with a shared history, but with absolutely nothing in common come 2016. Who knows what could've happened had I ignored all rules of decency and just held the risky contest, putting him into a sticky situation, or if I had walked into that edit bay and asked him to participate? But I do know two things: Kanye West knows the book exists, and he definitely now remembers the $300 he owes me. And that brings me *some* joy. Because, honestly, it's never been about the money. That's not the point, Ryan Phillippe.

20 Rap Albums That Influenced the Music of Hot Karl

Gravediggaz, *Six Feet Deep* (1994)

Wu-Tang Clan, *Enter the Wu-Tang (36 Chambers)* (1993)

Grand Puba, *2000* (1995)

Ras Kass, *Soul on Ice* (1996)

Camp Lo, *Uptown Saturday Night* (1997)

Cypress Hill, *Cypress Hill* (1991)

Nas, *It Was Written* (1996)

De La Soul, *Stakes Is High* (1996)

Chino XL, *Here to Save You All* (1996)

A Tribe Called Quest, *Midnight Marauders* (1993)

3rd Bass, *The Cactus Album* (1989)

Das EFX, *Dead Serious* (1992)

Ice Cube, *The Predator* (1992)

Fu-Schnickens, *F.U. Don't Take It Personal* (1992)

Prince Paul, *A Prince Among Thieves* (1999)

Aesop Rock, *Labor Days* (2001)

Beastie Boys, *License To Ill* (1986)

The Fugees, *The Score* (1996)

Jeru the Damaja, *The Sun Rises in the East* (1994)

The Roots, *Do You Want More?!!!??!* (1995)

10 Actresses My Mom Thinks Can Play Her in a Movie or TV Show Based on This Book (As Told to Me by My Mom)

Susan Sarandon

Sandra Bullock

Goldie Hawn

Julia Roberts

Sarah Paulson

Natalie Portman (When asked about the age logic here, my mom didn't have much of an explanation.)

Jessica Lange

Maura Tierney

Minnie Driver

Michelle Pfeiffer

For additional Extra Libris content from your other favorite authors and to enter great book giveaways, visit ReadItForward.com/Extra-Libris.

ESSAYS, READER'S GUIDES, AND MORE